The Nightingale's Burden

To Neda —
who is one of
my favorite artists
and what's more
a woman artist too!

Cheryl Walker

THE
Nightingale's Burden

*Women Poets and American Culture
before 1900*

CHERYL WALKER

INDIANA UNIVERSITY PRESS
Bloomington

Library of Congress Cataloging in Publication Data

Walker, Cheryl, 1947–
    The nightingale's burden.

    Bibliography: p.
    Includes index.
    1. American poetry—Women authors—History and
criticism.   2. American poetry—19th century—History
and criticism.   3. Women in literature.   4. Feminism and
literature.   I. Title.
PS147.W27   1982   811'.009'9287   81-48514
ISBN 0-253-34065-9   AACR2
ISBN 0-253-20301-5 (pbk.)
1   2   3   4   5   86   85   84   83   82

For Virginia Marilyn Iversen *and* Adrienne Rich,
the women poets who inspired this work

A knowledge of history gives the literary critic a sixth sense.
—PHILIP RAHV

Contents

Preface

In the spring of 1972 I entered Widener Library at Harvard University with a blue notebook under my arm. I was about to begin the research that has become this book, and so I was in search of material on American women poets. In the card catalog I found, much to my surprise, that there was almost nothing written on the subject, no book that attempted to relate one woman poet to another in terms of time period, shared experience, subject matter, influence, or style. There were two file cards that seemed pertinent to my interests. They directed me to two then recent works: Rosemary Sprague's *Imaginary Gardens: A Study of Five American Poets* (Chilton, 1969) and George Brandon Saul's *Quintet: Essays on Five Women Poets* (Mouton, 1967).

These books were curiously similar—both a series of five essays, both concentrating most of their attention on a generation of poets who emerged in the early years of this century. Sprague dealt with Emily Dickinson, Amy Lowell, Sara Teasdale, Edna St. Vincent Millay, and Marianne Moore. Saul concentrated on Teasdale, Elinor Wylie, Hazel Hall, Winnifred Welles, and Abbie Huston Evans. Neither book attempted to establish a context for comparing these poets, so each essay was an independent foray into the poet's life and work. Neither writer raised the question of what it has meant to be a woman poet in America. Each book apologized for itself. Turning its pages one felt oppressed by a sense of failure: the writer's, the poet's, one's own. Without intending to, these critics implied that what they were doing was a minor endeavor. Both were enthusiastic about their subjects. Neither seriously believed that others would be.

Since then cataloguers have been busy adding cards to that file and category. The field has virtually exploded. To begin with, numerous anthologies of women's poetry have made their way into print: Florence Howe and Ellen Bass's *No More Masks*, Ann Stanford's *The Women Poets in English*, Bulkin and Larkin's *Amazon Poetry, Psyche, Rising Tides, Salt and Bitter and Good, The Penguin Book of Women Poets*, Louise Bernikow's *The World Split Open*, and numerous others. Black women poets are now available in Erlene Stetson's *Black Sister*. Pattie

Cowell has just come out with *Women Poets in Pre-Revolutionary America: 1650–1775.*[1] Some of these anthologies, like Cowell's and Bernikow's, contain extensive critical introductions.

In addition to these anthologies, we now also have books of criticism about women poets, such works as Emily Stipes Watts's *The Poetry of American Women from 1632 to 1945,* Suzanne Juhasz's *Naked and Fiery Forms,* Sandra Gilbert and Susan Gubar's *The Madwoman in the Attic* as well as *Shakespeare's Sisters* which they edited. These have provided needed commentaries on the relation of women poets to one another. Essays continually appear in scholarly journals as well. Because of all this, the field is no longer underpopulated. In fact, there is so much material coming out all the time that one has difficulty keeping up with it.

At the time of this writing, however, there has yet to appear a full-scale, in-depth analysis of American women poets in terms of their literary traditions and historical experience. Emily Stipes Watts comes closest to achieving this goal, and Watts does make an attempt to argue tradition. However, her desire to cover so many poets within so few pages limits her ability to make comparisons and to situate her poets firmly in their historical time periods. This also leads to some misjudgments of particular poems, even to overvaluing the importance of some themes because they are looked at out of context.[2] Watts's survey demonstrates extensive scholarship. Yet it somewhat obscures the questions of literary tradition and women's culture. This is the liability, it seems to me, of negotiating literary history as a survey. Though Watts makes many good points, her readers tend to forget them and their applications because of the lack of an organizing vision.

I have chosen the opposite approach and hope that I do not err too heavily on the other side. Since Watts's book is useful in many ways, hers and mine may complement one another. My aim is to delineate a single approach to tradition and to deal only with those poets who have made the most significant contributions to its progress. I do not believe that all women poets by virtue of their sex have been driven to write the kinds of poems I describe here as belonging to this women's tradition. To say that would be tantamount to saying that biology leads to a particular destiny. I do believe that all the poets in this tradition were influenced by considerations of gender to write these kinds of poems and that this tradition is quintessentially female rather than male, not because of biology but because of shared experience.

I also feel that this is the dominant female tradition at least through the nineteenth century. The fact that Sarah Helen Whitman (1813–

1878) seems to have avoided personal subjects, devoting herself to themes derivative from Bryant and Poe, simply makes her an exception.[3] Frances Harper (1825–1911), as a black woman poet, lacks the ambivalence of most of these middle-class white women for reasons I speculate about in chapter 3. In the twentieth century one finds competing traditions such as those established by the experimentalists (Stein, Loy, Crapsey, and Moore, e.g.) and the populists (Taggard, Ridge, Rukeyser). Many of the poets who can be classified within this tradition also wrote poems belonging to other movements: Amy Lowell, H. D., and Edna St. Vincent Millay are obvious examples. Yet, until the second world war what was understood to be "women's poetry" was still essentially poetry belonging to this tradition: ambivalent, personal, passionate lyrics claiming some special wisdom derived from female experience.

The project here begun is an attempt to uncover the internal and external imperatives that have led American women to write these kinds of poems. Of first importance is the existence of such poems themselves, as a known body of work by women. This is my justification for beginning the major part of my discussion in the first half of the nineteenth century. We need to know what kinds of poems women were writing when women's poetry was for the first time widely disseminated. Popular conceptions of female poets have also exerted a certain kind of pressure on the young woman just starting to write verse, and the expectations of male editors should not be overlooked either. Most disturbing of all, however, is the way so-called "internal" and "external" become confused as women's conceptions of themselves are mediated through patriarchal language. Thus, Caroline Gilman feels humiliated at the publication of her poems, as though she had been caught in public "wearing man's apparel." Her statement, discussed further in chapter 2, is a classic example of the problems women poets face.

As this research got under way, I was struck again and again by the effectiveness of these imperatives, the regularity with which one can find their imprint on generations of writers' works. I also realized that a monumental task confronted me. I needed to look at male poets for purposes of comparison. I had to ask myself why such an important break occurred at the end of the nineteenth century and again after World War II. I even found myself sifting through controversies in American women's history.

The result of these considerations was a decision to divide the project in half. This volume constitutes the first part of my examination of this women's tradition. It stops at the end of the nineteenth century. Chapter 6 offers an introduction to the second volume, where I will concentrate on twentieth-century American women poets in much greater depth, again considering history, biography, and literary influences.

Ultimately, these books are less concerned to prove literary tradition than they are interested in the phenomenon of women's poetry as a sign of women's culture. This is why my discussion of this tradition deals explicitly with poetic autobiography, with the way women have expressed cultural norms in their self-representations. This is also why history becomes so important. One cannot ignore the fact that Anne Bradstreet saw herself as a Puritan, that Emily Dickinson lived in the era of "the cult of true womanhood," that Ella Wheeler Wilcox fancied the freedom of the "new woman" in the 1890s.

Nevertheless, what I find so fascinating is that despite great changes in some aspects of American society, certain deep-rooted female preoccupations persist, so that Anne Bradstreet shares with Louise Guiney a line of poetic feeling. Women's themes and self-representations have been more homogeneous across time than a superficial historical account of women's roles might suggest.

There are opportunities here to consider both change and continuity. One also needs a sense of the norms for women poets before one can assess an individual like Emily Dickinson as extraordinary. Most of these poets were conventional in some ways and eccentric in others. A feminist semiotics of American women's poetry must consider not only the way an individual piece refuses assimilation in the puzzle but also the way it demands such assimilation. From this point of view, popular poets must be considered side by side with serious ones. What we are after is a picture of how self-representation occurs and, when it does, the laws governing its intelligibility.

There is a fundamental narrative design at the core of the women's tradition I examine, and it must be illuminated by looking first at the conditions that give rise to it and second at its particular configurations in literature. For the former task I have used historical accounts. For the latter I have designated several archetypal models, such as the sensibility poem, the free bird poem, the sanctuary poem, and the poem of secret sorrow. One need not believe that these poems reflect in uncomplicated ways the "true" feelings of their authors to assert that their existence helps us imagine more fully the nature and dimensions of women's experience in American culture. However, many of these women did use their poetry as their "letter to the world," and like letters these poems both reveal and conceal. They demand interpretation.

The crux of the matter seems to me the relation between these poets and patriarchal determinants of social order, the structures of power. As Sandra Gilbert and Susan Gubar have admirably shown in *The Madwoman in the Attic,* authority lends a writer the ability to speak.[4] Lacking authority in this culture, American women poets have still spoken, but they have spoken obliquely, sometimes in cramped forms, and often without the confidence to range widely. In order to hear them, we must reconstruct much of the background their poems assume. Thus sociological, psychological, and historical factors as well as literary ones belong to this investigation.

Since I have chosen to focus on the relationship between art and power, I have avoided certain kinds of poems traditionally associated with women: conventionally religious poems, poems on the deaths of children, etc.[5] Every writer must limit herself in some fashion. I hope I have not done so at the expense of important issues.

This book was a long time in the making. Many people influenced its final form in ways neither they nor I could any longer specify with precision. However, I would like to acknowledge my debt to the following individuals. Those who read earlier versions or separate pieces of the whole and gave me substantive comments helped the book take shape. Thus I would like to thank Helen Vendler, Elaine Beilin Brown, Paul Gaston, Gloria Bowles, Ann J. Lane, the late Sylvia Wright Mitarachi, Vivian R. Pollak, Eileen Gillooly, Daniel Horowitz, Hayden White, Ann Douglas, Virginia Lawson, Catharine Stimpson, and Carolyn Heilbrun. I am especially indebted to those who helped me put the finishing touches on the entire final manuscript: Steven Schlossman, Alicia Ostriker, Robert Fossum, and Mary Anne Ferguson.

J. V. Cunningham was the person who started me on this project in 1972 and to him I owe a great deal. Adrienne Rich has been friend, consultant, harsh critic, and generous supporter through many stages of this work, and this book is unimaginable without her.

My typist, Nancy Burson, was always reliable and good-humored. To her and to my friends, who supported me through dark moments, go my love and gratitude.

My husband, Leonard de Heer, and my son, Ian, know how the ideas in this book have been thrashed out in daily life. They have provided comfort, courage, and inspiration.

I am also grateful for the support I have received from Scripps College, the National Endowment for the Humanities, and the Bunting Institute of Radcliffe College. Without their financial and personal assistance I would have found this project harder to complete.

Institutional support for examining rare books and manuscripts at the Huntington Library in San Marino, California, the Amherst College Library, and the Houghton and Schlesinger Libraries at Harvard University helped me delve into the fascinating alcoves of the past.

Acknowledgments

Grateful acknowledgment is made for permission to include the following:

Lines from "A Household," by W. H. Auden, from *Collected Poems*, edited by Edward Mendelson. © Random House, Inc.; poem copyrighted 1951 by W. H. Auden. Reprinted by permission of Random House, Inc.

Lines from "Henceforth from the Mind," "I Saw Eternity," "Women," "Kept," and "Masked Woman's Song" from *The Blue Estuaries* by Louise Bogan. Reprinted by permission of Farrar, Straus, and Giroux, Inc. Copyright © 1923, 1929, 1930, 1933, 1934, 1935, 1936, 1937, 1941, 1949, 1952, 1954, 1957, 1958, 1962, 1963, 1964, 1965, 1966, 1967, 1968 by Louise Bogan.

Lines from poems 398, 745, 1247, 1354, 1401, 1567 by Emily Dickinson in *The Complete Poems of Emily Dickinson*, edited by Thomas H. Johnson. Copyright 1914, 1929 by Martha Dickinson Bianchi; Copyright © 1957 by Mary L. Hampson. Reprinted by permission of Little, Brown and Company.

Lines from poems 44, 80, 260, 398, 421, 540, 713, 732, 745, 1036, 1176, 1209, 1247, 1354, 1401, 1567, 1683, 1734 by Emily Dickinson. Reprinted by permission of the publishers and the Trustees of Amherst College from *The Poems of Emily Dickinson*, edited by Thomas H. Johnson, Cambridge, Mass.: The Belknap Press of Harvard University Press, Copyright 1951, © 1955, 1979 by the President and Fellows of Harvard College.

Lines from poem 1401 by Emily Dickinson from *Emily Dickinson Face to Face: Unpublished Letters With Notes and Reminiscences*, by Martha Dickinson Bianchi. Copyright 1932 by Martha Dickinson Bianchi. Copyright renewed © 1960 by Alfred Leete Hampson. Reprinted by permission of Houghton Mifflin Company.

Lines from "Orchard" and "The Islands" by H. D. (Hilda Doolittle) from *Selected Poems of H. D.*, Copyright 1925, 1953, © 1957 by Norman Holmes Pearson. Reprinted by permission of New Directions Publishing Corporation.

Lines from the elegy for Thomas Parson, "Borderlands," "Tarpeia," "Knight Errant," and "Astraea," by Louise Imogen Guiney, reprinted by permission of Louise Drew-Wilkinson.

Lines from "La Vie de Boheme" and "Granadilla," by Amy Lowell, from *The Complete Poetical Works of Amy Lowell*. Copyright © 1955 by Houghton Mifflin Company. Reprinted by permission of the publisher.

Lines by Edna St. Vincent Millay from *Collected Poems*, Harper & Row. Copyright 1934, 1962 by Edna St. Vincent Millay and Norma Millay Ellis. Reprinted by permission of Norma Millay Ellis.

Lines from "Tulips" by Sylvia Plath in *Ariel*. Copyright © 1962 by Ted Hughes. Reprinted by permission of Harper & Row, Publishers, Inc. and Olwyn Hughes. (Originally appeared in *The New Yorker*).

Lines from "Snapshots of a Daughter-in-Law" in *Poems, Selected and New, 1950–1974*, by Adrienne Rich; reprinted by permission of the author and W. W. Norton & Company, Inc. Copyright © 1975, 1973, 1971, 1969, 1966 by W. W. Norton & Company, Inc. Copyright © 1967, 1963, 1962, 1961, 1960, 1959, 1958, 1957, 1956, 1955, 1954, 1953, 1952, 1951 by Adrienne Rich.

Lines from "Eros Turannos" by Edwin Arlington Robinson. Reprinted by permission of Macmillan Publishing Co., Inc. Copyright 1916 by Edwin Arlington Robinson; renewed 1944 by Ruth Nivison.

Lines from "Wisdom" by Sara Teasdale in *Collected Poems*. Reprinted with permission of Macmillan Publishing Co., Inc. Copyright 1917 by Macmillan Publishing Co., Inc., renewed 1945 by Mamie T. Wheless.

Lines from "On Imagination" by Phillis Wheatley in *The Poems of Phillis Wheatley*, edited by Julian D. Mason, Jr. Copyright 1966 by The University of North Carolina Press. Reprinted by permission of the publisher.

Lines from "A Crowded Trolley Car," "Malediction Upon Myself," "Heart's Desire," "Sanctuary," and "The Eagle and the Mole," by Elinor Wylie in *Collected Poems of Elinor Wylie*. Copyright 1921, 1923, 1924, 1925, 1926, 1927, 1928, 1929, 1932 by Alfred A. Knopf, Inc.; 1949 by William Rose Benet; 1956, 1957, 1960 by Edwina C. Rubenstein. Reprinted by permission of Alfred A. Knopf, Inc.

For permission to use the photographs, I am grateful to the Enoch Pratt Free Library, Baltimore, Maryland (Lizette Woodworth Reese); the College of the Holy Cross, Worcester, Massachusetts (Louise Imogen Guiney); the Amherst College Library, Amherst, Massachusetts (Emily Dickinson); the Schlesinger Library, Radcliffe College, Cambridge, Massachusetts (Lucy Larcom, Frances Osgood, Lydia Sigourney, and Elizabeth Oakes-Smith); and the Princeton Photographic Division, Library of Congress, Washington, D.C. (Ella Wheeler Wilcox).

Cheryl Walker teaches literature, American Studies, and Women's Studies at Scripps College, Claremont, California.

The Nightingale's Burden

Methodology and Mystery

Anne Bradstreet

1 Alone, frustrated, writing poems that could never be printed because they were too strange or too angry, a great woman poet may be lurking in our past whom we know nothing about. But in the period between 1632 and 1945, there are many women poets we do know something about. The problem is we don't know how to read their poems.

So much is missing that was important to the birth of these poems. We need information about both personal and public histories, to provide an informing context for a large rather than a merely literate act of reading. In the first place our knowledge of women's history is not full enough. Some of the difficulties arise from the fact that the reports we have about women poets are often filtered through the viewpoint of those who accepted or enforced the subjugation of women. Furthermore, the patriarchy has not only established negative criteria for judging women poets, it has also excluded their work from serious scrutiny.[1] We know very little about the real day-to-day-experiences of women themselves. We are only beginning to uncover women's diaries, journals, and letters detailing lives not lived in the public eye. The most difficult problem of all, however, is that we don't know how to analyze the effect of patriarchal domination on the way women themselves described their experience.

As historians go to work on women of the nineteenth and twentieth centuries, it becomes especially clear that we know in comparison very little about what early colonial women felt and thought. How do we know, for instance, what Lucy Downing really had in mind when she wrote to her brother John Winthrop, "whilst men make our lawes they are fitest to judge them"? Was this a genuine abdication of judgment on the issue of a woman's rebellion against her husband (the Mrs. and Mr. Peters she has just been describing), or was this an expression of anger against the legal system, set up by men to protect men?[2]

These questions are important because poems develop out of the most complex matrix of feelings and circumstances. The subconscious is deeply vulnerable to the impact of social norms, often more vulner-able—as we shall see—than the conscious mind. In their poems we have some of the most dramatic expressions of the longings and the fears, the anger and the compromises with which American women have struggled. Because the creative process involves an important degree of nonrational, nonconscious, nonintentional contact with the essential movements of the heart and mind, its products are often less refined, less thoroughly self-censored, than are letters, essays, even diary entries. Poems are one great untapped source of American women's history. They are cultural documents rich with information about women's psyches and women's lives.

This book attempts to provide a framework to make possible a new reading of these poems. It has not been written in defiance of those who are concerned with language, with structure or genre or any of the many approaches that populate the literary world. It has been written as a supplement to them. In fact, one task that this book undertakes is that of providing a theoretical framework for under-standing particular poems as signs of women's culture—what we might call a feminist semiotics of American women's poetry. It re-quires considering the mutual influence of literature and history.

The kind of reading that this book proposes asks that one keep constantly in mind one fact: the act of writing poetry has been a fundamentally different experience for women than for men. To be poets women have risked alienation from the one group into which the patriarchy has allowed them free entry, the caste of sex—defined for women in terms of the duties of caring for others. If it is true to some degree that men have also been ostracized from the world of their sex for writing poems, the psychic costs have been considerably less. For men have always had women to turn to; they have always had an established set of literary ancestors and the symbolic support of economically successful men of their own profession. Women, on the other hand, have rarely had men to turn to. Even more important, they have not had an established set of literary ancestors. They have only occasionally been economically self-sufficient. Furthermore, women have had to deal first with the prejudice against their becom-ing poets at all and second with the expectation that women's poetry must be trivial, undistinguished, and of interest only to other women. Though American history has seen a number of men assume the role of elder statesman in the world of poetry, no woman has ever achieved that kind of protected status in her lifetime. As against the general patriarchal acceptance of poets like Henry Wadsworth Long-fellow, John Greenleaf Whittier, even Emerson and Whitman in their old age, and certainly Robert Frost, one can only place the fragile eminence of Amy Lowell and Edna St. Vincent Millay, both of whom were more widely known for their rebellion against traditional female roles than for their poetry. No president has ever honored a woman poet at his inauguration. No women poet has ever had sufficient influence so that her word alone could make or break a reputation.

These facts have been so universally accepted as the way things are and should be that they have remained unexamined, and the most basic question we ask ourselves when reading a poem—what is going on in this work—is usually answered without taking them into account. This book attempts to reawaken what has been the political unconscious of readers of poetry by asking: How is what is going on in this poem better understood by knowing that this poet was a woman? And: How is this individual woman's work better understood by seeing it in relation to other women's work? In order to prepare for this act of reading, we must consider not only literary history but women's history, the nature of women's lives.

Sometimes, as in Anne Bradstreet's case, the facts are few. Though her father Thomas Dudley alternated with John Winthrop as governor of the Massachusetts Bay Colony, and though her husband Simon Bradstreet would become governor after her death, we have no letters and very little except demographic data—her various residences, the births and deaths in her family—with which to understand her life.[3] Here is where information about the role of women in the society-at-large must help to fill in the gaps. We know that Anne Bradstreet grew up not in America but in England, at the Earl of Lincoln's estate. In the aftermath of Elizabeth's reign, she and other gentlewomen were still allowed an education. She read Guillaume du Bartas (in Sylvester's translation), Sir Philip Sidney, Sir Walter Ralegh, Dr. Helkiah Crooke—poems, histories, and science texts—as well as the Bible. However, as David Latt points out, following the liberalization of attitudes toward women that occurred during Elizabeth's reign, there came a backlash. After a period of relative restraint, literally dozens of openly misogynist works were published in the seventeenth century. During the 1640s and '50s—when Bradstreet wrote most of her poems—there was an outpouring of especially virulent misogyny in the mother country. Latt suggests that this spate of hostile sentiment created a ferment in the world of publishing that raised the status of works both defending and attacking women to the level of a minor genre.[4] Heightened interest on both sides of the "woman question" may have been partially responsible for the enormous English interest in Anne Bradstreet's poems, published in 1650.

Bradstreet was praised on both sides of the Atlantic. However,

Thomas Powell's *Art of Striving*, a characteristically reactionary document, predicts how some of the more caustic spirits of the age must have responded to Bradstreet's work. In his book, published in 1635, Powell reprimands women for precisely the kind of self-education Bradstreet had undertaken just a few years before. He finds such learning impractical and advises: "Let them learne plaine workes of all kind, so they take heed of too open seeming. Instead of song and musick, let them learne cookery and laundry, and instead of reading Sir Philip Sidney's *Arcadia* let them read the grounds of huswifery. I like not a female poetesse at any hand."[5] After 1620 Powell's point of view was more the norm than the exception. We learn from it that women were allowed at this time to read and study poetry, but we also learn that there was beginning to be a new rash of articulate opposition to their doing so. Indignant men not only mourned the loss of housewifely skills in the new female generation, they also warned against "too open seeming"; educated women were becoming less submissive in the confidence of their newfound education. Yet clearly this confidence belonged only to a few. Its appearance in women's history is brief. Though Bradstreet migrated in 1630 with women who had tasted the fruits of an age of reform, the next generation of colonials were not much concerned with women's education. It has been estimated that 50 percent of the women of this generation were illiterate, and "dame schools," where they could be found, rarely went beyond the level of an eighth grade or poor high school education.

To understand American Puritan attitudes toward women we must examine the hierarchical context in which the founding fathers viewed all social order. Women were subject to men, wives to their husbands, just as citizens were subject to the will of the magistrate, and all, even governors, were made to feel impotent before the will of God. Any individual act of disobedience had communal repercussions because the American colony was founded as "a city on a hill," meant as an example to the world, and every Puritan was to be a "visible saint." Many women had to face public humiliation for violating this code. Acts of rebellious "carriage" or rash moments of insolence in defiance of their husbands brought women duckings, whippings, and hours in the stocks.[6] Separation and divorce were almost never sanctioned even when a husband was crude, wayward, or abusive, impotence being one of the few circumstances considered a just cause for living apart. Though husbands could and did divorce wives for committing adultery, infidelity on the husband's part was not considered grounds for divorce in the wife's case.

The concept of hierarchy sanctioned even the intellectual oppression of women, who were regarded as weaker than men both mentally and, in light of Eve's guilt as the first to fall, morally. John Cotton, for instance, took advantage of the controversy surrounding the trial of Anne Hutchinson to preach a sermon arguing that women should not be allowed to speak in church. Citing St. Paul, he warned: "The woman is more subject to error than a man, *ver. 14,* and therefore might soon prove a seducer if she became a teacher. . . . It is not permitted to a woman to speak in the Church by way of propounding questions though under pretense of desire to learn for her own satisfaction; but rather it is required she should ask her husband at home."[7] As Milton described the hierarchical structure for Adam and Eve: "He for God only, she for God in him."

John Winthrop, as much as any single individual, represented the thinking of the Puritan patriarchy of Bradstreet's day, and his famous journal entry concerning Ann Hopkins is revealing. He criticizes Hopkins's husband for letting his wife devote herself to intellectual work, an error which, Winthrop felt, led to her loss of sanity: "For if she had attended her household affairs, and such things as belong to women, and not gone out of her way and calling to meddle in such things as are proper for men, whose minds are stronger, etc., she had kept her wits, and might have improved them usefully and honorably in the place God had set her."[8] Not nearly so prominent but equally indignant was Thomas Parker, whose response to finding that his sister had emerged in print was to compose a public letter in which he said: "Your printing of a Book beyond the custom of your sex, doth rankly smell."[9] Lyle Koehler in *The Search for Power* concludes: "As a general rule, the specter of male overlordship is so apparent in institutional, economic, and family life throughout the seventeenth century that it leaves little room to doubt women's difficulty in achieving, much less exerting, a sense of their own assertive independence."[10]

In light of these attitudes, reading Anne Bradstreet's elegy for Queen Elizabeth I becomes a different experience than it might have been otherwise. Many English poets wrote poems praising Queen Elizabeth, and one might see Bradstreet as simply a member of the "Saint Elizabeth" cult that survived the queen's death by many years. The fact that Bradstreet places Elizabeth in an honor roll of famous women makes this poem no different from several others written by men. However, the one fact that does differentiate it—the fact that the poet was a woman—is revealed in the climactic moment of the poem when Bradstreet says:

> Now say, have women worth? or have they none?
> Or had they some, but with our Queen is't gone?
> Nay Masculines, you have thus taxt us long,

But she, though dead, will vindicate our wrong.
Let such as say our Sex is void of Reason,
Know tis a Slander now, but once was Treason.
But happy *England* which had such a Queen;
Yea happy, happy, had those days still been.[11]

The first word, "now," is important because it announces that the whole foregoing list of the queen's accomplishments has been leading up to this moment, to this point. The queen is a representative of what women can do. Anger against patriarchal prejudice is vibrant in that line, "Nay Masculines, you have thus taxt us long. . . ." And surely the seventeenth-century background of liberalization and backlash is part of Bradstreet's meaning when she mourns the passing of the Elizabethan age: "Know tis a Slander now, but once was Treason," "Yea happy, happy, had those days still been." Not only is the queen herself missed. The loss of her influence, her power, is also keenly felt because during Elizabeth's reign, Bradstreet implies, some acts of oppression were kept in check. In the final moments of the poem Bradstreet confesses that she looks forward to the millennium as a time when "*Eliza* shall rule *Albion* once again."

"The woman is more subject to error than a man. . . ." "I like not a female poetesse at any hand." "Your printing of a Book beyond the custom of your sex, doth rankly smell." ". . . usefully and honorably in the place God had set her." Surely comments such as these wound themselves unpleasantly in and out of Bradstreet's thoughts when she was writing her poems. Her clearest expression of personal outrage comes in her Prologue to the long Quaternion poems she wrote for her father where she admits:

I am obnoxious to each carping tongue
Who says my hand a needle better fits,
A Poets pen all scorn I should thus wrong,
For such despite they cast on Female wits:
If what I do prove well, it won't advance,
They'l say it's stoln,or else it was by chance.

But sure the Antique Greeks were far more mild
Else of our Sexe, why feigned they those Nine
And poesy made, *Calliope's* own Child;
So 'mongst the rest they placed the Arts Divine,
But this weak knot, they will full soon untie,
The Greeks did nought, but play the fools and lye.

Let Greeks be Greeks, and women what they are
Men have precedency and still excell,
It is but vain unjustly to wage warre,

> Men can do best, and women know it well
> Preheminence in all and each is yours;
> Yet grant some small acknowledgement of ours.

However straightforward these verses may at first appear to be, they are perplexing upon closer examination. The problem lies in the last stanza. When Bradstreet imagines that "they" will disparage the reference to the Greeks, we know that she is being ironic. With her, we are meant to agree that the Greeks did more than "play the fools and lye." However, when she says that "men have precedency and still excell," she is hardly any longer using irony. For her not to have believed this would have required an ability to sustain an almost constant assault upon her culture. Furthermore, in her time men did have precedency and did excel, precisely because of that ambiguous "precedency." They had a literary past, and they were past masters at defending their right to precede women in all branches of the arts. But acknowledging precedency is not the same thing as saying, "Preheminence in all and each is yours." Is Bradstreet being ironic here or serious? Ann Stanford reads these lines straightforwardly but to me they sound disingenuous, especially after "Men can do best." The effect of putting these two lines together is to make the second one sound as if it were uttered in order to soothe a temperamental child. It is as though Bradstreet were cutting short her opposition by an insincere capitulation, turning to the men with her reassurance that she is not trying to compete. She seems to want to get on to her final request for recognition, not just from men but from great men, the "high flown quills" she asks to give her "Thyme or Parsley wreath," a woman's crown, instead of the conventional laurels. Throughout our reading of women's poetry we must pay careful attention to tone, which is sometimes the first signal of buried anger or an unsettled mind.

These lines remind us of one of the critical factors we need to consider in our reading. The greatest danger women artists have faced has been, not oppression and hostility toward them, but their own internalization of the attitudes of the oppressors. This has caused women, even in moments of greatest aspiration and expansiveness, to feel secretly inadequate or inferior. Their poems include the impulse to achieve, the hope for recognition, and a confession of failure, the urge to renounce not only the world but also their own ambitions.

In the Prologue we can see the poet being self-aggrandizing one moment and self-effacing the next. She cannot simply come forward with her anger and her hopes. She must make the required bow toward the patriarchy: "Men can do best, and women know it well." In Bradstreet's poetry we can find other evidence of this kind of bow where she takes on a patriarchal voice, particularly in "David's Lamentation for Saul and·Jonathan" and the "Choler" section of her poem on the four humors.[12]

The Lament is the only place, as far as we know, where Bradstreet chooses to paraphrase a Biblical passage rather than integrating a Biblical reference into her own text. The passage, which begins at 2 Samuel 1:19, is David's elegy for his lost friends, Saul whom he revered and Jonathan whom he loved. The poet says:

> Distrest for thee I am, dear *Jonathan*,
> Thy love was wonderfull, surpassing man,
> Exceeding all the love that's Feminine.

In the Geneva Bible, used by the Puritans, the passage reads: "Woe is me for thee, my brother Jonathan: very kind hast thou been unto me: thy love to me was wonderful, passing the love of women."

We don't know why Bradstreet chose to paraphrase this passage. Elizabeth Wade White suggests that this poem was the poet's way of dealing with her turbulent feelings about the beheading of Charles I. (To the American Puritans Charles was, like Saul, a king cut down by scoundrels.) No matter what the occasion of the poem, however, Bradstreet's rendering of the Biblical text shows her caught between her patriarchal text and her sex. The Geneva Bible quotes David as saying that Jonathan's love surpassed the love of women. Possibly to deflect any suspicion of homoerotic feeling here, this Bible glosses "passing the love of women" by adding "either toward their husbands or their children." Bradstreet adds a tell-tale phrase— "surpassing man"—as though to equalize the comparisons. The love between David and Jonathan becomes extraordinary in both male and female realms. Yet her rendering of "passing the love of women" turns out to be even less ambiguous and more sweepingly dismissive than her Bible's. "Surpassing man" might be understood to mean transcending the usual level of human intercourse. But whereas "passing the love of women" is ambiguous and even in the gloss somewhat restricted, "exceeding all the love that's Feminine" seems to take in all the love that women are capable of giving. It is as though, having taken the heretical step of adding "surpassing man," Bradstreet feels she must make up for her little subversion of the text by making the dismissal of female love even stronger.

The poet's ability to lay aside for the moment her membership in this group she is dismissing and to take on the man-to-man voice of a warrior mourning his comrade is significant. It suggests an underlying truth about the entire enterprise of poetry as it has been understood by women. For many, the act of writing poems has been an initiation ceremony into the world of male power. In Bradstreet's day many important male magistrates wrote poetry: Roger Williams, William Bradford, John Cotton, Cotton Mather, even Bradstreet's father, Thomas Dudley. Though Pattie Cowell has recently revised the previously held belief that few colonial women wrote verse, poetry was conceived of as a primarily masculine occupation.[13] Bradstreet, for instance, acknowledges her father as her first real model. Because poetry was male-identified, Bradstreet and other women poets seem to feel that they must express the views of the masculine world even when such views diminish the status of women. In this passage Bradstreet no sooner allows her sex to intrude than she conceals it again and takes on the voice of the Other.

In "Of the four humours of Man's Constitution" Choler, speaking in a female voice, refers to the transformation she and her mother, Fire, have undergone.

> We both once Masculines, the world doth know,
> Now Feminines awhile, for love we owe
> Unto your Sisterhood, which makes us render
> Our noble selves in a less noble gender.

Of course, Choler's arrogance provides much of the amusement in this poem, but it is worthwhile noticing that such commonplaces of the patriarchal world as the superiority of manly fellowship to feminine love and the inferiority of the female to the male gender find their way into the poetry of even a woman like Bradstreet. They go unreproved in these poems by countervailing voices or sentiments, though most of Choler's other instances of arrogance are disputed by her sisters. Once again, we don't know what was going on in Bradstreet's mind when she wrote these lines. In a sense, we don't know how to read them, but, even though they are voiced by a persona rather than by the poet herself, they indicate a willingness to represent the views of the patriarchy. As we will see, this phenomenon occurs in the poetry of other women besides Anne Bradstreet.

The core of this vacillation—here described in terms of sexual politics—is what I call the female poet's ambivalence: such vacillation is the one fundamentally pervasive feature of American women's poetry up to 1945. In addition to the gender ambivalence described above, women poets have been prone to other variants of the same basic dis-ease: ambivalence toward the desire for power, toward their ambitions, toward their need to say "I am" boldly and effectively in the creative world.[14] The vital appetite for life that too readily turns into the death wish, aspiration that dissolves into renunciation— these are some of the characteristic movements which, when understood in a female poetic context, reflect women's uncertain standing in the patriarchal world. Let us consider Anne Bradstreet further in light of these more general statements, once again reading the poetry in the context of women's history.

Bradstreet was a member of two powerful families in the colony: the Dudleys and the Bradstreets. She was also related to the Winthrops. All power in the Puritan community derived from the family unit. Even extended kinship ties were very important. Single persons were not allowed to live alone. If they arrived from England without relatives or friends to house them, they were assigned by the magistrates to a family unit. The Church itself was seen as a family of saints, the first church being the offspring of the family of Abraham, and the state was organized to reflect this structure with a patriarch at the head and citizens who were supposed to remain loyal even to a leader they did not approve.

Despite her membership in these powerful colonial families, however, Anne Bradstreet's position was nowhere near as strong as it would have been were she a man. Wives played a dual sexual role that we may think of as reinforcing ambivalence by its very structure. On the one hand, wives were given full authority over children and servants. On the other, they were expected to defer to their husbands, to make themselves subservient, and, when agreement could not be achieved, to surrender their desires utterly to their masters'. Bradstreet captures the ambiguity of this role in her elegy to her mother where she praises her for being "an obedient wife" but remembers that she was "to Servants wisely awful."[15] Dorothy Dudley's force is conveyed in the lines:

> A true Instructor of her Family,
> The which she ordered with dexterity.

But Bradstreet does not go on at much length about her mother, whose virtues as presented in the elegy do not exceed a conventional list of feminine duties. The elegy for her father, however, gave Bradstreet the scope to talk about colonial affairs. It is twice as long and considerably more interesting than the elegy for her mother.

For women in the Puritan colony, motherhood had to substitute for political influence. Attendance at public meetings, limited voting privileges, and occasional chances at unusual careers in no way elevated the status of women generally: the mother remained the archetype of female power. In a community in which the importance of childbearing was enjoined upon Church members almost as a religious duty, women regarded their children as proof of their legitimation in the eyes of God and society. After a painful childless beginning, and agonizing self-doubt, Anne Bradstreet had eight.

Bradstreet chronicles her experience as a mother in the poem "I had eight birds hacht in one nest." One is moved by her catalog of cares and fears and amused by her wit almost to the point of ignoring the lines in which she makes writing poetry contiguous with motherhood. Toward the end of the poem she wishes her children well ("So happy may you live and die") and then proceeds to suggest that in the absence of her offspring, poetry will provide a substitute satisfaction.

> Mean while my dayes in tunes Ile spend,
> Till my weak layes with me shall end.
> In shady woods I'le sit and sing,
> And things that past, to mind I'le bring.

To ignore these lines is to ignore an important truth about the fundamentally reciprocal value of being a mother and being a poet for someone like Bradstreet. Both were creative acts in some way inviting immortality, and both provided a woman with a degree of power unavailable in other realms. In the eight birds poem, the poet hopes her words will be passed down to her children.

> Thus gone, amongst you I may live,
> And dead, yet speak, and counsel give.

In "Before the Birth of one of her Children," she asks her husband to grant her two favors if she should die in childbirth. First he must "look to my little babes my dear remains." But there is more he must do.

> And if chance to thine eyes shall bring this verse,
> With some sad sighs honour my absent Herse;
> And kiss this paper for thy loves dear sake,
> Who with salt tears this last Farewel did take.

Bradstreet did not die in childbirth, but she continued to draw upon the association these two poems make—the association between self-representation in children ("my dear remains") and self-perpetuation in art, the verses she asks her husband to kiss in her absence.

Probably the most well-known poem Anne Bradstreet wrote on this theme is "The Author to her Book." In 1650 her poems appeared in England under the title *The Tenth Muse Lately Sprung Up in America*, etc. Her brother-in-law, John Woodbridge, had apparently found a publisher for them in the mother country without her knowledge; they were an instant success. Bradstreet herself, however, reflected on her mixed feelings at seeing her work in print by composing "The Author to her Book" in which she calls her poems the "ill-form'd offspring of my feeble brain." At first the poet claims she was half-unwilling to acknowledge her "rambling brat." However, in the end she comes to hope the child will succeed and carry her name abroad.

> In Criticks hands, beware thou dost not come;
> And take thy way where yet thou art not known.

She undercuts the importance of male influences and declares in effect that this is a woman's work:

> If for thy Father askt, say, thou hadst none:
> And for thy Mother, she alas is poor,
> Which caus'd her thus to send thee out of door.

We have no evidence of the sense of frustration Bradstreet must have felt when motherhood and art came into conflict. Woodbridge, in his address to the reader, claims: "these Poems are the fruit but of some few houres, curtailed from her sleep and other refreshments." There must have been many times when one child, so to speak, threatened to displace the other. It is worth noting that women do not seem to mention their frustrations at not having enough time to write until writing becomes a more legitimate occupation for women and motherhood ceases to be regarded as a divinely imposed duty.

Although Bradstreet repeatedly calls her work a "simple mite," she admits its importance to her in terms of personal satisfaction. She was especially concerned that others recognize her work as original. Although her father was an inspiration to her, she wanted others to know that her poems had no "father." To Thomas Dudley himself she wrote: "My goods are true (though poor) I love no stealth." Emily Stipes Watts notes that one colonial woman poet (Martha Brewster, whose *Poems on Divers Subjects* was published in 1757) was forced to paraphrase a psalm extemporaneously in order to prove that she was learned enough to be the author of her own poems.[16]

Bradstreet wrote numerous poems thanking God for delivering her or some member of her family from illness. In one, "My thankful heart with glorying Tongue," she exclaims:

Accept, O Lord, my simple mite,
For more I cannot give.

Those simple words, "for more I cannot give," offer us a brief glimpse at how much she had invested in her poetry. It may have been "poor," but she was poorer without it. In several poems she offers God the tribute of her art as though this were her greatest gift.

However, she also sees her craft as a form of temptation.

O Lord, thou know'st my weak desire
Was to sing Praise to Thee.

In earlier days she seems to have been attracted to the idea of writing poetry for reasons more complicated and worldly than devotional. Some of her earliest tributes suggest that her admiration for Sidney and du Bartas, for instance, was entangled with admiration for their fame and worldly glory. Poetry, specifically understood as a powerful means to make an impression on other lives, captivated Bradstreet in this period. Her elegy for Sidney is almost entirely concerned with his fame and his influence. Very little is actually said about his poetry except:

Who knows the spels that in his Rhetorick lurks,
But some infatuate fools soon caught therein,
Fond *Cupids* Dame had never such a gin.

Similarly, the elegy for du Bartas emphasizes the relationship between poetic greatness and worldly glory transcending time.

Thy fame is spread as far, I dare be bold,
In all the Zones, the temp'rate, hot and cold.
. . . .
Immortal Bayes to thee all men allows,
Who in thy tryumphs never won by wrongs,
Lead'st millions chaind by eyes, by ears, by tongues.

She compares her muse to a child who, regarding the riches of another, wishes "some part (at least) of that brave wealth was his." Thus Bradstreet ends her Prologue to the Quaternions (written, like the tributes to du Bartas and Sidney, in the 1640s) with the previously mentioned request for recognition from the great.

And oh ye high flown quills that soar the Skies,
And ever with your prey still catch your praise,
If e're you daigne these lowly lines your eyes
Give Thyme or Parsley wreath, I ask no bayes.

She *is* ambitious, but her exaggerated modesty seems meant to hide the fact.[17] One might compare Anne Bradstreet's hopes for her poems with the carefully concealed hopes of an ambitious mother for her children. In both cases self-interest is operating behind the scenes and cannot be too openly admitted, either to oneself or to others.

The 1650s, however, were for Bradstreet a time of spiritual examination during which she rarely expressed worldly hopes. By the 1660s, if Stanford's chronology is accurate, the poet had renounced her early ambitions and was no longer in any sense advocating fame as an index of achievement.[18] Bradstreet's prose meditations (from the late '50s and the '60s) offer a perspective on this change. The poet claims God has chastened her through sickness and losses in order to turn her away from the world. "The Lord knows I dare not desire that health that sometimes I have had, least my heart should bee drawn from him, and sett upon the world" (August 28, 1656). In addition to religion, however, guilt for unwomanly aspirations may have played a part in this change. We cannot know her true feelings from this distance, though we can guess at the pressure she had been under, since she has left us her lines about "carping tongues."

It is my belief, however, that far too much has been made of Bradstreet's rebellion against the Puritan God. Ann Stanford first emphasized Bradstreet's refusal to submit by looking at some of the unresolved tensions in her lyrics. Wendy Martin speaks of her "subversive piety," comparing Bradstreet's acknowledgments of doubt with those expressed by Cotton Mather and John Winthrop, concluding that Bradstreet's, unlike the others', fail to mention the direct descent of grace. Emily Stipes Watts, however, makes the most far-reaching argument. After stating that "Anne Bradstreet could not transcend," she goes on to say: "Many American women poets would later follow just such a course—a belief in a God who refused to make any personal appearances."[19] The argument is compelling because it suggests the kind of political awareness about woman's place in patriarchal religion that we would like to ascribe to these women poets. However, I am not convinced. Bradstreet's doubts are very much in keeping with those expressed in perfectly conventional Puritan self-examinations. She (and later women poets by the dozens) wrote poems that convince me that they had a lively sense of personal proximity in their relations with a Creator. Emily Dickinson refused to join the church but she kept the Sabbath "staying at home," bringing God into her own personal space as Anne Hutchinson had done earlier. Whatever Bradstreet's former doubts, she came to sound at home with her religious beliefs. Poems like "As Weary Pilgrim" and "Contemplations" do suggest transcendence of a kind.

"Contemplations"—Bradstreet's greatest poetic achievement—was written in the 1650s. These meditations are Bradstreet's reflections on her spiritual journey, her pilgrim's progress, and they reveal a set of complicated motives. In the course of the poem, the speaker keeps vacillating between the natural world, whose creatures are often emblematic of earthly temptations, and the spiritual world in which these same desires are transformed and sanctified. The stream, for instance, represents a soul unswervingly set on its divine destination. Bradstreet complains:

> Thou emblem true, of what I count the best,
> O could I lead my Rivolets to rest,
> So may we press to that vast mansion, ever blest.

Her "rivolets" are her wayward desires and the undeviating stream, therefore, becomes her spiritual model. However, the poem itself is designed as a meditation, embodying the struggle that it serves (aesthetically at least) to resolve.

The climax of the poem occurs when the final temptation is presented, and the poet is attracted by the song of Philomel, the female bird of poetry. During the colonial period "Philomela" was used as a pseudonym for several women poets—no men, as far as I have been able to determine, called themselves by that name. Jane Colman Turell (1708-1735) mentions the English poet Elizabeth Singer Rowe in an address to her muse. She asks that "like sweet Philomela's be my name."[20] Elizabeth Rowe herself was known as Philomela, and more than a dozen editions of her works were published in America before 1800. We also know that Mercy Warren (1728–1814) sometimes signed herself "Philomela." What all of this serves to imply is that from the very beginning this women's tradition in American poetry has been a nightingale tradition, bound up with themes of aspiration and frustrated longing.

Bradstreet says:

> While musing thus with contemplation fed,
> And thousand fancies buzzing in my brain,
> The sweet-tongu'd Philomel percht ore my head,
> And chanted forth a most melodious strain
> Which rapt me so with wonder and delight,
> I judg'd my hearing better than my sight,
> And wisht me wings with her a while to take my flight.

The verb "rapt" reminds us of her earlier references to the power of Sidney's poetry to infatuate, and of du Bartas's to enchain, his readers. At first Philomel seems attractive because she "feels no sad thoughts, nor cruciating cares," a highly unconventional use of the nightingale in Renaissance poetry. But in the final stanza of this section we find Bradstreet once more equating the power of art with the power of motherhood. The overtones of this fantasy suggest that the real temptation of poetry, represented by this bird, lies in two of its effects: influence and immortality.

> The dawning morn with songs thou dost prevent,
> Sets hundred notes unto thy feathered crew,
> So each one tunes his pretty instrument,
> And warbling out the old, begin anew,
> And thus they pass their youth in summer season,
> Then follow thee into a better Region,
> Where winter's never felt by that sweet airy legion.

Philomel, in her capacity as a maternal influence, has a host of followers, and she and they escape the destructive effects of seasonal time.

In the final stanzas of the poem, however, the poet makes her bitterest and most impassioned case against "man's" stupidity in investing his hopes in earthly rewards. "Fond fool, he takes this earth ev'n for heav'ns bower." Besides making a general statement, she seems to be turning against that version of herself represented by her speaker. The speaker has also taken earth for heaven in the course of this poem. In fact, it seems that poetry itself has stimulated her to offer this bitter evaluation, perhaps because it represents her own fondest attachment to this world. Now she thrusts all her worldly longings aside and brings her poem to an orchestrated conclusion with this coda:

> O Time the fatal wrack of mortal things,
> That draws oblivions curtains over kings,
> Their sumptuous monuments, men know them not,
> Their names without a Record are forgot,
> Their parts, their ports, their pomp's all laid in th'dust.
> Nor wit nor gold, nor buildings scape times rust;
> But he whose name is grav'd in the white stone
> Shall last and shine when all of these are gone.

The poem has renounced her ambitions, her hopes for worldly eminence and the respect of "high-flown quills," in favor of divine prospects. Puritans, using the Geneva Bible, would have been familiar with the gloss on the white stone in Revelations: "such a stone was wont to be given unto them that had gotten any victory or prize, in sign of honour, and therefore it signifieth here a token of God's favor and grace."[21] She is still thinking about glory, but now she has in mind a "greater glory." That greater glory prefers transcendence.

Knowing the seventeenth century and the Puritans, we might not pause over the ambivalence in this poem and its ultimate religious resolution in the renunciation of worldly hopes, if these attitudes were not so prevalent in poet after woman poet. We do not know how to "read" Bradstreet's Puritan sentiments. Were they merely conventional, a function of her time and place? Did they stem from her particular nature? Or did her experience as a woman have something to do with the intensity with which she came to express her disillusionment with the world?

One fact is peculiarly suggestive. Long after Puritanism had declined in influence as a religious dogma, women poets like Emily Dickinson, Elinor Wylie, and Sylvia Plath continued to identify themselves with it. However, its attraction seems to lie not in its precise religious formulations nor in its historical influence in this country but in its offer of a way to transcend a restricted sexual role through the "tough"—therefore satisfying—means of self-discipline. Women have always longed to be heroes. In a world that limits female heroism to the domestic sphere, women turn to internal exploits. When Emily Dickinson writes, "Power is only Pain – / Stranded, thro' Discipline," she is expressing the Puritan psychology of these women poets.[22] By redefining and thus subverting the patriarchal conception of power, these women outwit their oppressors. Power for women becomes self-control instead of worldly supremacy.

Therefore, we should pause over Bradstreet's renunciation. We should pause and keep it in mind when we encounter similar renunciations in the work of a whole sequence of women poets. Why, for instance, were so many women writing about renunciation in the 1890s and 1900s—a period usually labelled progressive, optimistic, expansive?

Part of the aim of this book is to suggest possible reasons why. The main point, however, is to identify the preoccupations that repeatedly turn up in women's poetry, to place them in a historical context, and to establish the fact that women poets created their own tradition, a separable setting from the male tradition under which they are usually subsumed. Something has made American women poets adopt similar attitudes throughout a period of great external changes, a period of something like three hundred years. The contribution of this book is to identify these attitudes and to examine them in the context of women's experience. We are missing a great many facts. But our reading, if successful, should make the lack of these particulars less important. At the end of this study we should be able to identify more readily what kinds of poems women have written and what aspects of their generic experience are reflected in their poems.

Of course, the whole question of "women's poetry" is problematic, and the two-volume study begun here concentrates on only a limited number of individuals. Surveying poems by means of an overview means that certain poems, and certain women, will be left out. They do not reflect the archetypes and therefore they are put aside for another, for other readings. However, just as we examine Black literature, Jewish literature, Romantic literature, from a unifying perspective, and thus reduce a chaotic multiplicity of examples to a few defining exemplars, we may with women's poetry suggest the context "woman" and identify characteristics belonging to a large number of women poets. It means something particular to be a woman in American society, at least through the end of the nineteenth century—the period which is the subject of this volume. And that is why it is important to look at the way women's poetry begins to become identified with particular expectations about women's natures and lives.

The word that I have used to refer to the informing context established by this method of reading is "tradition." Tradition, however, is a slippery term that can mean many things. For our purposes tradition will refer to the context established by the comparison of women's poems with each other. This women's tradition does not imply that one woman was necessarily influenced by the others, although all the women in this study read other women poets and were deeply affected by their work. Emily Dickinson was transformed, as she tells us, by her reading of Elizabeth Barrett Browning. Amy Lowell wanted to write a biography of Emily Dickinson, and Sara Teasdale actually started one about Christina Rossetti. The nineteenth century saw women poets meeting together in literary salons, writing volumes of memorials about each other, establishing themselves as a group set apart. Louise Bogan, who would later write several essays on nineteenth-century women poets, reminds her generation: "It is a good thing for young women to bring to mind the fact that lost fragments of the work of certain women poets—of Emily Dickinson no less than of [Sappho] . . . —are searched for less with the care and eagerness of the scholar looking for bits of shattered human art, than with the hungry eyes of the treasure hunter, looking for some last grain of a destroyed jewel."[23]

Influences will be one of the concerns of this study but a lesser concern. More important will be the sense of tradition implied by the existence of a larger body of poetry to which an individual's work makes reference, consciously or unconsciously. Thus, the concept of tradition we will try to establish here will concern itself with the body of American women's poetry as a background and reference point for the work of individual women poets. It will examine consistencies more than influences. A woman poet need not be consciously invoking this tradition to be operating within its bounds. Her work, as it manifests the nature of women's experience and expresses what seems to be a generic point of view about "the way things are," brings her into the sisterhood.

Ultimately, it seems that these women poets have acted in a similar capacity to women prophets. They have constituted themselves as *"femmes sages,"* wise women, midwives of a sort, whose knowledge as it is passed on to others carries a female burden of dark and sometimes secret truths. This knowledge is part of the nightingale's burden. Thus, many of the poems we will consider will be philosophical, in the broader sense of that term. We will look at what has constituted women's poetic wisdom. In the eight birds poem, Bradstreet is partly enjoying her role as instructor, the role she also assigns to Philomel. The mother/poet figure is preemininently an advisor and a guide. Women poets throughout this tradition share with Bradstreet the delight of assuming an authoritative stance of this kind. With the same sense of exuberance they compose the female power fantasies discussed in the next chapter.

To be precise, however, one cannot say that the tradition I am describing begins in any real sense with the work of Anne Bradstreet. Though many of her poems were both successful and womanly, she was one isolated voice, and any definitive sense of tradition demands that there be numerous exemplars. The beginning of the nineteenth century witnessed the true hardening of the outlines of a woman's tradition, and Anne Bradstreet's voice was hardly heard in those years.

Evert and George Duyckinck's *Cyclopaedia of American Literature* (1855) presented Bradstreet as a Puritan poet of some importance, but they emphasized the flaws in her craftsmanship. They suggest their own preference for smooth, metrically regular lines in comments such as the following: "When we come upon any level ground in these poems, and are looking around to enjoy the prospect, we may prepare ourselves for a neighboring pitfall."[24] Little was made of Bradstreet's message to women, which may be why nineteenth-century women, so concerned with their status as an isolated group of poets, did not study her.

Nevertheless, we seem to have come full circle in our own time since two contemporary women poets, Adrienne Rich and Ann Stanford, have puzzled over the mystery of this Puritan forebear. Something in Bradstreet's work has survived "time's rust." Something speaks out to other women even in a world so completely changed. Today we tend to acknowledge the flaws in her style, the awkward inversions and occasionally halting meter, while at the same time marveling at the exuberance of her wit and the occasional sensitivity of her phrasing. Bradstreet's powers were extraordinary and her achievement remarkable given the obstacles she faced—lack of time, ill health, isolation. Modern women have discovered in her a female poet able to transcend the harassing problems of women's lives and distinguish herself in a world hostile to female achievement. Adrienne Rich admits:

> Reading and writing about Bradstreet, I began to feel that furtive, almost guilty spark of identification so often kindled in me, in [the middle sixties], by the life of another woman writer. There were real parallels between her life and mine. Like her, I had learned to read and write in my father's study; like her, I had known the ambiguities of patronizing compliments from male critics; . . . but above all, she was one of the few women writers I knew anything about who had also been a mother.[25]

Women poets have had a special importance for each other and for their women readers. They have been more than literary models. Women still ask themselves, can a woman do it? And they look for reassurance that a woman can, that she has. Even today one finds younger women combing the work of more mature poets, like Adrienne Rich for instance, for clues on how to live and how to understand a woman's experience. Women's poetry has thus served a political purpose quite in keeping with the prophetic and advisory strain in the poetry itself.

Something inheres in women's poetry that has the force of a secret kept alive by a clandestine group. The sharing of this secret, like the sharing of the past, is part of this book's undertaking.

Founding the Tradition
The Poetess at Large

2 "There is always something that violates us, deprives our voice, and compels art toward an aesthetics of silence," writes Geoffrey Hartman in "The Voice of the Shuttle."[1] In the myth Hartman refers to, Philomela, robbed of her voice, weaves her story into a tapestry and thus becomes a type of the poet, articulating a version of truth in defiance of the betrayals of language. The voice of the shuttle for Hartman is a genderless voice that, in trying to make itself heard plainly, must forever contend with the duplicitousness of meaning and the problematic relation of signifier to signified. Yet, for the woman poet, Philomela has a special significance, as those from Bradstreet on down suggest. Both as a defiled woman and as an artist urgently desiring to communicate through symbolic forms, Philomela is the type of American women poets in the nineteenth century. The aesthetic of silence, as Gilbert and Gubar point out, is quintessentially a female aesthetic. They remind us that "the girl child must learn the arts of silence either as herself a silent image invented and defined by the magic looking glass of the male-authored text, or as a silent dancer [or weaver] of her own woes, a dancer [or weaver] who enacts rather than articulates."[2]

Since the image of Philomela as nightingale is so important for this century of women poets, it is well to review the essentials of the myth. Philomela's sister Procne was married to Tereus, king of Thrace. Procne missed her sister and invited her for a visit, but Tereus sabotaged the sisters' reunion. Seized with a passion for Philomela, Tereus detoured Procne's sister, raped her, and cut out her tongue to keep her from exposing him. But Philomela embroidered the tale of her defilement in images that would "speak" to Procne. Edith Hamilton's *Mythology* comments: "She had a greater motive to make clear the story she wove than any artist ever had."[3] The whole truth, which might have eluded others, was as plain to Procne as if it had been written in words. Procne determined to avenge her sister's wrong, and the two joined forces. After sacrificing Tereus' son Itys, they served him up to Tereus at a banquet. The father, upon being told what he had eaten, determined to destroy the two women, but the gods intervened. Tereus was changed into a bird of prey (possibly a hawk), Procne into a nightingale forever mourning her son, and Philomela into a twittering swallow incapable of song. The Romans transposed the names of the birds, making Philomela the nightingale; English poetry has followed the Roman version. Philomela the nightingale is the sister who was raped, not the mother who sacrificed her child, and her melancholy song relates her injuries.[4] As the nightingale, she becomes the type of the poetess, who must use her ingenuity to overcome exile and mutilation. What is significant about this myth for our purposes is the way it records the burden of woe the nightingale carries and the peculiarly autobiographical emphasis of her art, an emphasis not lost upon another woman.

The nightingale tradition did not spring up overnight though there are traces of an equation of the woman poet with the nightingale in the colonial period, as we have seen. Still, we remember only a few of the women poets before 1800. Although Pattie Cowell in *Women Poets in Pre-Revolutionary America* tells us that "the numbers of women poets in colonial America seemed to increase exponentially in the eighteenth century,"[5] the books and magazines in which their poems appeared had a range of influence limited by the problems of distribution in eighteenth-century America. Though Cowell tells us that many of these women poets knew one another personally and exchanged their verses, few of them were remembered at all in the early nineteenth century. Those who were remembered were not the women that Cowell tells us wrote directly of women's experiences but those like Mercy Warren and Phillis Wheatley who expressed a view of American destiny that was of interest to the patriarchy.

Warren was preoccupied with political and intellectual rather than emotional experience; her models were all male. Wheatley, as Louise Bernikow comments in *The World Split Open*, is "more interesting as a phenomenon than as a poet." Because she was black and had been a slave, she had a brief vogue, but even her description of being brought from Africa in a slave ship sounds carefully tailored to please a white audience and dead to all anger. As Terence Collins has argued, Wheatley was caught in the double-bind of successful blacks.[6] She came to identify more with the white educated world that recognized her than with the black world of her origins. Wheatley was a student of Milton, with all the problems faced by women poets conceiving of their craft as sired by the patriarchy. Her poetry seems distracted both from black and from female experience. Thus it represents the compounded difficulties of being a black woman writer in America, caught between the origins of her sensibility and the expectations of her reading public.

Because of the fact that the more passionate women poets were lost to the nineteenth century, women poets of the new generation did not see themselves as carrying on a native tradition. For this reason Cowell's work is especially important, for it suggests the cycle of expression and suppression that we shall see again at the turn from the nineteenth century to the twentieth.

Yet by the end of the nineteenth century, everyone knew the figure of the American "poetess" and her tradition could not disappear entirely. For some her aesthetic seemed to be based on anything but reticence, as we see if we turn to Huck Finn's description of the poor, dead Emmeline Grangerford, a poetess *par excellence.*

> If Emmeline Grangerford could make poetry like that before she was fourteen, there ain't no telling what she could a done by-and-by. Buck said she could rattle off poetry like nothing. She didn't ever have to stop and think. He said she would slap down a line, and if she couldn't find anything to rhyme it with she would just scratch it out and slap down another one, and go ahead. She warn't particular, she could write about anything you choose to give her to write about, just so it was sadful. Every time a man died, or a woman died, or a child died, she would be on hand with her "tribute" before he was cold. She called them tributes. The neighbors said it was the doctor first, then Emmeline, then the undertaker.[7]

Twain's allusions may be obscure now but they would not have been so in their day. His humor depends partly upon their accessibility. Lucretia Davidson (1808–1825), for instance, was a child-poet like Emmeline Grangerford and wrote much of her work when she was fourteen. Her death two years later assured her instant renown in a century whose interest in death sometimes bordered on the necrophilic. She became a symbol of the frail female poet literally consumed by her own sensibility. Like Emmeline, most women poets were said to write spontaneously, without taking pains over their work and with an ability to manufacture verses "to order." Such women produced a staggering number of poems (at 71, Lydia Sigourney was still able to get down 850 lines in one spring), and they rarely revised. Finally, like Twain's character—who is the author of "Ode to Stephen Dowling Bots. Dec'd"—women poets were usually associated with elegies. One writer, Sara Lippincott (the famous "Grace Greenwood") was taunted by her brother who said: "First the undertaker, then the minister, then Sara." Twain plays with this phrase by putting Emmeline in before the undertaker.

What this passage suggests is that by the 1880s conceptions about women poets had crystallized sufficiently for Twain to feel he could depend upon a laugh of recognition when his readers encountered this passage. In fact, a consensus about women poets had emerged considerably earlier. In his tribute to Frances Osgood written in 1851, the influential editor Rufus Griswold described women's poetry in these terms:

> We turn from the jar of senates, from politics, theologies, philosohpies, and all forms of intellectual trial and conflict, to that portion of our literature which they [women] have given us, coming like dews and flowers after glaciers and rocks, the hush of music after the tragedy, silence and rest after turmoil and action.[8]

He knew, or thought he knew, what the difference was between male and female poets. Lydia Sigourney in her tribute to Felicia Hemans also thought she knew what made the British poet's work "essentially feminine": It was the depiction of "the whole sweet circle of the domestic affections,—the hallowed ministries of woman, at the cradle, the hearthstone, and the death-bed."[9]

Women poets do not seem to have resented the patronizing remarks made about their peculiar nature; they themselves felt different. Women poets of the nineteenth century saw themselves particularly linked to those of their sex who were also currently engaged in writing poetry or who had preceded them in this effort. As Ann Douglas puts it: "While a female author at the beginning of the nineteenth century was considered by definition an aberration from her sex, by its close she occupied an established if not respected place."[10]

Poe wrote of some four of five cliques who controlled the whole American literary scene; the women mentioned by Poe include Maria Brooks, Lydia Sigourney, Sarah Helen Whitman, Frances Osgood, and Elizabeth Oakes-Smith. Thus, by the middle of the nineteenth century, literary women could find a set of worthy exemplars, the first requisite of a tradition. Furthermore, women poets wrote poems to each other and edited women's memorials.[11] They had their "ladies' magazines," in which for the first time their work was welcomed and, because of the transportation revolution, distributed to a wide readership. Close friendships developed among them similar to those described as common in the nineteenth century by Carroll Smith-Rosenberg and others. These friendships provided an important network of support for those women who were entering the literary field. In the words of Smith-Rosenberg, this was "a female world in which hostility and criticism of other women were discouraged."[12]

However, there is no doubt that such women sometimes felt competitive hostility toward one another. For instance, in her memoirs Elizabeth Oakes-Smith reminisces about parties at the poet Emma Embury's house at which the guests engaged in witty repartee. Oakes-Smith says: "I remember Fannie Osgood and Phoebe Carey rather excelled in this small game, but Margaret Fuller looked like an owl at the perpetration of a pun, and I honoured her for it."[13] Expressions of esteem for another woman writer may conceal competitive anger. Here Margaret Fuller seems admirable but only at the expense of Osgood and Carey who "carried the day." Another revealing item is the letter from Sara Lippincott to Osgood that Griswold quotes in *The Memorial*. Lippincott ("Grace Greenwood") wrote: "With an 'intense and burning,' almost unwomanly ambition, I have still joyed in *your* success, and gloried in your glory; and all because Love laid its reproving finger on the lip of Envy" (p. 18). Lippincott makes no attempt to deny the possibility of competitive envy; it is merely repressed by the intervention of that maternal reproving finger. Perhaps the critical factor in her admiration for Frances Osgood lay in the fact that though each dabbled in the other's medium, Osgood (like Elizabeth Oakes-Smith) was primarily a poet whereas Lippincott (like Margaret Fuller) was primarily a prose writer. There was safety in their difference.

Tradition always presupposes feelings of both mutuality and competition, support and oppression. These writers knew their success was precarious, and as is often the case with oppressed groups, they deflected some of their feelings of hostility against the Other onto members of their own group. We know women poets had hostile feelings toward the male literary lions of their time by their surviving comments. Elizabeth Oakes-Smith, for instance, has this to say about Rufus Griswold, who helped to make her reputation: "That he was capricious and allowed his personal predilections and prejudices to sway him, is most true, for he had the whims of a woman coupled with a certain spleen he took no pains to conceal" (*Autobiography*, p. 113). Here Oakes-Smith's anger against Griswold, who dominated the literary scene, is turned back into a peculiar slap in the face of women. Her reference to "the whims of a woman" is predictable in the same way that Bradstreet's occasional expression of patriarchal views is predictable: these were commonplaces that did not invite looking into. One used them especially when one was suggesting something negative or limited about the patriarchy.

The fact that the nineteenth century saw women poets as different from men poets meant that women were always making comparisons among themselves. One result of such comparisons was the identification of significant precursors like the British poet Felicia Hemans. Hemans's influence on American women poets was enormous. Although Hemans was no feminist, she represented literary success and female independence. In 1836, a year after her death from tuberculosis at the age of forty-two, her completed *Poetical Works* were published in this country. They subsequently went through so many editions that American women poets like Lydia Sigourney sometimes saw themselves displaced by the British poet; Sigourney was saddled with the title "The American Hemans." In her essay Sigourney would have us believe that "sympathy, not fame, was the desire of [Hemans's] being" (p. xiv), but like Sigourney herself, and like the later poet Amy Lowell, Hemans was an energetic manager of her own career. Married at an early age to a young captain in the military, she gave birth to five sons. But her marriage was not successful. Rufus Griswold says, "An unhappy marriage embittered the larger part of her life."[14] Her husband was probably with her only intermittently during the years of her first publications and her growing maternal responsibilities. When his health forced him to retire to Italy, "the literary pursuits of Mrs. Hemans rendering it ineligible for her to leave England," as the guarded American introduction puts it, she stayed to pursue her career and raise her five sons in the company of her mother and sister.[15] Hemans was financially extremely successful, and she was praised by Byron, Shelley, and Wordsworth.

Although Hemans is still vaguely remembered for her famous line "The boy stood on the burning deck," we can no longer imagine the way her name was cherished and her work admired by women on both sides of the Atlantic. Undoubtedly influential on American women poets, she set the example for them by writing long poems on the "affections" and on famous female figures of the past. "The Forest Sanctuary," which she considered her best work, offers an example of a theme that became standard in the American female canon, a retreat to a "bower of refuge" in order to escape some violent assault, whether upon the body or the consciousness, and to experience a creative sense of freedom impossible in the world left behind. The kind of poem that explores this theme—I call it the sanctuary poem— will be discussed more fully later. Here I simply want to say that Hemans's subjects, her melancholy tone, and her ambivalence toward freedom are also characteristic of American women poets of the same period. She was looked upon as a kind of sacrosanct model and eulogized by Elizabeth Barrett Browning, among others.

A sense of tradition, then, developed among women based upon their membership in a separate sexual caste. Unlike American men who were preoccupied during this period with establishing a national literature distinct from British traditions, American women poets in the nineteenth century were perfectly willing to acknowledge solidarity with their English sisters, first with Felicia Hemans and later with Elizabeth Barrett Browning. As long as women's lives have been less concerned with commerce and the state than with a certain predetermined set of domestic expectations, their poetry has recognized affinities extending across national boundaries. In *Literary Women* Ellen Moers says that after 1850 women poets everywhere wrote love sonnets like those of Elizabeth Barrett Browning in frank acknowledgment that they recognized a female literary tradition. Similarly, after Hemans's poetry began to be published in this country in the early nineteenth century, American women poets started seeing their work in terms of a line of women writers going all the way back to Sappho.[16] Hemans herself had written on Sappho and a number of American women followed suit. In her "Ode to Sappho" Elizabeth Oakes-Smith asks her great precursor:

> What hast thou left, proud one? what token?
> Alas! a lyre and heart—both broken!   [G][17]

Nothing defines so well the perspective women poets had on both themselves and their art as the notion of separate spheres. Oakes-Smith's pairing of the lyre and the heart is a reference not merely to Sappho but to a complex of theories about women familiar in the nineteenth century. Men think, women feel. The male poet describes "all forms of intellectual trial and conflict," as Griswold tells us. The female poetic sensibility equates the strings of the lyre with heartstrings. At no other time in America's history have categorical distinctions dividing male and female natures been so universally accepted and so energetically reinforced by the culture. Several excellent studies of this phenomenon exist.[18] From our semiotic approach, we can see women's poetry as a sign of this culture. Felicia Hemans wrote: "Is not the life of woman all bound up / In her affections?" Sigourney quotes this poem approvingly, noting that Hemans captures the dual nature of woman's lot when she says, "*we* were made / For love and grief" (*The Works of Mrs. Hemans*, p. xiii). Julia Ward Howe's poem "Woman" presents the full panoply of virtues associated with "the cult of true womanhood": her ideal self is pious, pure, submissive, and domestic. The poem begins:

> A vestal priestess, proudly pure,
>   But of a meek and quiet spirit;
> With soul all dauntless to endure,
>   And mood so calm that naught can stir it,
> Save when a thought most deeply thrilling

> Her eyes with gentlest tears is filling,
> Which seem with her true words to start
> From the deep fountains at her heart.   [G]

Still, there is poignancy in the way some of the very women who
express their admiration for this model being confess to their own
sense of inadequacy and guilt. Howe ends her poem by crying, "Alas!
I would that I were she." Even the independent Lucy Larcom, whose
life is given in greater detail in the next chapter, tells us in her autobiography that the true task of woman is to be a helper, her real
power displaying itself in receiving and giving inspiration rather than
in performing heroic actions.

Probably the most intriguing poem on the subject of womanhood is
Frances Osgood's "Woman." Here we find not only conventional
attitudes regarding women but also one of the clearest expressions of
internal conflict concerning the female role. In the beginning of the
poem, it looks as if Osgood is expressing feminist sentiments.

> Taught to restrain, in cold Decorum's school,
> The step, the smile, to glance and dance by rule;
> To smooth alike her words and waving tress,
> And her pure *heart*'s impetuous play repress;
> Each airy impulse—every frolic thought
> Forbidden, if by Fashion's law untaught,
> The graceful houri of your heavenlier hours
> Forgets, in gay saloons, her native bowers.

Although the poem is addressed to men, the poet's perception of the
repressive aspects of patriarchal culture seems polemical here. As one
reads on, however, one recognizes the familiar belief that love re-
leases woman's soul and makes her more herself. We are told that
Love from above "plays on her pinions shut" and restores woman to
her real nature.

> No longer then the toy, the doll, the slave,
> But frank, heroic, beautiful, and brave,
> She rises, radiant in immortal youth,
> And wildly pleads for Freedom and for Truth!

However, freedom and truth, it turns out, do not mean the opportunity to engage in the "sterner" occupations allotted to men, but
something more like the opportunity to express selfish caprice. Osgood rejects feminist demands for independence, "The cold re-
formers know not what they ask." She especially doesn't want

women to "forgo the poetry of life, / The sacred names of mother, sister, wife!" Man, she says, needs woman to remind him of his higher nature. Having once said this, however, her underlying resentment breaks out once more: "Yet men too proudly use their tyrant power." They chill, bind, and silence women. What is to be the resolution of this conflict? In the most peculiar moment of all in this poem, Osgood ends by answering:

> Smile on, sweet flower! soar on, enchanted wing!
> Since she ne'er asks but for *one trifling thing*,
> Since but *one* want disturbs the graceful fay,
> Why, *let* the docile darling *have—her way!*[19]

The numerous words that are italicized reveal the strength of Osgood's feeling here and her felt need to overcome ambiguities. But one can't help noticing the choice of words that seem in context condescending, words like "trifling," "the graceful fay," and "the docile darling." Who is it that the poet is ridiculing? Who is the joke on? At one level it seems to be on the very woman for whom she has provided a spirited defence in other parts of the poem. Here she is once again "the toy, the doll, the slave." Her willfulness is to be indulged but only, one senses, in order to keep her from asking for more than "one *trifling* thing." But perhaps this is only a way of manipulating the men the poet is addressing. There is an implicit condemnation of them in the way the language of the last stanza parodies patronizing male attitudes. But finally, since the description of what the woman deserves is quite close to fantasies the poet elsewhere identifies as her own (see "Caprice," for example), one suspects the presence of some form of self-contempt. After struggling with the implications of this seemingly light-hearted work, we are reminded that elsewhere Osgood replied to a person who told her to write from her heart, by saying:

> Ah! woman still
> Must veil the shrine,
> Where feeling feeds the fire divine,
> Nor sing at will,
> Untaught by art,
> The music prison'd in her heart!
>
> ["Ah! Woman Still," *Poems*]

Lately it has been asked whether we should attempt to get at the truth content of women's poetry at all or whether, entering a woman's poem by another means, we should confine ourselves to the poet's use of figurative language. This argument disdains the auto-biographical content of poetry, claiming that, since language is inherently fictive, it creates masks no matter how "true" it attempts to be. Margaret Homans, for instance, considers what she calls "a feminine tradition" in *Women Writers and Poetic Identity* without making any real attempt to connect poems with biography. Her tradition is based on a theory that women poets belong together because they have faced the same obstacles. She cautions:

> With the aim of countering traditional illusions about femininity, the prevailing feminist opinion is that poetry by women must report on the poet's experience as a woman, and that it must be true. Although it is appropriate that readers learn to expand their notions of what constitutes acceptable poetic subject matter . . . this emphasis on truth implies a mistaken, or at least naive, belief about language's capacity not just for precise mimesis but for literal duplication of experience. . . . They assume that telling the truth without any sort of mask is both possible and desirable. . . . It is chasing phantoms to expect that language will suddenly work for the expression of women's truth. This aim is *fundamentally antithetical to the aims of poetry,* and it dooms itself by denying itself the power that poetry offers.[20] [Emphasis mine]

Like Osgood, Homans believes that the essence of women's poetry lies not in its revelations but its dislocated and dislocating rhetoric, what we might call its dislocutions.

I have quoted Homans's argument at length because I think it important. Elsewhere she reminds us, quite rightly, of the impact of patriarchal literature on the woman poet. Reading, she says, is for the poet what living in society is for the novelist—the essential nurturing experience. She points to the difficulties women poets have faced in expressing themselves, even in possessing to any real extent their own subjectivity because the literature in which they encounter themselves is so masculinist. However, to say that language and tradition inflict special wounds on the woman poet, making it necessary for her to maneuver and thus exploit the fictive capacities of her medium, is to say something akin to what Osgood says above. What Homans does not seem to concern herself about is that women poets, much like Philomela, have wanted their poems to convey autobiographical messages and these messages, for all that they come veiled and "slant," are part of these poets' aims. Homans errs, I think, in assuming that the "aims of poetry" are somehow inherent in the medium itself, separable from culture and not influenced by considerations of gender. The "intentional fallacy" cautions us not to confuse the poet's conscious desires for the poem with the full meaning of the poem itself. Nevertheless, the poet's meanings are and should be part of our consideration of the poem.

If we take Frances Osgood as an example, we are led to conclude that part of her intention in writing poetry was to express the burden of an overwrought sensibility that had few satisfactory outlets. Osgood had some sort of relationship with Edgar Allan Poe, possibly a sexual affair, and his appeal for her seems by her own account to have been just this understanding of her nature and her art. The major proponent of the sexual affair theory, John Evangelist Walsh, says: "As a writer of short fiction, even in most of her poetry, Fanny was relentlessly autobiographical, frequently including at least a portion of herself in the picture, and more often she was at center stage."[21] However, a poem like "Woman" tantalizes because of its uncontrolled tensions, which suggest that the tamed autobiographical impulse is one that often sublimates a deeper need to express unconventional and therefore unacceptable feelings. In "To the Spirit of Poetry" Osgood confesses that this spirit (perhaps connected with Edgar Allan Poe) knows how "to woo and win me from my grief's control" (G). Osgood's lack of a secure hold upon herself was noticed by many. Walsh says: "Seemingly in a moment, Fanny would pass from a smiling, mature woman to a capricious child, producing an effect little short of grotesque" (p. 10).[22]

There is considerable evidence that other women also used poetry as a way of giving form to what would otherwise be a shaky sense of subjectivity. Elizabeth Oakes-Smith became famous for her long poem "The Sinless Child." In her *Autobiography* she admits that "The Sinless Child" was written to communicate her feelings about "some things in my own life and experience."[23] Lucy Larcom's "Loyal Woman's No" (discussed in the next chapter) represented her feelings about a real suitor who had proposed marriage. Lavinia Stoddard's "The Soul's Defiance" impressed Rufus Griswold as a poem worthy of George Herbert. In his introduction to Stoddard's work, he writes: " 'The Soul's Defiance,' " her brother informed me, 'was interesting to her immediate friends for the truthfulness with which it portrayed her own experience and her indomitable spirit, which never quailed under any circumstances' " (G). My point is not that these poems represent the "whole truth" about the poet or that their language could or should be transparent, any more than we can believe that Lavinia Stoddard "never quailed under any circumstances." What these poems do represent is a sort of palimpsest. The second writing, so to speak, gives us the version of a self made acceptable to nineteenth-century patriarchal society, and it is interesting for the information it gives us in this regard. Society as well as reading plays a central part in the choice of a self to reveal. The deeper and less accessible script points to the part of the self that has been violated, almost rubbed out, but that speaks nevertheless. Twain's voluble poetess is consistent with an aesthetic of silence and the voice of the shuttle after all.

There is ample evidence that women poets in the nineteenth century felt unable to express their true feelings directly, whether because of internal or external pressures or some combination of both. In Emily Dickinson's words, they "tell all the truth but tell it slant." To make this poetry intelligible today we must recover the grounds of its being, which include the historical factors that inhibited free speech to begin with.

One of these factors is the theory of separate spheres. Women are defined by their relationship to love. In Emma Embury's poem "Oh! Tell Me Not of Lofty Fate" the argument runs:

> Man's sterner nature turns away
>   To seek ambition's goal;
> Wealth's glittering gifts, and pleasure's ray,
>   May charm his weary soul;—
> But woman knows one only dream—
>   That broken, all is o'er.   [M]

In "Widow at her Daughter's Bridal," Lydia Sigourney sums this up in the line, "The soul of woman lives in love." As Nancy Cott and others have noted, the idea that women should be submissive, long-suffering, other-worldly figures, both inspiring and redeeming the coarser natures of men by ministering to them in the home and devotedly educating their children, sometimes seemed to the women of the period less a repressive than a sustaining notion. Cott says, "The demarcation of women's sphere from men's provided a secure, primary, social classification for a population who refused to admit ascribed statuses, for the most part, but required determinants of social order" (p. 98). The cult of domesticity also gave women a sense of importance, satisfaction, and solidarity with other women. We should not underestimate the attraction of an identity model that seemed to provide both security and status.

Furthermore, the rhetoric concerning woman's place reinforced the idea that woman's role represented real power. In an article titled "The Rights of Women" by John L. Clark, which appeared in the December 1853 issue of *Godey's Lady's Book,* Clark insists:

> Oh, that women would be true to themselves, and consider the exalted position they occupy! Consider how far it transcends that of men! What an influence they possess in controlling popular will!

> Then they will not stoop to mingle in the strifes and petty jealousies that clamor so loudly for "Women's Rights"; but, from their high station, frown upon everything so repugnant to a high-minded and true-hearted woman. [p. 544]

Although we might object to the clearly defensive and self-serving position which this male writer takes, it was a position also shared by many women. An eighteen-year-old girl, reading Hannah More's *Strictures on the Modern System of Female Education,* wrote: "oh every man of sense must humbly bow before woman. She bears the sway, not man as he presumptiously supposes" (Cott, p. 99).

Catharine Beecher, one of the most highly vocal of the theoreticians who concerned themselves with woman's role in society, advised:

> Let every woman become so cultivated and refined in intellect, that her taste and judgment will be reverenced; so unassuming and unambitious, that collision and competition will be banished; so "gentle and easy to be entreated," that every heart will repose in her presence; then, the fathers, the husbands, and the sons, will find an influence thrown around them, to which they will yield not only willingly but proudly.[24]

Beecher consistently advocated a position that, while seeming to yield all authority, would subvert male power and, quite without appearing to do so, dominate through the force of subtle influence. Under cover of operating in a separate sphere, women were actually establishing goals and asserting their claims to prominence in ways that tried to parallel those of male society. They talked of their "ambition" to please their husbands. They used metaphors from politics and business to describe their domestic roles.[25] For the first time, domesticity was seen as an occupation, a career.

However, in reality a symmetrical struggle was going on. Under the guise of submission and self-sacrifice, women were actually asserting their rights to power and making their wills felt. Men, under the guise of acknowledging this power, were, like John L. Clark, desperately hoping that women would "not stoop to mingle in the strifes and petty jealousies that clamor so loudly for 'Women's Rights'; but, from their high station, frown upon everything. . . ." The pedestal, that "high station," had now been built.

It is easy to see that the reason Catharine Beecher was rarely attacked by men, whereas the Grimké sisters, Elizabeth Oakes-Smith, and other feminist lecturers often were, was that this new elevation of women in reality protected men from having to take them seriously "down here" where life was actually carried on. The result of this struggle was that, unlike men, women felt guilty when they undertook literary careers, even when literary work had been incorporated into "women's sphere." The reassurance of "supporters" like Rufus Griswold must have seemed hollow. Griswold was willing to support women like Frances Osgood because "she had no need to travel beyond the legitimate sphere of woman's observation." In other words, she limited herself to a set of perceptions that in no way challenged patriarchal power. Griswold was incensed with women who "quit their sphere" and ventured into politics or "rude or ignoble passion" (*The Memorial*, p. 29).

Thus, although the woman writer may not have been seen as standing in overt competition with literary men, it was still obvious to many women that they were doing something not quite feminine in entering the literary world. When Caroline Gilman discovered that one of her poems had been secretly passed to a Boston paper for publication, she cried half the night. Later she admitted to being "as alarmed as if I had been detected in man's apparel."[26] Women poets knew they must be careful. Sara Josepha Hale put it: "The path of poetry, like every other path in life, is to the tread of woman, exceedingly circumscribed. She may not revel in the luxuriance of fancies, images and thoughts, or indulge in the license of choosing themes at will, like the lords of creation."[27] This explains the shyness of many women who chose pseudonyms rather than appear in print under their own names or who simply avoided publicity altogether. Lucy Larcom wrote: "I could never understand a girl feeling any pleasure in placing herself 'before the public.' The privilege of seclusion must be the last one a woman can willingly sacrifice."[28] Often women's families objected to publicity, if they didn't. Lydia Sigourney's husband insisted that she use a pseudonym until she finally rebelled and took her own name in print. He wrote: "Who wants or would value a wife who is to be the public property of the whole community?"[29]

For all the influence it was said women had, to "give or withhold a literary reputation," or to "exercise the ultimate control over the Press,"[30] they knew how fragile and circumscribed their power really was. Although women like Sara Josepha Hale were nominal editors of the ladies' magazines, they were in fact controlled by their publishers, who were male. These women were deeply influenced and deeply debilitated by their own internalized sense of guilt over their desire for power. One can see this in the many poems that denigrate ambition such as Emma Embury's "Oh, Tell Me Not of Lofty Fate." In direct contrast to this attitude are the typically positive portrayals of ambition one finds in male poems of the period, such as Park Benjamin's "To One Beloved." In this poem the speaker loses his love but ends by looking forward to achievement in the world as a substitute.

> The future vast
> Before me lifts majestic steeps on high,
> Which I must stand upon before I die!
>   For, in the past
> Love buried lies; and nothing lives but fame
> To speak unto the coming age my race and name.[31]

This kind of poem could not have been written by a nineteenth-century woman. Although critics like Ann Douglas have tried to argue for the dominance of a feminine sensibility over the literary scene, this mode influenced a limited number of male poets. The poems of writers like Nathaniel Willis and Henry Tuckerman, a few moments in Longfellow's work, the gothicism of Poe, these might be the result of "feminine" influences, but in the main the attitudes toward power, fate, and duty expressed by men were different from those expressed by women. The nightingale's burden had a specifically feminine tone.

It is interesting to compare, for instance, the poems on poets and poetry that women wrote with those written by men. As Douglas says, "Much of the contemporary writing on the stereotypic feminine figure suggests that, if woman precipitates and represents sensibility, she must inevitably prove this precisely by her sensitivity to pain" (*Feminization of American Culture*, p. 46). Women poets incorporated this notion into their definition of the poet. In "The Bard" Elizabeth Oakes-Smith describes the origin of the poetic impulse in these lines:

> Chained to our rock, the vulture's gory stain
>   And tearing beak is every moment rife
>   Renewing pangs that end but with our life.
> Thence bursteth forth the gushing voice of song,
>   The soul's deep anguish thence an utterance finds,
>   Appealing to all hearts.   [G]

But in some poems guilt, conflated with the whole project of literary self-declaration, announces itself in the implication that women must pay for their presumption as poets by suffering. Thus, in "The Picture of a Departed Poetess," Elizabeth Eames breaks out:

> Yet oh, thy expression tells us that thou hast sorrowed,
>   And in thy yearning, human heart, *atoned*
> For thy soul's lofty gifts.   [Emphasis mine. G]

And in her essay on Hemans, Sigourney carefully tells us that Hemans's genius was educated by "the infusion of sorrow," a necessary addition to allow her sympathy with those who mourn.

During this phase of American women's history, it is hard to find a woman expressing pride in her success. Countless women's poems tell us that a poet must refuse to think of fame. Similarly, Elaine Showalter allows us to see that women novelists in England were also experiencing internal pressures which made them fearful of their own ambitions. In *A Literature of Their Own* she says: "By working in the home, by preaching submission and self-sacrifice, and by denouncing female self-assertiveness, they [the feminine novelists] worked to atone for their own will to write" (p. 25). The same could be said for American women poets.

American male poets of this period almost never associate the poet with a highly developed capacity for pain. Nor do they denounce fame to the same degree or with the same intensity. Men usually talk about perceptions of nature, order, aesthetics, or humanitarianism as the critical capacities of the poetic nature. Women poets like Catherine Warfield and Eleanor Lee write of grief:

> I feel that I have sorrows wild
>   In my heart buried deep—
> Immortal griefs, that none may share.
>   ["I Walk in Dreams of Poetry," G]

Dreams of poetry for these women meant dreams of sorrow. Even Margaret Fuller reminds us, "Each Orpheus must to the abyss descend."[32]

Nevertheless, sorrow was literary capital. The new opportunities for literary expression provided by the availability of education and the rise of ladies' magazines opened a door for women that had been closed before. Women formed the bulk of the reading public and publishers were quick to see the market potential in this new semi-educated class. Magazines like *Godey's Lady's Book, Lady's Magazine,* and *Graham's Magazine* were highly successful ventures. Lucy Larcom records that the factory girls at the Lowell mills read them avidly. So did a wide range of women from many parts of the country. Because of the outlets they provided for women writers, it became possible for women to sell their literary productions and thereby support not only themselves but their families. Both Lydia Sigourney and Elizabeth Oakes-Smith did this. Oakes-Smith estimated that 500 women in the country were then engaged as authors, editors, and contributors to the field. It was, after all, the great era of the poetess. The wives of eminent intellectuals were often poets. Emerson's first wife, Ellen, wrote poetry; Maria Lowell, James Russell Lowell's wife, was one of the poets T. W. Higginson recommended to Emily Dickinson. Alice B. Neal, in an article titled "American Female Authorship," wrote: "The time is gone past when literary tastes or pursuits are admitted as a stigma upon the social relation of any woman."[33] Walt Whitman, for his part, was not so sanguine. In the Brooklyn *Daily Times* of July 9, 1857, he wrote: "The Majority of people do not want their daughters trained to become authoresses and poets. We want a race of women turned out from our schools, not of pedants and bluestockings. One genuine woman is worth a dozen Fanny Ferns."[34] Though they differ, both views suggest that women were experiencing new urges in the direction of self-assertion and the will to literary power. The struggle was on.

However, with equal force, women reminded themselves that they shouldn't expect too much. Insofar as they desired power, they felt guilty.[35] They knew that these new opportunities were entailed, and often they reinforced their own sense of powerlessness by admitting the justice of such restrictions. Many women poets express a longing for freedom, but in an equal number of cases they reject this aspiration. Pessimism pervades women's poetry during this period to a much higher degree than it does men's. Fearful of what might follow an open declaration of ambition, women poets generally expressed their demands for fulfillment in terms of a belief in an afterlife. Elizabeth Oakes-Smith asks:

> Life-Giver! who hast planted in the soul
> This seed-time dread of hopes too high for earth,
> Emotions, yearning, time may not control,
> In heaven alone, Oh! hath the harvest birth?
>
> ["Stanzas," G]

For every cry for life there is a corresponding surrender to renunciation. Indeed, in at least one archetypal poem of the period—the "free bird" poem—one finds aspirations for freedom and renunciation in the same work. Through an analysis of this composite body of verse, one is led to the conclusion that women poets' primary attitude toward experience is an ambivalent combination of fear and desire. Reflecting on their own fears, these poets speak for many gifted women. What Kathryn Kish Sklar has written about Catharine Beecher might as easily be said about women poets as a group. Catharine Beecher's sensibility included "a rich mixture of affirmation and denial. Her own attitude toward her abilities alternated between a desire to succeed and a will to fail. Her talents were profoundly shaped by the channels of self-doubt they passed through and the restricted openings she permitted them."[36]

One is sometimes tempted to be irritated with Catharine Beecher.

Like these women poets she was inclined to be self-indulgent and she
stopped short of a radical political analysis of women's position in the
culture. But to wish women writers had written other books, or to
speak unsympathetically of their narcissism, as some critics do,
seems to me a serious failure to acknowledge the vulnerability and
terror women experienced in their creative lives. Some of their dilem-
mas will be considered in the next chapter. Here a discussion of three
basic categories of poems will allow us to explore poetic manifesta-
tions of the uncertainty such women obviously felt. These poems
may be classified as identifications with power, identifications with
powerlessness, and reconciling poems that attempt to establish a
ground for power in the midst of powerlessness itself.

The three categories I have proposed for examining the ambivalence characteristic of women's poetry are in no way meant to be
exhaustive. They are merely useful as models for a particular set of
attitudes. The nineteenth century itself thought in terms of discrete
categories, and therefore it seems appropriate to use these tools to
explore the female poetic vision it established. However, in the same
way that we feel annoyed when we examine early editions of Dickinson's poems and find them divided into poems on "nature" or "love,"
we chafe at these categories because they reduce the differences
among poets and poems in order to make a general point. What is
useful about having the "power fantasy" or the "free bird" poem or
the "sanctuary" poem as discrete types to look at is not the way they
establish patterns of influence, nor even the way they reflect the
cultural experience of the nineteenth century. Ultimately, these
poems are useful as paradigmatic reflections of what continue to be
feminine patterns of thought even far into the twentieth century.
Some of the *topoi* suggested here will be transformed as women return to them at a later period. The sensibility poem, for instance,
becomes "the burden of beauty" that Lizette Reese, Sara Teasdale,
Edna Millay, and even Sylvia Plath suffer under. We hear the earlier
description of the poet as a person who must be tormented in many
twentieth-century women's poems that detail the cost of writing
poetry, what H.D. calls "the cold splendour of song/and its bleak
sacrifice" ("The Islands").

I have throughout this chapter culled examples from various
women poets as though their works could be treated without distin-
guishing one poet from another. This is not true if we look at the way
the poems reflect the biographies, and in the next chapter we will
make some attempt to do this. Here it seems useful to begin by
examining what is shared among these women poets. The selves
revealed here have all been declared acceptable by nineteenth-

century editors, and thus at one level they may be considered stamped with the signature of their times. At another level, however, these poems may provide insights into conflicts the poets themselves had no intention of revealing.

To the first category of identifications with power belong some of the most fascinating and overlooked of nineteenth-century women's poems. We are accustomed to thinking of these women poets as renunciatory or lamenting, but we must also be careful to acknowledge that what Barbara Welter found in young girls' diaries is also present in women's poems. In *Dimity Convictions*, Welter says: "The young girl, however much she is warned against ambition, might eschew fame and wealth as unsuitable for females, but she was quite explicit in her desire for power" (p. 7). Welter finds this desire for power deflected through the medium of marriage. In women's poems we also find deflections, projections, or displacements. One of the most prevalent derives from the cult of sensibility. Women were often praised for their lively sensibility by men. Griswold says of Osgood: "She always had the quick sensibility of childhood" (*The Memorial*, p. 17). But ambitious women like Margaret Fuller and Catharine Beecher tried to refashion this quality to make it not childlike but the key to mature transcendence. Frances Osgood herself wrote numerous poems that carry a subversive message to the patriarchy, challenging the male perspective on feminine sensibility and its particular genius, the Fancy.

In the nineteenth century Romantic and Neo-Romantic critics often distinguished between Fancy and Imagination, giving the latter powers to perceive universal laws. (For Emerson in "Nature," "Imagination may be defined to be the use which the Reason makes of the material world.") Fancy, in contrast, simply produces images spontaneously without recourse to absolutes. Remembering the distinctions made between male and female poets, it is easy to see why women poets would find themselves left to the realm of Fancy. At times the words are used interchangeably, but some women poets seem to demand the distinction, attempting to overturn the status implications. We find Elizabeth Oakes-Smith, for instance, in her "Farewell to Fancy" saying that some had called Fancy a lower creature but it was her poetic muse nonetheless. The notion of universal absolutes sometimes conflicts with the notion of separate spheres. When women fantasize about power, they stumble against this conflict.

In Osgood's "A Flight of Fancy," one discovers a typical feminine fantasy. Here Fancy is the female principle, a force not unlike caprice for Osgood. She claims the right to her freedom but in so doing she subverts the reigning order. Placed on trial, she must be caught by a lawyer who appeals to her narcissism.

> He held up a *mirror*, and Fancy was caught
> By her image within it,—so lovely she thought.

Her crime is that she has completely bedazzled Reason. She seems at the same time to be a female sexual principle, because she scandalizes the old spinsters, "maidens of uncertain age." As is typical of the sensibility poems, she has the attributes of a bird. Arrayed against her are the forces of the patriarchy and its supporters, who try to jail her and make Reason her keeper. But true to the power-fantasy form, she escapes (through "the hole in the lock, which she could not undo").[37] This final line is the most suggestive. If women are going to be caught and held captive by the patriarchy, their only escape—the poem implies—may be through the very image of their sexuality (this ardent sensibility) that has been used to defeat them. Here this is represented as the lock which contains this mysterious hole. It is a lock women cannot undo entirely, though they may be able to turn it to their own advantage.

Another power fantasy that expresses its references to feminine sensibility through images of flight is Margaret Fuller's "Dryad Song." In this poem the speaker claims she feels immortal. She is "running on air, mad with life, dizzy, reeling." Love is the source of this feeling, but its effect on the speaker is to make her disown all vulnerability. "Chance cannot touch me! Time cannot hush me! / Fear, Hope, and Longing, at strife / Sink as I rise, . . ."[38] The normal difficulties of life fall away, and the speaker escapes into a world where she has infinite power, where she can in fact fly—an accomplishment which, when fantasized, is connected by Freud with latent sexual longing. Obviously here it is meant to suggest fulfillment of a more general sort.

Sexuality rarely makes a full appearance in these women's poems but highly charged language sometimes invites one to read certain poems as having a sexual content. Osgood's "The Cocoa-Nut-Tree" is a perfect example. In this poem the speaker identifies herself with the tree—"it loves like me"—and yet this tree is strikingly masculine in its form,

> With its stately shaft, and its verdant crown,
> And its fruit in clusters drooping down.

Lest one jump too quickly to the conclusion that Osgood uses this poem to confess a latent longing for a masculine sexual identity, the poem advises us that the advantages to be derived from the tree are possible only at the expense of its sexuality. Palm wine, we are told in the fourth and fifth stanzas, is made by tying up the embryo bud to prevent the plant from producing its sexual parts: the flower and the nut. The poet goes on to say:

> Ah, thus to the child of genius too,
>   The rose of beauty is oft denied;
> But all the richer, that high heart, through
>   The torrent of feeling pours its tide,
> And purer and fonder, and far more true,
>   Is that passionate soul in its lonely pride.
>   Oh, the fresh, the free,
>   The cocoa-nut tree,
>   Is the tree of all trees for me! [G]

It is hard not to feel that this woman, and in fact many women of the eighteenth and nineteenth centuries, saw feeling and poetic sensibility as means for transcending their sexual role. Sex itself seems frightening in their frankest reflections on it, a tool for humiliating women and subjugating them by brute force.[39] Thus, the speaker in "The Cocoa-Nut Tree," who identifies herself with a fundamentally male symbol, seems to be fantasizing possibilities of freedom and power accorded to "the passionate soul in its lonely pride" rather than seeking any real sexual transformation or sexual power.

Osgood wrote many passionate love poems, and it was rumored that she had had an affair with Poe. She may even have borne his child, the elusive Fanny Fay who died before the age of two. If so it may have been Poe's seduction of Osgood that turned Griswold so violently against him. She was considered naively pure and childlike. In her autobiographical story "Ida Grey," she described herself as "too pure, too aerial, too finely organized for [her husband's] rougher and warmer temperament."[40] Everywhere her expressed attitude toward genital sexuality is negative. As for Elinor Wylie, passion is for Osgood an affair of the soul not the body. One need only read "The Triumph of the Spiritual over the Sensual" or "Reflections" to find this expressed. In the latter poem Osgood maintains that woman's sensibility is more elevated than man's:

> For God taught her—but they had learned of men
> The meager task of how to mete out love,
> A selfish, sensual love, most unlike hers.
> . . . .
> And yet that he should let a lyre of heaven
> Be played upon by such hands, with touch so rude,

> Might wake a doubt in less than perfect faith,
> Perfect as mine, in his beneficence.   [G]

Although the "she" in the poem is supposed to be woman in the abstract, the tone implies a very personal involvement with this issue. The lyre, at once an image of female sexuality and poetic sensibility, must be protected from the rude touch of men and their "coarser sense." The assertion of faith in the patriarchial deity is defensive, unconvincing: merely public. The last line pulls her back from rebellion just in time.

One of the most curious power fantasies is A. R. St. John's "Medusa." Later this mythological figure would suggest herself to both Louise Bogan and Sylvia Plath. Gilbert and Gubar suggest that the Medusa is the monster counterpole of the angel image of woman in patriarchal literature. Both must be subdued. St. John in this odd poem captures the attraction of the monster's power and at the same time the guilt associated with that attraction. For the speaker in this poem, the Medusa awakens ambivalent feelings: she calls her "demon goddess, power divine." Unlike so many poems by nineteenth-century women about classical figures, this poem does not moralize. Although the speaker seems to desire some simple explanation of the Medusa's nature, she acknowledges the impossibility of finding one and provides us instead with a clear picture of the conflicting feelings this figure arouses in her.

> Fatal beauty, thou dost seem
> The phantom of some fearful dream;
> *Extremes of horror and of love*
> *Alternate o'er our senses move,*
> As, wrapt and spell-bound, we survey
> The fearful coils which round thee play,
> And mark thy mild, enduring smile,
> Lit by no mortal fire the while.   [Emphasis mine. G]

Curiously, the speaker seems to want to identify with the Medusa as a symbol of endurance ("Oh couldst thou unto mortals give / Thy strength to suffer, grace to live"), but she also feels the necessity of projecting onto the Medusa human feelings of remorse for the destruction she has caused. Taken as a whole, this is a fascinating and highly ambivalent poem, one that looks forward to Sara Teasdale's portrayals of Guenevere and Helen as women whose female power is both alluring and destructive. As an image of the poet, Medusa represents that violated wild self whose power is felt as the spirit of poetry, "the phantom of some fearful dream."

In a lighter vein, Lucretia Davidson's "Auction Extraordinary" makes use of the dream frame to play out her fantasy of power. The speaker dreams that the town's bachelors are being taxed "in order to make them all willing to marry." When the bachelors refuse to pay the tax, they are all sold off at auction.

> The auctioneer then in his labor began,
> And called out aloud, as he held up a man,
> "How much for a bachelor? Who wants to buy?"
> In a twink, every maiden responded, "I,—I."
> In short, at a highly extravagant price,
> The bachelors all were sold off in a trice:
> And forty old maidens, some younger, some older,
> Each lugged an old bachelor home on her shoulder.   [G]

What is being challenged here is the hierarchy of power in which women must wait for men to make marriage proposals, wait for men to make the important decisions. Although within the dream the women seem perhaps too eager to purchase their men, the speaker maintains an ironic distance in her judgment that the price is "highly extravagant" and her implication that the bachelors are a burden to lug around. Through her distance she manages to share both the power achieved by reversal that the dream represents and a higher order of power that can subjugate both the maidens and the bachelors beneath its irony. The whole poem, written by a girl less than seventeen years old, expresses in a humorous way some of the feelings of ambivalence women had concerning marriage, a relationship perceived to represent both power and powerlessness. Davidson herself, like many talented young girls her age, had sworn never to marry. More will be said on this subject in the next chapter.

It is relatively easy to locate poems that proclaim helplessness, powerlessness, and the inability to affect one's destiny. Frances Osgood, for instance, balances her numerous poems of self-proclamation and escape with others that present the images of confinement frequent in women's poems: chains, fetters, cages, and prisons. One typical example is Osgood's "The Fetter 'Neath the Flowers." Reflecting the ambivalence women felt toward relations with the opposite sex, this poem describes love as a seemingly weightless chain that a young woman first tolerates and then decides to break.

> Vain resolve! the tie that bound her
>   Harden'd 'neath her struggling will;
> Fast its blossoms fell around her,
>   But the fetter linger'd still.   [*Poems*]

In her poem "Eros" Anne Lynch (Botta) vows to tear her worshipped human idols from her shrine and free herself from their hold. "Help me to cast away each earthly chain," she begs (G). Elizabeth Oakes-Smith's poem "Stanzas" welcomes the insensitivity of the world, which allows her to protect herself, in another image of confinement:

> So pass they all, and it is well!
> I would not such should read the mind
> Where hidden tenderness may swell,
> Like gem in icy cave confined.   [G]

All see the central experience of female life as one of limitation or confinement. Gilbert and Gubar go so far as to say: "Dramatizations of imprisonment and escape are so all-pervasive in nineteenth-century literature by women that we believe they represent a uniquely female tradition in this period" (*Madwoman*, p. 85).

An untitled poem by Margaret Fuller perhaps best captures the potential for frustration in the experience of limitation. It will be obvious again later in Edna Millay's "Renascence," which begins: "All I could see from where I stood / Was three long mountains and a wood." Fuller's poem begins with a vision of potential freedom but soon subsides into frustration:

> Let me but gather from the earth one full-grown fragrant flower,
> Within my bosom let it bloom through its one blooming hour;
> Within my bosom let it die, and to its latest breath
> My own shall answer, "Having lived, I shrink not now from death."
> It is this niggard halfness that turns my heart to stone;
> 'Tis the cup seen, not tasted, that makes the infant moan.[41]

Poems of this variety abound, pointing to an archetypal female category of "the unattained." Elizabeth Oakes-Smith includes one sonnet called "The Unattained" in her sequence of six sonnets on "The Poet's Life." Her poem seems a cry of frustrated rage. "And is this life? And are we born for this?" She repeatedly questions:

> Must still THE UNATTAINED beguile our feet?
> The UNATTAINED with yearnings fill the breast?
>
>   [Emphasis hers]

Athough this poem, like so many of Oakes-Smith's, tries to find a ground of optimism in religion, it leaves us without hope concerning this world:

> High hopes and aspirations doomed to be
> Crushed and o'ermastered by earth's destiny!   [G]

Although Oakes-Smith expresses herself straightforwardly in this poem, we must discern, in a poem like "Fern-Life" by Lucy Larcom, the hidden commentary behind the seemingly innocent description of plant life. The poem opposes two categories of plants, ferns vs. flowers, an innocent enough distinction apparently. However, the ferns seem to be images of women and the flowers (although some attempt is made to deflect this towards the human vs. the divine) become an image of men, not "man."

We are first told that the ferns are overshadowed by the more powerful "flowers of the glen."

> And we pencil rare patterns of grace
> Man's footsteps about:
> A charm in our wilderness-place
> They find us, no doubt.

However, the last line's bitter irony is immediately surrendered in the helpless cry of the next stanza:

> Yet why must this possible more
> Forever be less?
> The unattained flower in the spore
> Hints a human distress.

The poem even seems sensitive to the distortions of nature that occur in the attempt to imitate the more powerful "flowers." Men, she suggests, have freedoms denied to women, "While our dumb hope through fibre and vein, / Climbs up to be free." Men are endowed with the liberty to use language without restriction, the freedom to be.

> To fashion our life as a flower,
> In weird curves we reach—
> O Man, with your beautiful power
> Of presence and speech!

Sarah Josepha Hale reminds us that women did not have this liberty. Although this poem ends with the usual diversionary action, displacing aspirations essentially earthly toward the divine realm, it leaves us with clear testimony concerning the frustration of the unattained. However we may be told, we do not feel that "the soul can be glad in a bliss / It may never attain."[42]

Aspiration in these poems is excited only to be repressed. The mostly highly concentrated and most common expression of this pattern is the archetypal free-bird poem referred to previously. Felicia Hemans provides an early model of this class of poems in "The Wings of the Dove." At first, the poet aspires to imitate the bird, which is a symbolic representation of freedom.

> Oh! for thy wings, thou dove!
> Now sailing by with sunshine on thy breast;
>   That, borne like thee above,
> I too might flee away, and be at rest!

But immediately the poet sees the impossibility of choosing the bird as a model,

> Wild wish, and longing vain,
> And brief upspringing to be glad and free!
>   Go to thy woodland reign!
> My soul is bound and held—I may not flee.
>
> For even by all the fears
> And thoughts that haunt my dreams—untold, unknown,
>   And burning woman's tears,
> Poured from mine eyes in silence and alone;
>
> *Had* I thy wings, thou dove!
> High midst the gorgeous Iles of Cloud to soar,
>   Soon the strong cords of love
> Would draw me earthwards—homewards—yet once more.
>
> [*Poetical Works*]

It is a mistake, however, to see this as the Ur-poem that all American women poets took as their model. We must remember Anne Bradstreet's early use of Philomel as a solicited and then rejected model of power. Phillis Wheatley's eighteenth-century poem "Fancy" also follows this structure. Fancy is portrayed as a bird who can transcend the barrenness of winter.

> Fancy might now her silken pinions try
> To rise from earth, and sweep the expanse on high.

Ultimately, however, the poet must disavow her connection with Fancy.

> Winter austere forbids me to aspire,
> And northern tempests damp the rising fire.   [G]

Emily Judson's "My Bird," Maria Lowell's "Song," Elizabeth Ellet's

"O'er the Wild Waste," and Amelia Welby's "The Freed Bird" provide other versions of this structure. I quote here in full Elizabeth Oakes-Smith's "An Incident" because it presents in condensed form the essentials of the free-bird poem. As in Hemans's version, this poem includes a bird who first suggests power, through the speaker's identification with freedom, and then powerlessness, through the rejection of this identification. This poem will be the subject of later references.

> A simple thing, yet chancing as it did,
>   When life was bright with its illusive dreams,
> A pledge and promise seemed beneath it hid;
>   The ocean lay before me, tinged with beams
> That lingering draped the west, a wavering stir,
>   And at my feet down fell a worn, grey quill;
> An eagle, high above the darkling fir,
>   With steady flight, seemed there to take his fill
> Of that pure ether breathed by him alone.
>   O noble bird! why didst thou loose for me
> Thy eagle plume? Still unessayed, unknown
>   Must be that pathway fearless winged by thee;
> I ask it not, no lofty flight be mine,
>   I would not soar like thee, in loneliness to pine.   [G]

One asks oneself why this structure seems so compelling for nineteenth-century women poets. Why did they slap down the hand that reached out for fulfillment, for freedom, for power? The answer, I think, lies in their well-founded fears. A commentary on the poem quoted above is provided by Elizabeth Oakes-Smith in a later, highly emotional, work called "Farewell to Fancy," where she begins:

> I, who have shrunk in terror from a flight
> That leaving lowlier things, too oft hath left
> The aching heart of all its love bereft. . . .[43]

Inherent in these lines is a suggestion that a woman must choose between love and poetry, that a commitment to both is somehow impossible. We will see that this motif preoccupies twentieth-century women even more than it did nineteenth-century women. However, here we encounter a sentiment rarely expressed in the next century, the terror of jeopardizing relationships with men. Surely this terror has something to do with the fact that most women in the nineteenth century perceived themselves to be economically, socially, psychologically, and politically dependent on males.

For comparison one can look at Charles Fenno Hoffman's "The Farewell." Independent of relations with women, this male speaker is

able to turn his back on love with an equanimity unavailable to
women of the period in similar situations.

> The conflict is over, the struggle is past,
> I have looked—I have loved—I have worshipped my last,
> And now back to the world, and let fate do her worst
> On the heart that for thee such devotion hath nursed.
>
> [G, *Poets and Poetry*]

Women simply did not feel themselves able to say, "And now back to
the world." Twentieth-century women certainly experience a version
of nineteenth-century terror, but they are less likely to express it so
baldly in their poems. The ladies' magazines that nineteenth-century
poets read were filled with stories of women who disregarded the
strictures of patriarchal authority and came to bad ends. Ostracized
and poverty-stricken, they learned the lessons of powerlessness to
their own sorrow.

Barbara Welter discusses the prevalence of anxiety and guilt in
women's diaries. The fears she lists are numerous, like Catharine
Beecher's fears described in Sklar's biography.[44] Such fears suggest a
feeling of powerlessness in the world. William Chafe adds another
dimension to our understanding of the dynamics of fear in women's
lives by suggesting that anxiety over potential male violence may be a
basic component. As long as women see themselves as physically
inferior to men in a world where physical struggles arise, they will be
fearful. Chafe argues that women, like blacks, need not have experienced a threat of brutality personally to be haunted by it. "Nor is the
fear with which women view the potential of being struck or raped by
a male lover, husband, or attacker an insignificant reality in determin-
ing the extent to which women historically have accepted the dominance of the men in their lives."[45] The stories of battered women in
our own time certainly support this idea.

Whether we ascribe such fears to economic, social, political, physical, or psychological factors, it is clear that women's poems have
expressed considerably more anxiety with respect to freedom and the
desire for power than men's poems. Male poets of the nineteenth
century also wrote numerous bird poems. However, the structure
outlined above is not in the least characteristic of their works. In
Richard Henry Dana's "The Little Beach-Bird," the poet finds the
bird's voice melancholy like the sea and advises it to "come, quit with
me the shore" and dwell instead in gladness and light. James G.
Percival's "To the Eagle" uses the wild and free creature as a way of
celebrating America. In Park Benjamin's "The Stormy Petrel" the
speaker identifies his soul with a bird who rides out storms coura-

geously. But often the male poet refrains from identifying with the bird he apostrophizes, as in John Brainard's "The Sea-Bird's Song" or William Cullen Bryant's "To a Waterfowl." The male poet may use the bird to represent felicities that the speaker may not have been aware of. Thus, Bryant's waterfowl reminds him that a divine guide protects him.

In what seems almost a parody of the feminine model, Theodore S. Fay's "Song" gives us this structure: the bird, representing a man, is at first made captive but ultimately reasserts his freedom in defiance of female power. Like Osgood's "The Fetter 'Neath the Flowers," Fay's bird falls "in a cruel trap which lay / All hid among the flowers." However, unlike Osgood's maid who finds to her sorrow that she cannot extricate herself, this bird gets free by "pressing through a tiny hole," and the poem ends with a taunt.

> And now from every fond regret
>   And idle anguish free,
> He, singing, says, "You need not set
>   Another trap for me,
>   False girl! Another trap for me."
>
> [G, *Poets and Poetry*]

However we interpret bird poems by nineteenth-century males, they do not reflect the vulnerability or ambivalence toward freedom characteristic of women's bird poems. It is worth noting that at the end of the century Kate Chopin used a bird in *The Awakening* to represent first the possibilities of Edna Pontellier's freedom and ultimately the defeat of her aspirations, at least in the context of this world. As Edna is about to kill herself, she sees a bird with a broken wing fluttering back to earth.[46]

The free-bird poem provides a structure in which defeat, one might say, is snatched from the jaws of victory. I place these poems in the category of identification with powerlessness. However, there is a third category of ambivalence in which the opposite is suggested; victory is snatched from the jaws of defeat. These are reconciling poems, but the reconciliation is suggested in terms of a triumph. Unlike Lucy Larcom's "Fern-Life," for instance, where the poem mostly anguishes over the experience of limitation and then at the end tells us "the soul can be glad in a bliss / It may never attain," these poems begin with a premise of defeat and then move on to show the advantages inherent in this position. Emersonian compensation takes on a particularly feminine cast in this poetic genre. Dickinson, as we shall see, made the concept of value through deprivation a major theme in her poetry. She wrote:

> Satisfaction – is the Agent
> Of Satiety –
> Want – a quiet Comissary
> For Infinity.   [P. 1036]

Like Dickinson's, the vision in this category of poems is implicitly renunciatory. Yet these poets always salvage something from their dispossessions. Usually, it is some sense of superiority through self-control, dignity, transcendence of the mundane or vulgar—all maneuvers familiar to the Puritan mentality expressed by these women. The word especially associated with the wisdom promulgated in the poems of renunciation is "maturity." For these women, maturity is achieved by a rite of passage, often by marriage or a surrogate for the marriage experience.[47] In this rite of passage, girlish self-indulgence is laid aside and one hears talk of "girding on" adult responsibility as though it were an uncomfortable but necessary burden. Numerous poems of the period pertain to this transition. One by Lydia Sigourney, which concerns leaving her female friends because of marriage, looks forward to Louise Bogan's "Betrothed" and to the letters of Emily Dickinson. Sigourney begins:

> Sweet, sweet band of sisters! Ah, how could I sever
> The bright, golden chain that encircling has charmed?
> How shall I write the words, Parted forever!
> On the casket our friendship so long has embalmed?[48]

A more penetrating look at the feelings evoked by this rite of passage is offered by Elizabeth Oakes-Smith's "Duty," in which the hopes of youth, like guests, all depart.

> Till cold and desolate—a calm pale face
> Looks in, then enters the despoiled heart,
> And all is hushed and still, for Duty fills the place.   [G]

In her memoirs Oakes-Smith tells us that her husband was exacting, not in the least disposed to allow his new wife "to let up on any point of duty." Marriage and duty are often synonymous for these women, and both at times represent self-sacrifice and suffering.

Characteristically, these women suppress anger and accept; this is what their poetry tells us. But the reader, informed of the difficulties of adjusting, forced to acknowledge the energy needed for sublimation, is left to wonder how satisfying these maneuvers actually were. In Maria Brooks's poem "The Obedient Love of Woman Her Highest Bliss," there is something macabre in the vision of love we are asked to accept.

> To every blast she bends in beauty meek;—
>   Let the storm beat,—his arms her shelter kind,—
> And feels no need to blanch her rosy cheek
>   With thoughts befitting his superior mind.
>
> Who only sorrows when she sees him pained,
>   Then knows to pluck away pain's keenest dart;
> Or bid love catch it ere its goal be gained,
>   And steal its venom ere it reach his heart.   [M]

The elements to mark are the renunciation of intellectual life in the third and fourth lines, the negation of self implied in "who only sorrows when she sees him pained," and the conception of obedience. Clearly, the power this woman describes, a masochistic power available only to the victim, is gained through an indulgence, almost a revelling, in powerlessness.

Women of this period are rarely content to paint a purely negative vision of experience, however. Although they continually tell us that life defeats one's aspirations, they also provide grounds for hope. The shrine of hope for these women poets is the sanctuary, and the archetypal poem of deliverance is the sanctuary poem.

Mary "Hewitt" (Stebbins) in "The Hearth of Home" describes the locus of feeling that will, throughout this study, be called the sanctuary; it is a refuge.

> Thither, when overwhelmed with dread,
> The stranger still for refuge fled,
>   Till he might fearless thence depart:
> And there the slave, a slave no more,
> Hung reverent up the chain he wore.

Later in the poem, the speaker associates herself with the slave, just as many white women joined the abolitionist movement because of their own identifications with the lack of freedom experienced by black people.

> My humble hearth though all disdain,
> Here may I cast aside the chain
> The world hath coldly on me lain.   [G]

Important to this conception is the fact that the seeker of sanctuary is vulnerable and desires safety. Often, though not always, the emotion she associates with the outside world is fear. Lucretia Davidson's poem "On Solitude" summarizes:

> 'Tis sweet to draw the curtain of the world.
> To shut out all its tumult, all its care;

Leave that dread vortex, in which all are whirled
And to thy shades of twilight calm repair.

[Emphasis mine][49]

Nancy Cott provides an informative discussion of the way home became synonymous with a certain kind of refuge in the nineteenth century. "In an interesting development in language usage in the early nineteenth century, 'home' became synonymous with 'retirement' or 'retreat' from the world at large" (p. 57). However, for women home is sometimes a refuge in itself, or it may embody a further need to find some retreat from the constant duties, accessibility, and assaults upon the consciousness which domesticity became for them. We find numerous women exclaiming like Sophronia Grout, "A retired chamber is one of the choicest blessings I enjoy. . . . Here may I review my feelings, mourn over my numerous imperfections. . . . Veiled from the world I vent my feelings on paper for I do find relief in recording the exercises of my mind" (Cott, p. 16). Even Abigail Adams confesses the desire for such a retired chamber. Writing in August 1776 to her husband John, she exults in the possession of her aunt's "pretty closet with a window": "I have a pretty little desk or cabinet here where I write all my letters and keep my papers *unmolested by anyone*. I do not covet my Neighbours Goods, but I should like to be the owner of such conveniences. I always had a fancy for a closet with a window which I could more peculiarly call my own" (emphasis mine).[50] Louisa May Alcott wrote that without her room "I don't exist." Virginia Woolf's "room of one's own" seems to have been coveted by women long before Woolf formulated her idea of it.

However, the sanctuary we are concerned with need not be represented by a chamber in the house. Caroline Sawyer's "The Valley of Peace" is a seductive death-wish in which the cemetery speaks, enticing the hearer to find sanctuary there.[51]

> Poor outcast! too long hast thou wandered forlorn,
> In a path where thy feet are all gored with the thorn;
> Where thy breast by the fang of the serpent is stung,
> And scorn on thy head by a cold world is flung!
> Come here, and find rest from thy guilt and thy tears,
> And a sleep as that of thine innocent years;
> We will spread thee a couch where thy woes shall all cease:
> Oh, come and lie down in the Valley of Peace!   [G]

It is important that the world is represented as not merely irritating but threatening to the self, having caused both physical and emotional torture. Commonly in these poems, renunciation of a world at least potentially destructive to the vulnerable self is advised. Power, freedom (often associated with childhood, "thine innocent years"), may be expressed paradoxically in terms of "sleep." Still, as the poem goes on to say, "the weak, the oppressed, all are safe in its fold." The vision of real triumph, however, belongs to the world beyond: "We shall rise—we shall soar where earth's sorrows shall cease." Sanctuary poems are an index to the degree to which women have felt oppressed or vulnerable in our culture, and they often imply a kind of death—the Womb/Tomb conjunction Showalter mentions.

That even the desire for sanctuary may arouse feelings of guilt is shown in M. St. Leon Loud's "A Dream of the Lonely Isle." After describing her fantasized bower of bliss, Loud details the reasons for seeking sanctuary.

> My heart had grown, like the misanthrope's,
> Cold and dead to all human hopes;
> Fame and fortune alike had proved
> Baseless dreams, and the friends I loved
> Vanished away, like the flowers that fade
> In the deadly blight of the Upas' shade.
> I longed upon that green isle to be,
> Far away o'er the sounding sea,
> Where no human voice, with its words of pain,
> Could ever fall on my ear again.
> Life seemed a desert waste to me,
> And I sought in slumber from care to flee.   [G]

Ultimately, the speaker discovers that she has made a pact with evil in bartering life's ties to gain her own peace. She awakens "with a heart redeemed from its selfish stain." Chastened, she vows "to mingle in scenes of the world again / With cheerful spirit," despite the "pains and sorrows" that she expects to encounter there.

Are there no sanctuary poems by men in this period? There are numerous tributes to the home, such as John Howard Payne's "Home, Sweet Home," James Percival's "Home," and, to a certain extent, Longfellow's "The Children's Hour." Typically, however, men find rest and refreshment rather than safety or protection in the home. Nancy Cott quotes a New Hampshire pastor who in 1827 summarized the attractions of home for men: "It is at home, where man . . . seeks a refuge from the vexations and embarrassments of business, an enchanting repose from exertion, a relaxation from care by the interchange of affection" (Cott, p. 64). How different this pleasant repose between exertions is from the desperately attained refuge of the slave or the woman in "The Hearth of Home."

In the same way, male poems on solitude, rest, or retirement may describe the vexations to the spirit that the outside world presents, but their havens are usually chosen with a cool head rather than with the beating heart belonging to one whose anxieties are newly relinquished. Here is William Burleigh's "Solitude," a characteristic example of this male Romantic motif:

> The ceaseless hum of men, the dusty streets,
>   Crowded with multitudinous life; the din
>   Of toil and traffic, and the wo and sin,
> The dweller in the populous city meets:
> These have I left to seek the cool retreats
>   Of the untrodden forest, where, in bower
>   Builded by Nature's hand, inlaid with flowers,
> And roof'd with ivy, on the mossy seats
>   Reclining, I can while away the hours
> In sweetest converse with old books, or give
> My thoughts to God; or fancies fugitive
>   Indulge, while over me their radiant showers
> Of rarest blossoms the old trees shake down,
> And thanks to HIM my meditations crown!
>
> [G, *Poets and Poetry*]

This is certainly not to say that men have written no desperate poems or that the sanctuary, as a political theme, has not had deep resonance in the masculine mind. However, the prevalence of this motif in women's poetry does reflect, I think, a female preoccupation with domestic affections, a preoccupation men do not share to the same extent. To the degree to which women have been discouraged from self-reliance and encouraged to orient themselves around others (to lay down gladly their "proud self-reliance" as Josiah Holland advises in *Miss Gilbert's Career*), to that degree they have been buffeted between desires for attachment and equally fierce longings to renounce all human involvements. The sanctuary poem usually reflects a longing for isolation from the demands of others. However, as such, it is testimony to the strength rather than the weakness of female responses to such demands. William Burleigh, on the other hand, wants to run away from "toil and traffic."

The escape to the sanctuary, like all defensive maneuvers, increases the power of the thing it seeks to avoid. The reason sanctuary poems, in the terms I have used to describe them, are more characteristic of women is that the patriarchal world has been to them both a seeming source of power and an assurance of powerlessness. Indeed, the sanctuary, though repeatedly invoked, never seems wholly satisfactory. It represents a moment of visionary transcendence which the reader can see fading at the edges to mortal despair.[52]

One final type of poem which belongs here is the renunciation poem that undermines its own premises in a tone of bitter self-contempt. Julia Ward Howe's "Lees from the Cup of Life" is a good example, but I quote "Song" by Mary E. Brooks because it so precisely parallels twentieth-century works by Millay, Wylie, Bogan, and Plath. To a certain extent, this kind of poem has affinities with "the experienced woman" poem that so many poets of the 1920s and '30s write. Its cynicism suggests: I've looked life full in the face so at least I know the worst now. Similarly, Mary Brooks's immunity to life seems hard-won rather than celebratory in this poem:

> Here's to the heart's cold iciness,
>   Which cannot smile, but will not sigh;
> If wine can bring a chill like this,
>   Come, fill for me the goblet high.
>
> Come, and the cold, the false, the dead,
>   Shall never cross our revelry.
> We'll kiss the wine-cup sparkling red,
>   And snap the chain of memory.   [M]

Even without the sudden confession of despair that Julia Ward Howe ends her poem with, we know how transient this moment of glory will be. This fantasy of power lasts only until the next hangover.

We may, I think, justly judge most of this poetry as amateurish. But we must also remember that this is precisely what women were encouraged to be. The *North American Review* praised Lydia Sigourney for lacking the ambition to attempt the highest level of poetry; therefore hers was "true feminine genius." Griswold repeatedly reinforces the idea that the best women poets spent no time trying to perfect their art. Frances Osgood is admired because "for the most part her poems cost her as little effort or reflection as the epigram or touching sentiment that summoned laughter or tears to the group about her in the drawing room" (*Memorial*, p. 21). Anne Lynch's poems "are the natural and generally unpremeditated effusions of a nature extremely sensitive, but made strong by experience and knowledge, and elevated into a divine repose by the ever active sense of beauty" (G). Women poets themselves promulgated the view that they wrote quickly and artlessly. Alice Carey, sister of Phoebe, wrote to Griswold: "We write with much facility, often producing two or three poems in a day, and never elaborate. We have printed, exclusive of our early productions, some three hundred and fifty" (G). Thus, the attitude of the amateur became the key to professional success for women.

Poetry assumed its place as part of women's sphere once it was contrasted with history; poetry, in this case, was understood to deal with elusive feelings and states of mind, history with facts and fortunes.[53] However, the critical world never accepted the effusions, seen as natural to the feminine sensibility, as poetry in its most valuable form. Men were judged by a different standard. In attempting to defend Poe's exaggerated praise of Frances Osgood, Walsh comments: "It might be kept in mind that, as was the custom of the time, he rendered judgment on women poets mostly by comparing them with each other, not by applying the high canons invoked for male writers" (Walsh, p. 38). When Griswold comes to grips with John Brainard, he criticizes in him the same qualities he praises in women. "Brainard lacked the mental discipline and strong self-command which alone confer true power. He never could have produced a great work" (*Poets and Poetry*, p. 238). Griswold's comments on James Percival, another popular poet of the day, are even more revealing. Griswold says of Percival:

> He lacks the executive skill, or declines the labour, without which few authors gain immortality. . . . [He] writes with a facility rarely equalled; but when his thoughts are once committed to the page, he shrinks from the labour of revising, correcting, and condensing. He remarks in one of his prefaces, that his verse is "very far from bearing the marks of the file and the burnisher," and that he likes to see "poetry in the full ebullition of feeling and fancy, foaming up with the spirit of life, and glowing with the rainbows of a glad inspiration." If by this he means a poet should reject the slow and laborious process by which a polished excellence is attained, very few who have acquired good reputations will agree with him. [*Poets and Poetry*, p. 220]

Thus, Griswold's final separation of male and female poets placed only men in *The Poets and Poetry of America*. Women were relegated to a separate volume: *The Female Poets of America*. Poetry, as those serious about it knew, was not really a matter of effusion. Even Lydia Sigourney had some perspective on the value of her productions. She wrote:

> How to obtain time to appease editorial appetites and not neglect my housekeeping tactics was a study. I found the employment of knitting congenial to the contemplation and treatment of *the slight themes that were desired*. This habit of writing *currente calamo* is fatal to

literary ambition. *It prevents the labor of thought by which intellectual eminence is acquired.* If there is any kitchen in Parnassus, my Muse has surely officiated there as a woman of all work and an aproned waiter. [Emphasis mine][54]

She said that too often women writers were denied the opportunity of serious criticism. Of course, she was self-indulgent in many ways, and as Ann Douglas unsympathetically argues, she probably didn't want to know the bitter truth about her work. Yet she was smart enough to catch a glimmer of what Adrienne Rich in "Snapshots of a Daughter-in-Law" would later lament:

> Time is male
> and in his cups drinks to the fair.
> Bemused by gallantry, we hear
> our mediocrities over-praised,
> indolence read as abnegation,
> slattern thought styled intuition,
> every lapse forgiven, our crime
> only to cast too bold a shadow
> or smash the mould straight off.[55]

In fact, the magazines, for all that they opened up opportunities for women, encouraged the hack work, those "slight themes that were desired," which Sigourney mentions. *Godey's, Graham's,* and the *Lady's Wreath* published and applauded sentimentality. In these poems the sentimental is less a matter of self-dramatization (although that does occur) than a reliance on words like "sweet" and "the thorn," an over-fondness for idealizing children or the dead, a tendency to take comfort in simplistic conceptions of life and pious platitudes. If, as Douglas has argued, sentimentality is a matter of failed political consciousness, these poems are a manifestation of the fact that women were powerless and so deeply trapped in their own powerlessness that they were afraid to disappoint the very critical expectations that kept them mired in mediocrity. If it were really true that women were the literary powers of this period, they would have been free to violate these expectations.

So what is the value of this poetry? As an indication of what women may have felt, it is an invaluable resource, for in addition to representing the conventional view of women at the time, these poems lay bare their desire for power and their deep-felt experience of powerlessness. The cultural wisdom of the period claimed that women should not desire power and that, in fact, they had quite enough already—as underpaid teachers, as wives, and particularly as mothers. Read as poetry, the lack of compression, of originality, the rareness of fresh insight or humor in women's poems are disturbing. There were numbers of male poets, of course, who were no better.

On the whole, this body of work defies reassessment. The critical standards it invokes are so invariably those of its own time that one feels anachronistic in applauding or condemning it. These poems are not alive to the possibility of contemporary renewals: their language is too stilted, their convictions too predictable, their rhythms too monotonous. Nevertheless, at a deeper level of significance than perhaps they ever intended, these poets express attitudes still shared by women today. The ambivalence that clearly haunted (and haunts) women beginning to wonder about their rights finds its way into the poetry. However stumblingly or ploddingly, these women established a tradition in women's poetry, a tradition embodying a particular attitude toward their lives—a frustrated, renunciatory, fantasizing, conciliatory posture. In their poetry we can still hear their dissatisfaction even a century or more later. It suggests a struggle with their culture, and their lives—as the next chapter will show—demonstrate that this struggle was by no means merely literary.

Frances Osgood

Elizabeth Oakes-Smith

Lydia Sigourney

Lucy Larcom

Emily Dickinson

Ella Wheeler Wilcox

Lizette Woodworth Reese

Louise Imogen Guiney

A Composite Biography
Early Nineteenth-Century Women Poets

3 A recurring question in all literary times and places is what can poetry do? What is it the poet's duty to make it do? At the Modern Language Association convention of 1979, Seamus Heaney provided this answer: "I take it then that the one central, current, and indispensable assumption that still goes without saying is that poetry has a binding force, a religious claim upon the poet, and I take it that his ambitions will not be merely aesthetic, his activity not merely therapeutic or histrionic. I also assume that the poet still has in some sense a tribal role."[1] A further question arises in a study like this one: Are her ambitions, her activities, consistent with his? Can we speak of "the poet" as though the act of writing poetry itself erases at the point of origin the significance of gender, nation, race, class, time? Heaney, for instance, makes room for tribe but not for sex.

As his answer shows, theories, poems, and persons are never truly universal. Each is bound by the specificity of its signature, the rules of its code. Heaney's code—of universality, of masculinity, of religion broadly conceived—is the one most accessible to those grounded in our Western literary tradition. When he speaks of the religious claim, he undoubtedly means that the poet will feel the urge to transcend self in the fulfillment of his duty. Yet even Emerson in a revisionist moment suggests the limits of this theory when he says: "As I am, so I see; use what language we will, we can never say anything but what we are."[2]

American women poets in the nineteenth century were certainly encouraged to be merely histrionic. They were sometimes inclined to be merely therapeutic. They were not poets in Heaney's sense. With the exception of Emily Dickinson, none loved language enough to revise her literary conventions radically. Few bound themselves to Heaney's religious principle, and when they did, they wrote thoroughly undistinguished verse. And yet they are interesting, as much because of their attempt to reconcile art with life as for the opposite attempt, to reconcile life with art. Life predominated for most of them, life which demanded of them certain sacrifices—leisure, de-

67

velopment of their talents, serious attention to revising and perfecting. Yet they managed to uphold their tribal role, if gender can be understood as tribe here. In her autobiography Lucy Larcom wrote: "My 'must have' was poetry. From the first that meant life to me." And yet, "through my life, it has only been permitted to me as an aside from other more pressing employments" (*New England Girlhood*, pp. 10 and 60). In spite of such difficulties, the aesthetic impulse prevailed and became finally no longer personal but generic, transcending histrionics, therapeutics, and losing itself in the voice of the nightingale whose song is a song of women's refusal to be silenced as much as it is an acknowledgment of powerlessness and pain.

Alicia Ostriker has written: "When a woman poet says 'I' she is likely to mean the actual 'I' as intensely as her verbal skills admit."[3] What does this mean, why is this true, and how does this autobiographical impulse become a generic one? The women we are examining here were better poets than the general run of women writing verse in the nineteenth century. They were not just versifiers but women of some education (many had studied foreign literatures) who chose this art form because of certain needs and aims. Frances Osgood's plaint in "The Spirit of Poetry" captures the intensity of their commitment:

> Well do I know that I have wronged thine altar
>   With the light offerings of an idler's mind,
> And thus, with shame, my pleading prayer I falter,
>   Leave me not, spirit! deaf, and dumb, and blind:
> . . . .
> Heaven knows I need thy music and thy beauty
>   Still to beguile me on my weary way,
> To lighten to my soul the cares of duty,
>   And bless with radiant dreams the darkened day:
> To charm my wild heart in the worldly revel,
>   Lest I, too, join the aimless, false, and vain;
> Let me not lower to the soulless level
>   Of those whom now I pity and disdain.
> Leave me not yet—leave me not cold and pining,
>   Thou bird of paradise, whose plumes of light,
> Where'er they rested, left a glory shining;
>   Fly not to heaven, or let me share thy flight.   [G]

Immediately one feels the presence of an "actual I" in this poem. Poetry answers some desperate need in her and provides a way of being in the world that offers the only dignity she can claim.

The "actual I" Ostriker speaks of, then, was a woman with a certain history and background. Because of the nature of that history and background, this woman grew up with a secret store of aspirations and ambitions. Because of the nature of her society and its effect on a talent not wholly secure, these hopes became panders for the perversion of her talents. Yet the need to give the voice a self in the world remained. The poems declare it. And this is not the story of one woman alone. Thus, "the story," as it is told in bits and pieces, gains credibility for us and becomes the song of the tribe.

This "certain history and background," which was in its basic elements not so much particular to one individual as shared by a group, needs further exploration. We are hampered again by the insufficiency of materials.[4] Yet, with what we have, we can still construct the outlines of a composite biography, useful not only for a better sense of the past century but also for a wiser look at our own. Many of the experiences nineteenth-century women shared have their counterparts in the lives of twentieth-century women poets whom one might well expect to have lived very different lives. To put the nineteenth century into perspective, I have drawn on the lives of Maria Brooks, Lucretia Davidson, Lydia Sigourney, Frances Osgood, Elizabeth Oakes-Smith, Lucy Larcom, and Frances Harper, supplementing their stories whenever appropriate with information about the lives of other poets.

The purpose of the composite biography is to bring into focus the lives that governed these women's impulses to write, especially five categories of experience: education and early life, marriage, work, social activities, and health. The investigation covers the years 1797 (when Maria Brooks was born) to 1911 (when Frances Harper died). However, most of the materials are from the middle of the century. Several of the poets traveled (many went to Europe) or lived for a time outside New England, but the tradition they represent belongs to the Northeast.[5] Their values are indissolubly linked to Puritan values; though its landscape is one of moderate contrasts rather than extremes, its climate is unrelenting, and these are the features we also recognize as New England's.

When Edgar Allan Poe reviewed Rufus Griswold's anthology of female poets, he criticized the predominance of New England women in the book, and Poe may have had a legitimate complaint. Nevertheless, one cannot ignore the fact that the tradition we are considering was shaped by a New England cast of mind; most of its poets felt their strongest ties to its symbolic land, and even Amelia Welby, Catherine Warfield, Eleanor Lee, and the Carey sisters (all five, "Westerners") express its sentiments. Lucy Larcom wrote: "I am glad that I grew up under these wholesome Puritanic influences, as glad as

I am that I was born a New Englander; and I surely should have chosen New England as my birthplace before any region under the sun" (*Girlhood*, p. 10). Emily Dickinson said she saw "New Englandly." Amy Lowell in "Lilacs" spoke of

> Lilacs in me because I am New England,
> Because my roots are in it,
> Because my leaves are of it,
> Because my flowers are for it,
> Because it is my country
> And I speak to it of itself
> And sing of it with my own voice
> Since certainly it is mine.

And even Genevieve Taggard, a native of Hawaii, would later sum up her feelings toward her adopted New England by saying, "This, oddly, is my land."

A comment by a contemporary (Samuel Bowles's biographer, George Merriam) can help us to see how a nineteenth-century man would describe the "characteristic New-England type" of woman. The comment is usually quoted in connection with Emily Dickinson. Its language reflects the notions and stereotypes of the nineteenth century, but much of this description (written in 1885) is true of a whole group of American women poets. Merriam says:

> There is in that section a class of such who inherit a fine intellect, an unsparing conscience, and a sensitive organization; whose minds have a natural bent toward the problems of the soul and the universe; whose energies, lacking the outlet which business and public affairs give to their brothers, are at once stimulated and limited by a social environment which is serious, virtuous, and deficient of amusement. There is naturally developed in them high mental power, and almost morbid consciousness, while, especially in the many cases where they remain unmarried, the fervor and charm of womanhood are refined and sublimated from personal objects and devoted to abstractions and ideals. They are Platonic in their attachments, and speculative in their religion; intense rather than tender, and not so much soothing as stimulating.[6]

It is certainly true that their social environment both stimulated and limited them, giving rise to the pervasive ambivalence expressed in their poems.

These poetic women, who were "not so much soothing as stimulating," were inevitably precocious; some of them performed remarkable feats of intellect. Lucy Larcom was reading at two and a half.

Maria Brooks memorized many classical works as a young child, including all of Milton's *Comus*. Lucretia Davidson is described as covering pages with primitive poems in meter and rhyme before she had even mastered her letters. Lydia Sigourney had written a novel by the age of eight. Both Frances Harper's and Frances Osgood's juvenile literary productions attracted the attention of adults, who felt they showed promise of great things to come.

We may wonder whether such stories are exaggerated but there is surely a grain of truth in them. Of course, some male poets were also precocious, but evidence of precocious intellect had a particularly important value for these women in terms of domestic politics. Since a "normal" course of development inevitably brought a young female into the trap of domesticity, evidence of "difference," of more advanced intellectual capabilities than expected, was necessary in order to win these girls the time and freedom necessary for creative work.

One naturally wonders about the parents: How did they respond to these precocious daughters? How did the daughters regard their parents? To a certain degree, precocity was encouraged. Typically, the father emerges as the intellectual model of achievement, although he often seems distant and inaccessible. Lucy Larcom's father sounds startlingly like Emily Dickinson's in Larcom's description: "His reserved, abstracted manner—though his gravity concealed a fund of rare humor,—kept us children somewhat aloof from him" (*Girlhood*, p. 25). Larcom seems to have felt insecure about her father's love and longed for evidence of his approval. Maria Brooks's male parent was important to her, because he took her education seriously and encouraged her to read and study. Anna Peyre Dinnies is another woman whose father figured largely in her development. Margaret Fuller's father seems to have been a harsh taskmaster, but he treated his daughter like the son he had hoped to have, forcing her to master a classical education and thus expanding her mind beyond the limits of other women's.

For many reasons these daughters have special regard for their fathers. But none of the women I have studied expresses as fierce and passionate a degree of devotion as Lydia Sigourney, who writes of her father:

> I cannot recollect that he ever thanked me. I would not have had him; it would have troubled me. The holy intonations of his voice when he said "my child," was enough. The sweetest tears swelled under my eyelids when I thought of him. Methinks the love of a daughter for a father is distinct and different from all other loves.
>
> [Haight, p. 3]

These sentiments are peculiarly echoed by Elizabeth Barrett Browning in *Aurora Leigh*. Even those whose fathers are dead, or unwilling to enter into such an intense relationship, find substitute father figures. Elizabeth Oakes-Smith opens her autobiography with a tribute to her two grandfathers. Lucretia Davidson, we are told, died with the name of Moss Kent, her surrogate father, on her lips.[7] This preoccupation with the father may in part explain why a number of these women poets married older men, but the father's main importance was as an intellectual model, a figure of force operating in the world outside the home.

In contrast, the mothers of these women appear more accessible, less romanticized. They are also weaker figures, however. Like Emily Dickinson's mother, Lucretia Davidson's was educated and intelligent but subject to constant illnesses. Though her immense sensitivity and lively affections contributed to the most vivid experiences of Lucretia's family life, she, like Lucy Larcom, sought her father's approval more than her mother's.

Often these mothers are caught between a desire to support their talented daughters and a fear of defying convention. Thus, they exhibit conflicting tendencies. Davidson's mother encouraged her, at the same time counselling her against becoming too involved with literature. Catherine Sedgwick, Davidson's biographer, comments that Davidson's mother "very judiciously advised her to intersperse her literary pursuits with those domestic occupations so essential to prepare every woman in our land for a housewife, her probable destiny" (Sedgwick, p. 45).[8] Elizabeth Oakes-Smith's mother pressured Elizabeth into marrying at the age of sixteen a man twice her age. She refused to consider her child's desire to be given an advanced education so that she could open "a great school for girls." Later, this mother confessed that she had forced the marriage on Elizabeth because she had so much of her father's blood in her that if she didn't marry young, she probably wouldn't marry at all. However, one sometimes senses the presence of veiled hostility in such treatment of a daughter, as though, in their compliance with the patriarchy, these mothers were making sure that their girls would be unable to experience greater freedom than they themselves had had. Fear must not be overlooked as a motivation, however. Loss of male support in a male-dominated world was a specter many mothers recoiled from when counselling or directing their daughters.

Because of the pressures these daughters experienced, it is not surprising that we find evidence of childhood discontent, even of covert rebellion, in the biographies of these women. Lucretia Davidson often expressed the desire to spend a fortnight completely secluded in her room so that she could write. Although she did not refuse the domestic tasks imposed upon her, she sought to minimize their hold over her in her daily life. Sedgwick, a writer herself, shows her own ambivalence when she describes Davidson: "Her application to her studies was intense. Her mother judiciously, but in vain, attempted a diversion in favor of *that legitimate sedative to female genius, the needle;* Lucretia performed her prescribed tasks with fidelity, and with amazing celerity, and was again buried in her book" (emphasis mine; Sedgwick, p. 29). Lucy Larcom also chafed when she was forced to surrender herself completely to domestic tasks. Although she enjoyed sewing and taking care of her sister's baby, she felt: "These were not the things I had most wished to do. The whole world of thought lay unexplored before me,—a world of which I had already caught large and tempting glimpses, and I did not like to feel the horizon shutting me in, even to so pleasant a corner as this" (*Girlhood*, p. 192).

Clearly, these feelings have a great deal to do with the poetry of limitation and confinement mentioned previously. However, sometimes young girls accepted the restrictions placed upon their sex with the lassitude of despair rather than the energy of opposition. When Elizabeth Oakes-Smith was told she could not further her education beyond the secondary school level, she merely submitted. "With a weird feeling of 'what's the use,' I felt myself impelled, and yet cast longing eyes toward idealisms, vast and undefined, which I was not permitted to grasp. I was Puritan, blood, bone, and soul; by long descent trained to obedience" (*Autobiography*, p. 42).

The association in Elizabeth Oakes-Smith's mind of Puritanism with the discipline learned in early life is not an idle one. Although she later became a Unitarian, she was careful to point out that her Puritan grandfather was "more in accordance with my turn of mind" than the flamboyant and free-thinking Huguenot one. Julia Ward Howe's experience was similar. Puritanism, as I have said, is for these women less a creed than a psychology. Lucy Larcom mentions that the Puritan influences in her family were very strong; from them she learned to appreciate discipline, though, as she tells us, she was "naturally inclined to dally and dream, and . . . loved her own freedom with a willful rebellion against control" (*Girlhood*, p. 183). Lucretia Davidson and Frances Harper displayed, even in their early lives, the rigid adherence to duty associated with both female self-sacrifice and the American Calvinist tradition.

True to these allegiances, American women poets manifested an early and intense fascination with heroic sacrifice and martyrdom. Both Elizabeth Oakes-Smith and Lucy Larcom poured over Foxe's

Book of Martyrs (as did Anne Bradstreet) and longed to model themselves on these saintly figures. Oakes-Smith went to unusual lengths, however, to prove she could act courageously. At first, she tested herself by holding her fingers in a candle flame. However, when this led to fainting, she had to stop. Hearing that plasters applied to the skin caused a pain "like burning flame," she secretly applied a plaster to herself. She writes: "In the night pain wakened me, but I bore it without a murmur lest I should waken my sister. I was very happy, for I had learned that I could bear it" (*Autobiography*, p. 36). In the morning, she fainted from the pain, the plaster was removed, and she ceased torturing herself, but years later she said the discipline had been good for her as preparation for the greater torture of slander and abuse she received for her expression of feminist beliefs.

Except for Sigourney, all of these women came from what we would now call the middle class. Their fathers were generally merchants or lawyers. Even Lucy Larcom, who went to work in the Lowell mills, was a middle-class child. Only the death of her father, leaving eight children to support, compelled her to enter the working class, and at this time mill work was not yet regarded as evidence of membership in anything less than the middle ranks, since, when the Lowell mills opened, they were designed to offer work to farm girls who wanted to earn a little money before marrying and settling down.

Given their middle-class status, it is not surprising that many of these young women received an "advanced" education. It was common for the daughters of bourgeois families to attend a female academy for a few semesters, although they usually did not seek degrees. Lucretia Davidson, for instance, was first sent to Emma Willard's seminary in Troy, New York. After illness forced her to withdraw from this school, she attended Miss Gilbert's at Albany. Even Lydia Sigourney, whose father was a gardener, studied mental and moral philosophy, history, French, and Latin, as well as painting, embroidery, and music. At Lowell, Lucy Larcom, who was heartbroken when her father's death prevented her from attending secondary school, was tutored by her sister in history, literature, and German. Later, she attended the Monticello Seminary in Illinois, returning to Massachusetts to teach at another institution of higher education for women, Wheaton Seminary.

By mid-century, the legacy of Frances Wright, an early educational reformer, had taken hold to such a degree that many women felt it was their duty to develop their minds. Lucy Larcom reports that, though girls were expected to marry, there was a new feeling that they should not ignore their own mental development: "We were often told that it was our duty to develop any talent we might possess, or at least to learn how to do some one thing that the world needed, or which would make it a pleasanter world" (*Girlhood*, p. 190). In spite of the fact that Wright was vilified during her lifetime because of her belief in sexual freedom and her unconventional behavior, her ideas concerning female education were accepted by many more conservative women. Wright wrote: "Until women assume the place in society which good sense and good feeling alike assign to them, human improvement must advance but feebly. . . . Let women stand where they may in the scale of improvement, their position decides that of the race."[9]

The commonest sentiments expressed in ladies' magazines emphasized that a purely "ornamental" education was inappropriate for American women who, unlike their European sisters, prided themselves on raising their children without depending on governesses and tutors. Thus, they were the primary influences upon the minds of the next generation, and they should be properly educated or the race "must advance but feebly." Lydia Sigourney was a deeply conventional woman, and yet she echoes these sentiments in her *Letters to Young Ladies* (1837):

> Is it not important that the sex to whom Nature has intrusted the moulding of the whole make of mind in its first formation should be acquainted with the structure and developments of mind?—that they who are to nurture the future rulers of a prosperous people, should be able to demonstrate from the broad annals of history the value of just laws and the duty of subordination—the blessings they inherit and the danger of their abuse? [p. 10]

However, having been raised with the belief that it was their duty to develop their faculties, having experienced at a young age the attention of adults who admired their intellectual powers and creative efforts, many young women feared the subordination of intellect and the circumscription of freedom associated with marriage. In an unguarded moment Elizabeth Oakes-Smith calls it being "put into bondage." Therefore, we should not be surprised to discover that the women poets we are considering proclaim at an early age that they will not marry. Although Lucretia Davidson had a number of suitors, her mother relates: "She could not do justice to husband or children, while her whole soul was absorbed in literary pursuits; she was not willing to resign them for any man, therefore she had formed the resolution to lead a single life" (Sedgwick, p. 48). Although Lydia

Sigourney later accepted the marriage proposal of an older man, she had also vowed at an early age never to marry as she was the sole supporter of her parents.

Lucy Larcom reflects on the sense of freedom she felt when it suddenly occurred to her that she could lead a single life. "I heard somebody say one day that there must always be one 'old maid' in every family of girls, and I accepted the prophecy of some of my elders, that I was to be that one. I was rather glad to know that freedom of choice in the matter was possible" (*Girlhood*, p. 124). She later rejected a marriage proposal in part because she preferred her independence and literary career. She said of her suitor, "I am almost sure there are chambers of my heart he could not unlock" (Addison, p. 57). They disagreed violently over abolition. Out of her experience in this relationship she wrote "A Loyal Woman's No"—the poem that made her famous—in which she castigated the man for refusing to take an abolitionist stand. Implicit in at least one stanza of this poem, however, is a condemnation of marriage.

> I am not yours, because you love yourself:
> > Your heart has scarcely room for me beside.
> *I will not be shut in with name and pelf;*
> > I spurn the shelter of your narrow pride!
> > > > [Emphasis mine. *Poems*][10]

Of the women who did marry, not one seems to have led the happy existence portrayed in the ladies' magazines. Elizabeth Oakes-Smith was bitter all her life about being forced by her mother to marry at the age of sixteen. In her feminist essay *Woman and Her Needs*, she says: "It is not unusual for girls to be married and become mothers at sixteen, at the expense of health, happiness, and all the appropriateness and dignity of life" (p. 66). And: "It should be considered not only unwise to do so, but absolutely indelicate. It should affix odium to parents and guardians, if done by their instrumentality; or if by the will of the girl, be regarded as an *evidence of precocious development, as unchaste as it is unwise*" (p. 65). In her autobiography, Oakes-Smith tells us that she was glad she gave birth to four boys in a row, and had no girls.

> I felt painfully that had I been a boy, time and space would have been allowed me to fill up this arrested beautiful development, while marriage, which a girl must not refuse, was the annihilation of her. . . . And I was secretly glad not to add to the number of human beings who must be from necessity curtailed of so much

that was desirable in life; who must be arrested, abridged, engulfed in the tasteless actual. [p. 46]

Although her husband became taciturn and reclusive when her career began to occupy more and more of her energy, Oakes-Smith never ceased to oppose divorce on religious grounds. She felt that marriage was a sacrament that human beings could not violate.

Maria Brooks also married an older man at the age of sixteen. Her father had died, leaving her an orphan, when she was only fourteen, and she seems to have looked to this man to support her in the absence of her father. However, the marriage was a disaster. In *Idomen*, a frankly autobiographical work, Brooks reveals her feelings:

> My parents were dead, my few relatives in distant countries. . . . [Brooks] I had never loved other than as a father and protector; but he had been the benefactor to my fallen family, and to him I owed comfort, education, and every ray of pleasure that had glanced before me in this world. But the sun of his energies was setting, and the faults which had balanced his virtues increased as his fortunes declined. He might live through many years of misery, and to be devoted to him was my duty while a spark of his life remained. I strove to nerve my heart for the worst. Still there were moments when fortitude became faint with endurance, and visions of happiness that might have been mine came smiling to my imagination. I wept and prayed in agony. [Grannis, p. 35]

Brooks's biographer, Ruth Shepard Grannis, believes that Brooks had an affair that left her tortured with guilt all her life. L. W. Koengeter in *American Women Writers* reports that her lover was a Canadian officer whom she intended to marry. They parted for reasons unknown to us.[11] Robert Southey, who knew the poet well, wrote: "Mrs. Brooks, I doubt not, always has been and still is, haunted by the feeling, that, if she had been mated with one capable of esteeming and loving her as she deserved to be esteemed and loved, she would have been one of the happiest of God's creatures" (Gustafson, p. xviii). Frances Osgood wrote a poem "Had We But Met" (probably to Poe) describing a similar plight in very much the same terms.

Although Lydia Sigourney married by choice and kept up a fiction of domestic harmony, her marriage was no happier. Her husband intensely disliked her literary activities. As Ann Douglas relates: "In a long letter of 1827, he mercilessly described her career in terms of sexual desire: she evinced a '*lust* of praise, which like the *appetite* of the cormorant is not to be satisfied,' and was guilty of an 'apparently unconquerable *passion* of displaying herself'" (emphasis Doug-las's).[12] Although they did not separate, their relations were strained, and Sigourney seems to have focused all her familial affections on her son, Andrew, who died at the age of nineteen.

One of the causes of marital problems, clearly, was friction con-cerning the literary careers of these women. Reviewing the first twenty years of married life, Julia Ward Howe wrote: "In the course of that time I have never known my husband to approve of any act of mine which I myself valued."[13] Lucy Larcom and Lucretia Davidson chose literature and renounced marriage (although Davidson's case is moot because she died at the age of sixteen). Lydia Sigourney, Elizabeth Oakes-Smith, Maria Brooks, Frances Osgood, and Frances Harper all attempted to integrate marriage and a literary career with limited success. Osgood's husband left her to find adventure and his own means of support, returning from California and the gold-mines only shortly before her death. Frances Harper did not marry until she was thirty-five. She tried for a time to continue her literary career on the farm she had bought in Ohio. William Still says: "Notwithstand-ing her family cares, consequent upon married life, she only ceased from her literary and anti-slavery labors, when compelled to do so by other duties" (Still, p. 764). We don't know what these "other duties" were, but when her husband died four years later, she returned to her feminist and abolitionist field-work and never married again. Shortly before her marriage, she had published a short story, "The Two Offers," in which a white woman gives up marriage to devote herself to the abolitionist cause, perhaps a fantasy Harper herself entertained.

Throughout the biographies and reminiscences of these women, one finds an implicit assumption that literature is at odds with love, or that a literary career must be guiltily fitted in around domestic activities. Elizabeth Oakes-Smith arose hours before her husband (al-though he was also a writer) in order to read and study before her daily tasks began. She says: "I had no [other] hours of solitude in which I might dream and invent" (*Autobiography*, p. 73).[14]

Nevertheless, one senses enormous reluctance to give up paid work that allowed them a degree of dignity and self-respect, even when this work was not strictly literary. When for a period she was removed from the mill to perform domestic tasks, Lucy Larcom was overcome by a feeling of apathy. When she returned to the mill, she found the people and the excitement, the commotion around her, thrilling. "I felt that I belonged to the world, that there was something for me to do in it, though I had not yet found out what. Something to do; it might be very little, but still it would be my own work" (*Girl-*

hood, p. 193). Those words, "still it would be my own work," indicate the degree to which women like Larcom felt that "taking care" did not offer enough opportunities for self-expression and the expansion of their faculties to be considered their "own work." Even Lydia Sigourney mentions that she felt sad at the time of her marriage, knowing she would have to give up teaching, and supporting her parents, in order to be supported herself.

Frequently, what allowed these women to return to their literary work was the failure of their husbands' careers. The cycles of nineteenth-century economic life made business a risky venture, and bankruptcies were common. Sigourney's husband did not prosper in business, and ultimately she resumed her writing and became the primary support of the family, publishing 56 books and 2,000 articles in her lifetime! No wonder her husband was bitter about her career: she was paid as much as $100.00 for four poems, a fortune at that time, and *Godey's Lady's Book* sent her $500.00 just for the right to use her name on its title page. He must have felt her success as a perpetual reprimand.

Maria Brooks also turned to literature when her husband failed in business, but Elizabeth Oakes-Smith's case is the most dramatic. Her husband lost all their money in land speculation. Oakes-Smith says: "I saw the shipwreck before us, but made the best of it, and it was nothing I could in any way prevent. Internally, I vented my spleen upon the false position held by women, who seemingly could do nothing better than suppress all screaming and go down with the wreck" (*Autobiography*, p. 73). However, she had her revenge. Although Seba Smith had originally outdistanced her in the field of literature (he was the publisher of the first daily newspaper in Maine, the *Daily Courier*, and the author of the humorous "Jack Downing Letters"), she surpassed him after their financial difficulties. Oakes-Smith published numerous poems and stories, including a long poem called "The Sinless Child" that established her reputation. When her writing was insufficient to support the family of six, she became a feminist lyceum lecturer, travelling around the country and earning a living in this even more dramatic occupation.

However, it is incorrect to see these women as operating independently from men in any real way. All of their careers depended, to a greater or lesser degree, on the support and intervention of male figures. Maria Brooks is remembered by Lydia Sigourney and Elizabeth Oakes-Smith as being the preeminent woman poet of her day; but her reputation was to a large extent manufactured by Rufus Griswold who admitted that *Zophiël* (her most significant work) sold few copies in this country and was read by only a small group of admirers. Robert Southey, with whom she stayed in the summer of 1831, made sure that admiration was expressed for *Zophiël* in the *London Quarterly Review*, and it was he who engineered her fame in England.[15] (Charles Lamb is said to have commented on it: "Southey says it is by some Yankee woman: as if there had ever been a woman capable of anything so great!" Gustafson, p. vii.) After her death, her work was championed by Griswold, Whittier, and Stedman successively, without whom even her best poems would probably have been quickly forgotten.

For Lucretia Davidson, it was Washington Irving, and again Southey, who acted as male midwives to her career. She gained a reputation far greater than that of other equally talented women poets. In *Minor Contemporaries*, Poe says that her name was "familiar to all readers of poetry"; and the *Poetical Remains of the Late Lucretia Maria Davidson* became so popular that it was translated into German.

However, it was not always famous poets who were decisive for these women. Although Elizabeth Oakes-Smith maintained an important lifelong friendship with William Cullen Bryant, her first decision to be a serious writer was made with the encouragement of John Neal, editor of the *New England Galaxy*. Similarly, Lydia Sigourney knew many influential male poets in her heyday, but it was Daniel Wadsworth, "a wealthy and intelligent gentleman" of Hartford, who first convinced her at the age of twenty-four to collect and publish her early works. For Oakes-Smith and Osgood, participation in the literary circles frequented by Poe and Griswold was instrumental. Although Lucy Larcom avoided these "salons" (and was thus pretty much ignored by Griswold), she depended on Whittier to get her works into print. All of this serves to support the hypothesis that men not women controlled the literary scene. It was to Thomas Wentworth Higginson that Emily Dickinson thought to turn in 1862, rather than a woman poet or editor.

Nevertheless, one should not minimize the importance of female friendships to these women poets. Barbara J. Berg *(The Remembered Gate: Origins of American Feminism)* has argued that American feminism derives from the breakdown of barriers between classes of women that took place in voluntary societies of the nineteenth century. Except for Lucretia Davidson, who was too young, all of these women had experience with social causes that united them with other women. In 1834 Maria Brooks had an edition of *Zophiël* published to benefit Polish exiles. Lydia Sigourney joined the temperance movement, raised money for Greek relief, and cemented her friendship with Emma Willard by participating in the Willard Association for the Mutual Improvement of Female Teachers, founded in 1837. In addition to supporting efforts to aid working women, Elizabeth Oakes-Smith worked for abolition, prison reform, and proper care for the insane. She knew and admired Dorothea Dix, Lucretia Mott, and Susan B. Anthony. Discussing her visits to women's prisons, she said she "used [her] influence to ward off from women the extreme penalties of laws they had no voice in making" (*Autobiography*, p. 149). Because of her work, many women wrote to her, confessing their problems. She later admitted: "In this new field, designed to reveal woman to herself, I realized an inconceivable satisfaction" (*Autobiography*, p. 153).

Few of these involvements were directly advantageous to their literary careers. In fact, Elizabeth Oakes-Smith was cruelly abused by the press because of her feminist lyceum lectures. Even her friend Sara Josepha Hale refused to hear her speak. The poets Emma Embury and Charles Fenno Hoffman thought her ideas represented "dangerous fanaticism." Yet most of the poets under study here benefitted from the sense of sisterhood they felt after working with other women of similar beliefs. Julia Ward Howe was the founder of the first New England Women's Club and (with Lucy Stone) of the American Women's Suffrage Association. She noted in her reminiscences: "One of the comforts which I found in the new association [with other women] was the relief it afforded me from a sense of isolation and eccentricity" (N.A.W.). Sigourney, Larcom, Oakes-Smith, and Harper also became involved with the women's rights movement in some capacity, although not all of them supported women's suffrage. Lucy Larcom wrote about the cruelty of women who designated their working sisters as inferior or lower-class. She felt it was "the first duty of every woman to recognize the mutual bond of universal womanhood" (*Girlhood*, p. 200). Her views were fundamentally feminist as the following quotation shows:

> We may as well acknowledge that one of the unworthy tendencies of womankind is towards petty estimates of other women. This classifying habit illustrates the fact. If we must classify our sisters, let us broaden ourselves by making large classifications. We might all place ourselves in one of two ranks—the women who do something, and the women who do nothing; the first being of course the only creditable place to occupy. And if we should escape from our pettinesses, as we all may and should, the way to do it is to find the key to other lives, and live in their largeness, by sharing their outlook on life. [*Girlhood*, p. 102]

In the past it was thought that women were isolated from each other and undertook literary careers without the social interaction so readily available to literary men. In *Literary Women*, Ellen Moers says: "Women through most of the nineteenth century were barred from the universities, isolated in their own homes, chaperoned in travel, painfully restricted in friendship. The personal give-and-take of the literary life was closed to them" (p. 43). Recent scholarship in American women's history has proven this was not always so. Carroll Smith-Rosenberg and Lillian Faderman find much more feminine interaction on all levels: "Women helped each other with domestic chores and in times of sickness, sorrow, or trouble. Entire days, even weeks, might have been spent almost exclusively with other women."[16] "The personal give-and-take of the literary life" was precisely what Elizabeth Oakes-Smith enjoyed at the parties given by Anne Lynch and Emma Embury, or at her own literary gatherings which she held every fortnight. Maria Brooks's first book of poems is dedicated to a woman who cheered her, encouraged her, and gave her poetry discipline and art. Obviously, there was a good deal of literary interaction among nineteenth-century American women interested in poetry. For a time at least, the poems and letters flew back and forth between Susan Gilbert and Emily Dickinson; Susan seems to have provided the only sensitive, sophisticated criticism Dickinson received on her work.

However, with all the support furnished by friendships with other women, opportunities for publication, and involvement with social causes, nineteenth-century American women poets were no healthier as a class than their more frustrated sisters. The mortality rate for women generally was very high and, contrary to what actuarial tables show today, women did not live as long as men. Elizabeth Oakes-Smith finds women "past all joy, and beauty, and hopefulness, at a period when the other sex are in the perfection of their powers" (*Woman and Her Needs*, p. 66). Often, the dangers associated with childbirth led to early deaths or disabilities for women. Lydia Sigourney counted, out of 84 of her students, 27 who died before middle age.

The statistics for women poets are no more encouraging and may, in fact, be less so. Using a sample of 34 women poets for whom we have vital statistics, I have counted 15 who died at 40 or younger, 8 of whom did not survive past 30.[17] Even taking into account the fact that the reputations of some of these women were made by an early death (and thus their dates may skew the sample), it still appears that women poets were not a particularly healthy group. For them, death was more likely to occur because of consumption (which killed Frances Osgood, Maria Lowell, Alice Carey, Emily Judson, and the Davidson sisters) than childbirth, although it is hard to say why this is true. Perhaps it is because as a group these women poets had fewer children than the norm. Also, as Susan Sontag has written recently, consumption was regarded in the nineteenth century as a particularly literary disease, and therefore death may have been ascribed to tuberculosis in cases where something else really killed the poet.[18]

Nevertheless, of the six women to whom we are paying particular attention, five lived to be at least 50: Maria Brooks, Lucy Larcom, Lydia Sigourney, Elizabeth Oakes-Smith, and Frances Harper. A surprising number of the more prominent women poets lived to an advanced age: Anne Lynch (Botta) (76); Elizabeth Ellet (65); Caroline Gilman (94); Julia Ward Howe (91); Elizabeth Oakes-Smith (87); Lucy Larcom (67); Frances Harper (86); Sarah Whitman (75). Perhaps, as Sontag argues, it is not fair to make psychological judgments about disease. Yet it seems true that in the nineteenth-century many women used illness as a way of expressing self-hatred and/or anger against the patriarchy. The stronger their sense of self-esteem and their ability to participate in the world, the less likely they were to die at an early age of either consumption or childbirth. Women poets like Elizabeth Barrett Browning and Christina Rossetti seem to have used "delicate health" as a way of gaining power over their lives—illness exempted them from many of the trying duties assigned to women. Both lived beyond the age of 50, however ill they may actually have been.

Looking at patterns of disease and death is not the only way of evaluating health, however. Mental as well as physical health must be considered, especially since women poets in this phase seem concerned with the theme of madness. In *Aurora Leigh*, Browning's heroine specifically associates the decision to become a poet with madness. Aurora says:

> Am I such [a poet] indeed? The name
> Is royal, and to sign it like a queen,
> Is what I dare not,—though some royal blood
> Would seem to tingle in me now and then,
> With sense of power and ache,—with impostumes
> And manias usual to the race. Howbeit
> I dare not: 'tis too easy to go mad, . . .   [*Works*, I, ll.934–40]

There are numerous poems concerning madness in Griswold's collection, and we find a context for understanding these poems when we discover that Maria Brooks, Lucretia Davidson, and Lucy Larcom all dreaded the onset of "dark delirium." Maria Brooks attempted suicide twice. Daniel Addison tells us that Larcom avoided marriage partly because "at times she felt her mind might give way" (p. 57).

Elizabeth Oakes-Smith had at least one mental breakdown. It is no wonder that Poe, with his sensitivity to the dynamics of compulsive psychology, was more attractive to this generation of women than to its men. Of course, it is not fair to say that women poets are exceptional in having fears of mental instability; men have also shared them. However, for women the fear of madness is often connected in one way or another to their position of relative powerlessness in patriarchal society. We need not agree with nineteenth-century physicians, that women are governed by their wombs and thus prone to hysteria (from the Greek word meaning womb), to say that psychic illness is particularly connected in the nineteenth century to female sex roles. Charlotte Perkins Gilman explored this relationship in her autobiographical work *The Yellow Wallpaper.* And Gilbert and Gubar conclude: "It appears that the woman poet must literally *become* a madwoman, enact the diabolical role, and lie melodramatically dead at the crossroads of tradition and genre, society and art" (*Madwoman,* p. 545).

It is rare to find a personal poem on the fear of madness among nineteenth-century men. With the exception of Melville and Poe, this period seems a relatively sane one for American male poets, certainly for those who published alongside these women in the magazines.

For women, on the other hand, it was a period of great mental torment. One wishes there was more information about women poets and their mental health in this period. We are both balked and tantalized by the knowledge that Lucretia Davidson's last poem ends:

> Oh! may these throbbing pulses pause,
>   Forgetful of their feverish course;
> May this hot brain, which burning, glows
>   With all a fiery whirlpool's force
>
> Be cold, and motionless, and still—
>   A tenant of its lowly bed;
> But let not dark delirium steal. . . .   [G]

The poem was left unfinished and found at her deathbed. Given the inevitable pressures felt by women like Davidson who were torn between art and convention, it seems to me likely that the fear of madness among women poets was one of the less pleasant side-effects of trying to project a self into the world. Female guilt and female anger certainly both bear a part.[19]

In the process of sketching out this composite biography, certain experiences seem to be shared among these women poets. They were all precocious. They all associated themselves in childhood with strong male figures. For those about whom we have sufficient information, we can say that at an early age gender distinctions presented themselves as limiting the opportunities open to them as women. Although most tried, all were unsuccessful at carrying on both a happy domestic married life and an active literary career. Those who are on record regarded marriage (and men) at best ambivalently. They all looked to other women to furnish them emotional support, and some, like Elizabeth Oakes-Smith and Lucy Larcom, were disappointed by what they felt was evidence of feminine betrayals. Like Anne Bradstreet's, their works, more often than not, required a male midwife in order to reach the public. All were "successful" and yet all suffered disadvantages because of their sex, even Lydia Sigourney, who had to compose, *currente calamo*, against her own best judgment.

At this point a final comment on Frances Harper is in order. Harper became the most popular black poet in history when her *Poems on Miscellaneous Subjects* was published; it sold 12,000 copies in four years, and her first two books sold over 50,000 copies—an extraordinary count. Though her work is not considered by Rufus Griswold, she deserves mention in a study of American women poets. There is very little biographical data available on her but what there is supports a conclusion that she represents a different tradition than the one we are considering here, and this is probably due to her experience as a black. Although Harper like the others read and admired Felicia Hemans, her own poetry never recommends reconciliation, withdrawal, or renunciation. The picture William Still paints of her is one of a strong, self-determined woman with a firm sense of self-worth. For instance, she conveys in her letters complete fearlessness about lecturing on abolition in the deep South. Perhaps, like Frederick Douglass's, her moral energies were so clearly defined and intensely directed, that she felt none of the ambivalence toward power characteristic of the women poets I am mainly concerned with. She had seen the enemy, but he wasn't "us." This means that she, unlike Phillis Wheatley, somehow escaped the slave mentality.

In her poem "Vashti," rewritten by later black women poets, a queen is requested by the king's "wily counsellors" to come before the assembled crowd of feasting men and unveil her face.[20] She refuses and thus symbolically threatens the patriarchy. The counsellors say that if Vashti is allowed to remain queen, "the women, restive 'neath our rule, / Would learn to scorn our name." Therefore, Vashti must lay aside her crown.

> She heard again the King's command,
> And left her high estate,

Strong in her earnest womanhood,
    She calmly met her fate.

And left the palace of the King,
    Proud of her spotless name—
A woman who would bend to grief,
    But would not bow to shame.

This calm defiance is admirable, but it is uncharacteristic of both the poems and the lives of nineteenth-century American women poets, who usually attempt some form of reconciliation with male power and avoid open hostility. Even Lucy Larcom's "A Loyal Woman's No" is not as strong as this poem because its anger is so narrowly directed. This is a period in which we must read women's poems with a good deal of care, however. The fabric woven by day was often, like Penelope's, unwoven at night, in the realm of the subconscious, in dreams or in poems. It is the poems with which we will have most to do, and, as the next chapter on Emily Dickinson will show, it is the poems that are often the most tantalizing as well as the most revealing.

Tradition and the Individual Talent

Helen Hunt Jackson and Emily Dickinson

4   By mid-century the dominant members in this women's tradition must have seemed to younger women poets like an Establishment. From their point of view, Holmes, Whittier, Bryant, Lowell, and Longfellow were probably no more formidable than Brooks, Sigourney, Oakes-Smith, Whitman, and Osgood. Poetry had become so inbred that only an outsider like Emily Dickinson could revitalize it. Dickinson was not ignorant of women's poetry. She pored over the Brontës, Elizabeth Barrett Browning, and George Eliot, sending their poems as treasured presents to her favorites. Among American women poets, she probably knew something of Maria Brooks, Lydia Sigourney, Maria Lowell, Caroline Gilman, and Amelia Welby.[1] She may even have seen occasional copies of the ladies' magazines. Though we don't know to what extent she admired American women's poetry, one thing is certainly clear: she ignored its stylistic conventions.

However, she did not ignore the type of the poetess as a cultural phenomenon. She couldn't, because as a woman interested in literature, she had to come to terms with this model. At the age of fourteen, she mocks her tendency to become "poetical" in a letter by saying, "you know that is what young ladies aim to be now-a-days" (L. 8).[2] For the rest of her life, she toyed in her poems with that stock character, the poetess, craftily using the conventions of the role to serve her own purposes and then rewriting the part to suit herself.

In some ways Dickinson's persona had its origins in this literary drama. It is well-known that she became a recluse, but the poetess too was known to demand her share of isolation. Catherine Sedgwick, for instance, described Lucretia Davidson as "this little thoughtful and feeling recluse." Lucy Larcom says in her autobiography that she thought of herself as a solitary. And Anne Lynch in 1845 called her reflections on her own life, "The Diary of a Recluse." This last title had the perfect ring of poetic autobiography to this generation. Lynch, a famous hostess, was hardly a hermit. Still, she knew how to assume the proper pose.

Another part of "the myth" of Emily Dickinson concerns her vague, mothlike appearance in the white dress that became her constant garment. This has usually been seen as a sign of her eccentricity. However, it seems less so in light of this description of Maria Brooks given by her niece: "She *always* dressed in white or grey, wearing transparent sleeves through which her beautiful arms were seen" (her emphasis; Gustafson, p. xiv). On the other side of the Atlantic, Christina Rossetti was also reclusive and frequently dressed in white. Was this entirely because of her commitment to Christ or was it evidence of a different desire, less ethereal than earthly?[3]

George Whicher reminds us that in Emily Dickinson's girlhood "the notion of the poet as a beautiful soul standing apart from the crass occupations of life was widely accepted."[4] We have already looked at ways in which notions of feminine sensibility were incorporated into the image of the poetess. She was intense, spontaneous, effusive, ethereal. In particular, she was melancholy. Abigail Adams's famous cry, "Oh, why was I born with so much sensibility?" is echoed by a number of women poets who, like Frances Osgood, represent themselves as too vulnerable to suffer the coarseness of common life. Sometimes it is hard to distinguish the true feelings of these women poets from those dictated by the role they assumed to satisfy public expectations. For a woman like Dickinson the sense of difference from others, the intense feelings, were certainly real. But it is also important to remember that one's self-conception is determined in part by the social vocabulary of one's culture. Still, the poetess was more than a social norm. She was an accessible image for a literary self.

Nineteenth-century women poets reformed the conception of poetry that had previously existed. By defining the poet in terms of the capacity for pain, they implied that women had a special talent for verse. While men were out working in the marketplace, women, so the theory went, were at home suffering quietly and writing poems. Their feelings were more profound than men's; they were touched with tragic insight. Out of this conception of women, poets developed a motif that came to have considerable importance for this female poetic tradition. The term I will use for this motif is "the secret sorrow." Both as a literary device and as a way of understanding one's own experience, this motif served to structure women's thinking about their lives. It allowed them to feel heroic without forcing them to lay claim to the kinds of power jealously guarded by the patriarchy. It gave them a sense of self-importance and an object for contemplation that they could claim as their own. It inspired them to write poems. Even Emily Dickinson felt the power of its attraction, and her work, more than that of any other poet of this period, gave the secret sorrow an enduring form.

Numerous nineteenth-century works connected the secret sorrow with the female poetic temperament. In her introduction to *The American Female Poets*, Caroline May says:

> The themes which have suggested the greater part of the following poems have been derived from the incidents and associations of everyday life. And home, with its quiet joys, its deep pure sympathies, and its *secret sorrows*, with which a stranger must not intermeddle, is a sphere by no means limited for woman, whose inspiration lies more in her heart than her head. [My emphasis. M, p. vi]

It is interesting that May associates the home, woman's sphere, with secret sorrow. There is something charged and vaguely suggestive about the comment that domestic secrets are those "with which a stranger must not intermeddle," as though such sorrows had an erotic component. Often, as we shall see, they did.

If we turn to some of the poems written in this period, we find Lydia Sigourney, Elizabeth Oakes-Smith, and Lucy Hooper also associating the poetess with secret sorrow. In her "Monody on Mrs. Hemans" Sigourney exclaims:

> Yet was the couch
> Of thy last slumber in yon verdant isle
> Of song, and eloquence, and ardent soul—
> Which, loved of lavish skies, *though banned by fate,*
> Seemed as a type of thine own varied lot
> The crowned of Genius, and the child of Wo,
> For *at thy breast the ever pointed thorn*
> *Did gird itself in secret.*   [My emphasis. G]

Elizabeth Oakes-Smith uses the same image in "The Poet":

> Sing, sing—Poet, sing!
> With the thorn beneath thy breast,
> Robbing thee of all thy rest;
> *Hidden thorn for ever thine,*
> Therefore dost thou sit and twine
> Lays of sorrowing—
> Lays that wake a mighty gladness,
> Spite of all their mournful sadness.   [My emphasis. G]

The thorn image makes explicit the connection between this tradition of poets and the nightingale's sorrow. Lucy Hooper, in her "Last

Hours of a Young Poetess," reveals in startling and rather amusing terms, one attraction of the secret sorrow.

>   Oh, how much
>   The world will envy those whose hearts are filled
>   With secret and unchanging grief, if fame
>   Or outward splendor gilds them!   [G]

The secret sorrow was, for many women, poetic capital.

When Dickinson writes at the age of sixteen, "I find no rose without a thorn" (L. 10), we rather easily dismiss this statement as the posturing of a young girl. However, during her lifetime she composed dozens of poems on the theme of secret sorrow; these range from #126 ("To fight aloud is very brave") to #1410 ("I shall not murmur if at last"), covering a time span from 1859 to 1877. It is harder here to know what is literary pose and what is genuine feeling. Certainly Dickinson seems to have felt that this theme had special resonance for her.

Even Susan Gilbert Dickinson, Emily's sister-in-law, adopted the persona of the secretly suffering poetess in a peculiar letter she sent to Emily in October 1861. This letter has been cut into three pieces so we are left to wonder what else it contained. Susan writes:

> *Private* I have intended to write you Emily to day but the quiet has not been mine – I should send you this, lest I should seem to have turned away from a kiss –
> If you have suffered this past Summer I am sorry [cut] *I* Emily bear a sorrow that I never uncover – If a nightingale sings with her breast against a thorn, why not *we?* [cut] When I can, I shall write–[5]

Obviously, the nightingale image was particularly appealing to women of this period, even to women as extraordinary as Emily and Susan Dickinson.

In Longfellow's novel *Kavanaugh*, a favorite of the younger Dickinsons', Alice Archer is described in terms perfectly appropriate to the mid-nineteenth-century conception of the female poet. "A fair, delicate girl whose whole life had been saddened by a too sensitive organization and by somewhat untoward circumstances. . . . She was thoughtful, silent, susceptible, often sad, often in tears, often lost in reveries. She led a lonely life."[6] Alice is an avid reader of poetry, and she dies appropriately at an early age. Her secret sorrow has been her love for Kavanaugh, the village preacher, who marries her best friend, Cecilia Vaughan. Alice comes to seem heroic through her silence and her fidelity to this secret love even at the point of death.

One can readily see why this story appealed to Emily Dickinson, who would later write, "Mirth is the Mail of Anguish–" (P. 165).

Not all secret sorrow involves forbidden love. (Helen Hunt Jackson's, for instance, seems to have concerned only the memories of her dead husband and beloved child.) However, the theme of forbidden love is one of the most prevalent among women poets of the nineteenth century. One remembers Maria Brooks's "Song" in which the speaker thinks longingly of suicide because of the torture of keeping her feelings to herself. Brooks actually attempted suicide twice. We know that she was plagued by guilt because of her attachment to a man other than her husband. When she lost both her son and her stepson, she expressed in a letter her sense that "a dreadful atonement had been made—which again seems to hint," Grannis says, "at some secret, mysterious sorrow in her life" (p. 35).

Maria Brooks's torment was real, but the theme of the forbidden lover transcends biographical reference. It is a conspicuous feature of women's poetry from Emily Dickinson to Edna St. Vincent Millay. More needs to be considered than the biographical facts. As this theme takes on archetypal significance, we will need to probe its structural and psychological appeal for women poets operating out of different value systems and in different generations.

Why, we might ask, did Helen Hunt Jackson dwell on forbidden love (for instance, in "Esther Wynn's Love Letters") since, according to Evelyn Banning, she had no personal experience with such an attachment? Esther's story sounds remarkably like early accounts of Dickinson's love life. "It was plain that some cruel, inexorable bar separated her from the man she loved; a bar never alluded to—whose nature we could only guess,—but one which her strong and pure nature felt itself free to triumph over in spirit, however submissive the external life might seem."[7] Jackson uses the "inexorable bar" and secret passion again in her novel *Mercy Philbrick's Choice*. Mercy becomes a famous poet but only after rejecting both Parson Dorrance and Stephen White. When Dorrance dies, however, Mercy decides, rather belatedly, that he was her chosen one: "As confidently as if she had been wedded to him here, she looked forward to a reunion with him there, and found in her secret consciousness of this eternal bond a hidden rapture, such as has been the stay of many a widowed heart through long lifetimes of loneliness."[8] One suspects that Mercy prefers the dead lover to the live one because of the freedom this attachment allows her. Stephen, the remaining rejected suitor, is depressed at her insistence on a platonic relationship, but by not marrying Stephen, Mercy is free to pursue her career, a choice that is made to seem preferable, as long as her ability to love is not in question.

Both of these stories may be linked to Emily Dickinson, but Jackson herself was also fascinated with heroic secrecy and forbidden love.[9] Her interest in Dickinson does not wholly explain her concern with these themes. In a long poem called "The Story of Boon," Jackson recounts a tale told by Anna Leonowens, the English governess at the Siamese court. (It later became a subplot in *Anna and the King of Siam*.) "The Story of Boon" is one of martyred women and capricious men. Boon herself is tortured, not only by the king's men but by the Amazons who serve him. She finally dies without having revealed her secret, that her husband the duke is in love with the king's mistress. This mistress, Choy, does reveal the forbidden attachment, however, and she is scorned by all but the compassionate Boon. The tale disgusted T. W. Higginson, who called it "made-up nonsense," but it clearly fired Jackson's imagination. She framed her poem at the beginning and the end with an impassioned personal statement of its power over her.

> It haunts my thoughts morn, night, and noon,
> The story of the woman, Boon,—
> Haunts me like a restless ghost, until
> I give myself to do its will.   [*Poems*]

The implication is that the attraction of this story goes beyond conscious choice. Its appeal seems to be the appeal of a female archetype, whose power is linked to the subconscious.

From one point of view, the secret sorrow and the forbidden love operate as justifications for renunciation. Women's wisdom here tells us the world is more beautiful to those who are not entirely of it; we learn how much we loved the dead only after they are gone; value increases through deprivation. As Dickinson says, "To disappear enhances," and "impotent to cherish / We hasten to adorn." There is in Dickinson always an attraction to "the extatic limit / Of unobtained Delight ." (P. 1209). Secret sorrow and especially forbidden love may become excuses, from this point of view, for a rejection of the world, for closing "the valves of [one's] attention / Like stone." These images may be used to hide failed political consciousness, cowardice, or escapism.

However, as we have noted in our previous discussions of ambivalence, women have chosen renunciation, because often it represented the only form of power available to them. This issue of power is a vital one, to both Dickinson and Jackson. In "To an Unknown Lady" Jackson apostrophizes:

> O sweetest immortality, which pain
>   Of love's most bitter ecstasy can buy,
>   Sole immortality which can defy
> Earth's power on earth's own ground, and never wane. . . .

It is the immortality of poetry which, Jackson tells us, is bought of "love's most bitter ecstasy" and can "defy / Earth's power on earth's own ground." Out of the resources of the secret sorrow, the poet develops her special talents. Poetry becomes power, or, as Dickinson says:

> To pile like Thunder to it's close
> Then crumble grand away
> While Everything created hid
> This – would be Poetry –   [P. 1247][10]

However, one must always remember that the power claimed by these poets is presented as a triumph of the powerless. The philosophy of renunciation develops as a strategy for dealing with balked ambition. One remembers Lucy Larcom's "Fern-Life" and Elizabeth Oakes-Smith's "An Incident." Dickinson's point of view that value is achieved through deprivation has often been labelled "compensation" by critics. However, as Vivian Pollack says, the term "compensation" as derived from Emerson becomes misleading when applied to the works of poets like Dickinson, "since it fails to take account of the vulnerability and threatened deterioration of the self" implicit in their poems.[11] Preoccupation with compensated value fascinates women poets because they feel themselves deprived. "I had been hungry all the years," Dickinson writes. Out of this experience of deprivation, this secret sorrow, this desire for the forbidden (which is really a desire for forbidden power), they construct—though not necessarily consciously—a value system that applauds displacements of appetite. Dickinson's attitude toward her own ambition furnishes us with numerous examples of this mechanism. Jackson's "Memoir of a Queen," in which her royal highness rules a kingdom unrecorded on "written page or stone," offers a similar instance of displacement.

In judging Helen Hunt Jackson and Emily Dickinson, we want to consider the ways in which these poets and their poems belong to a women's literary tradition. It is important to analyze motifs like the secret sorrow and the forbidden love in terms of the poet's attitudes toward both power and poetry. Ultimately, one must acknowledge, however, that for Jackson the culturally determined literary sensibility she inherited was definitive. For Dickinson, it was merely provocative. Very early Dickinson began to express a prophetic sense of her own worth and her future success as a poet. "I think that what we *know* – we can endure that others doubt, until their faith be riper," she writes in 1862 (L. 277). If we read the following poem anachronistically, and perhaps perversely, we can use it as a metaphorical comparison between her poetry and Helen Hunt Jackson's, though at this time Dickinson did not yet know of Jackson's work. The "you," then, might represent no single person but rather the generation with which Dickinson contended and which so universally misjudged her worth. The poem was sent in a letter to Samuel Bowles, who might well have stood for this forbidden love, the world of fame and temporal power, in Dickinson's mind.

> If she had been the Mistletoe
> And I had been the Rose –
> How gay upon your table
> My velvet life to close –
> Since I am of the Druid,
> And she is of the dew –
> I'll deck Tradition's buttonhole –
> And send the Rose to you.   [P. 44]

Helen Hunt Jackson's work represents what her era regarded as the finest flowering of the female poetic tradition. Yet this work was indeed a kind of rose, exquisite in its way but fading quickly. One might say it was "of the dew." We no longer read her.

Although personally rebellious, Jackson was not a renegade as a poet. Dickinson, on the other hand, was personally conservative and poetically heterodox. It is to Jackson's supreme credit that she recognized the genius of a woman like Dickinson and wrote to her, "You are a great poet—and it is a wrong to the day you live in, that you will not sing aloud" (L. 444a). Dickinson, however, knew better. Jackson, whom Thomas Johnson calls the leading woman poet of her era, and whom T. W. Higginson praised as "the most brilliant, impetuous, and thoroughly individual woman of her time," was better suited to the world of Lowell and Bryant than Dickinson could have been.

In the first place, Jackson's life was lived in the world. When newly married, she was introduced to Washington society by her first husband. Later, when the couple moved to Newport, Rhode Island, she made a lifelong friend of Anne Lynch—the woman who wrote "The Diary of a Recluse" and whose home became "the first important salon in the history of American Letters."[12] Lynch's parties were attended by Ralph Waldo Emerson, Edgar Allan Poe, Rufus Griswold, Margaret Fuller, Elizabeth Oakes-Smith, Frances Osgood, and the

Carey sisters. They were a meeting-ground for well-known women poets. Jackson knew this and spent time with Lynch and her husband in New York. In the 1860s we find her seeking out the friendship of T. W. Higginson. Later, when she moved to the West, she developed another kind of commitment to the world by becoming deeply involved in the cause of the American Indians. On July 7, 1882, she was appointed Commissioner of Indian Affairs in Southern California. Obviously her life bore little external relation to Emily Dickinson's.

However, like Dickinson, she knew suffering from the inside. Her first child, Murray, died at the age of one of "brain fever." She was emotionally shattered, but this was only the beginning of her troubles. Her husband, having survived his commission as a major in the Civil War, was overcome by poisonous gas in a freak accident in the Brooklyn Navy Yard; he died before his wife could reach him. One person whom she thoroughly adored was left to her, her second son, Rennie. Two years after his father's death, he died of diphtheria, at the age of nine. All three members of her family were buried at West Point. "And I alone," she said, "am left, who avail nothing" (Banning, p. 65).

However, in the next few years with Higginson's encouragement, she began to write poetry in a serious way, also singing—as Dickinson claimed to do—"off charnel steps." Her career as a writer began to occupy her full attention. Thus, when she received a proposal of marriage from William Jackson, she demurred. But finally when Jackson agreed not to interfere in any way with her writing, she accepted him. She lived the last ten years of her life in Colorado Springs and Los Angeles, writing both poetry and prose but concentrating her attention primarily on the Indian cause. In her day she was more famous for having written *Romona* and *A Century of Dishonor*, both books about abuses perpetrated against the Indians, than she was for her poetry. She died only a year before Emily Dickinson, on August 12, 1885.

Jackson was an intelligent, self-reliant woman who had acted independently in carving out for herself an unusually successful professional career. There is every reason to suppose that she might have been sympathetic to the women's movement. But she wasn't. In 1873 she expressed herself unequivocally as an opponent of "the Women's Right Movement": "There is an evil fashion of speech which says it is narrowing and narrow life that a woman leads who cares only for her husband and children; that a higher, more imperative thing is that she herself be developed to her utmost. . . ." Jackson, however, wanted to go on record as believing that a woman "who creates and sustains a home, and under whose hands children grow up to be strong and pure men and women, is a creator, second only to God" (Banning, pp. 99–100). One does pause over the fact, however, that she refused to marry Jackson until he agreed to allow her the freedom she claimed women did not need, the freedom to develop herself "to her utmost." It is also true that though Jackson may have been unsympathetic to the women's movement, she was sensitive at some level to the situation of women in patriarchal society, and thus her refusal to support the fight for women's rights becomes more poignant. Her poems reveal a sensitivity she was unwilling to express politically. They also reflect a thorough grounding in the dominant female poetic tradition of her time.

Jackson's work contains numerous tributes to famous women: "Vashti," "Esther," and "Charlotte Cushman" are examples.[13] She also considers the sanctuary which, with typical moralistic fervor, she rejects:

> With what a childish and short-sighted sense
> Fear seeks for safety; reckons up the days
> Of danger and escape, . . .

Like many women before her, she counsels in "Renunciation" our forbearance with the divine timetable. We should suppress our impatience. In "Covert" the heart must contain itself lest it reveal its secret. Unlike the "small brown mate / Of some melodious, joyous, soaring bird," which suddenly bursts into flight and song at her step, she tells her own heart:

> Fly not at sound of strangers' aimless feet!
> Of thy love's distant song drink all thy fill!
> Thy hiding-place is safe. Glad heart, keep still!

This poem would even make a good comparison with Louise Bogan's "Men Loved Wholly Beyond Wisdom" where the speaker advises her heart to be wise "like a thing gone dead and still" and to imitate the cricket whose music is "terrible" and "dissembling"; its message cannot be precisely located. In the nineteenth-century poem, however, we recognize the insistence on curbing aspiration so often suggested by the free-bird poem, of which Jackson's poem is a variant. This phenomenon is also what distinguishes forbidden-lover poems from, say, the male tradition of courtly love. The real "forbidden lover" for these women was worldly power.

Oliver Wendell Holmes and James Russell Lowell were not writing poems about the dangers and benefits of secrecy. Jackson was. In fact, her sorrow poems are often very revealing. In "The Loneliness of

Sorrow," for instance, she personifies grief but carefully does not reveal its sex. Throughout this poem sorrow is referred to as an "it," a neuter creature. However, the poem indicates in spite of itself the suppressed gender of this figure.

> Friends crowd around and take it by the hand,
> Intruding gently on its loneliness,
> Striving with word of love and sweet caress
> To draw it into light and air. Like band
> Of brothers, all men gather close, and stand
> About it, making half its grief their own,
> Leaving it never silent nor alone.

Further on, sorrow is described as a "hermit whom mere loneliness defends," as "majestic in its patience, and more sweet / Than all things else that can of souls have birth." Surely there is a female hidden in this supposedly neutral image.

The grief Jackson describes is secret, unexpressed; its presence is like that of "one born dumb / From whose sealed lips complaint can never come." Most startling of all, however, is the way Sorrow seems to be endangered by male figures. There are no female sympathizers here and the men who "gather close," like a "band of brothers," seem to be torturing this muted figure inadvertently. By making "half its grief their own / Leaving it never silent nor alone," they are forcing attentions on Sorrow that she doesn't want.

However, in an interesting role reversal, the defenseless woman is protected by her innate isolation, "like hermit whom mere loneliness *defends.*" Her power, however, is an otherworldly, a displaced, power, achieved only at the expense of this world.

> Bearing the one redemption of this earth
> Which God's eternities fulfil, complete,
> Down to its grave, with steadfast, tireless feet
> It goes uncomforted, serene, alone,
> And leaves not even name on any stone.   [Poems]

The sanctuary she consciously rejects in "Danger" returns unsolicited in her notion of feminine renunciation. In "Acquainted with Grief," which T. W. Higginson thought one of her best poems, Jackson makes sorrow explicitly female but gives her a more ambiguous nature. At first, she seems a deceitful, malicious creature, assuming disguises to stab the unwary and pursuing her victims relentlessly. However, in the second half of the poem, our sympathies are intentionally aroused for her. The poem begins "Dost know Grief well?" Its last six stanzas conclude:

Then dost thou know, perchance, the spell
    The gods laid on her at her birth,—
The viewless gods who mingle well
    Strange love and hate of us on earth.

Weapon and time, the hour, the place,
    All these are hers to take, to choose,
To give us neither rest nor grace,
    Not one heart-throb to miss or lose.

All these are hers; yet stands she, slave,
    Helpless before our one behest:
The gods, that we be shamed not, gave,
    And locked the secret in our breast.

She to the gazing world must bear
    Our crowns of triumph, if we bid;
Loyal and mute, our colors wear,
    Sign of her own forever hid.

Smile to our smile, song to our song,
    With songs and smiles our roses fling,
Till men turn round in every throng,
    To note such joyous pleasuring.

And ask, next morn, with eyes that lend
    A fervor to the words they say,
"What is her name, that radiant friend
    Who walked beside you yesterday?"

Although from one point of view, sorrow appears to be powerful,
in fact she is a slave, the image of female oppression.

She to the gazing world must bear
    Our crowns of triumph, if we bid;
Loyal and mute, our colors wear,
    Sign of her own forever hid.

The punishment for her power is repression, "that we be shamed
not." Who is the "we" in this poem? The sex, both of the speaker and
the person spoken to, is ambiguous. But the men who turn around to
look at her once again seem to be a "band of brothers." The person to
whom the poem is addressed sounds like the male object of a female
pursuit, a member of this band perhaps. And the speaker? He addresses the person spoken to like a fellow, as though they were two
men involved with the same woman. The irony, of course, is that
once this female succeeds in overtaking and wounding the heart she
pursues, she becomes a slave, forced to give up her own identity,

silenced. The secrecy forced on sorrow here is not the route to power but the badge of powerlessness. Thus, Jackson, like many of her contemporaries, conveys ambivalent feelings about the nature of patriarchy, about women, about their desire for authority and the displacement of their power. Her choice of what seems to be a male speaker is more eloquent than she probably realized. She is willing to identify with secrecy but not with powerlessness.

Although these two poems do not provide the best examples, Jackson's greatest strength lies in her graceful conclusions. Her weakest poems are marred by sentimentality (that badge of failed politics) and by archaic diction or loose, nerveless lines. However, she knows how to make last lines count. For instance, in "Danger," while she postures ("Oh, vain pretence!") and falls back on clichés ("The winds blow where they list"), she nevertheless manages to make the poem dramatic because of her last line.

> The winds blow where they list, and will disclose
> To no man which brings safety, which brings risk.
> The mighty are brought low by many a thing
> Too small to name. Beneath the daisy's disk
> Lies hid the pebble for the fatal sling.   [*Poems*]

These effects would become standard in women's poetry around the turn of the century. One finds in Lizette Woodworth Reese, for instance, these endings that suddenly, by force of specificity, hit hard. But Jackson went first. She was good at dialogue. She had an ear and a fine sense of dramatic movement. It is perhaps too bad that now we concentrate, in the secret-sorrow poems, on effects she probably did not intend. However, her work has become merely historical. It is like the rose whose original bloom has faded and is now pressed into the album, precious for other reasons.

Emily Dickinson, on the other hand, was "of the Druid." Her reputation increased magically, dramatically, as Helen Hunt Jackson's faded away to nothing. Writing about Dickinson, Allen Tate comments that the best poetry does not dispense with tradition but rather probes its deficiencies.[14] This is exactly what Dickinson's did. She decked "Tradition's buttonhole" by offsetting the empty spaces in this feminine tradition with the contrast of her own mysterious and potent talent.

Her biography has been written and rewritten. Yet few of her biographers have paused to comment on the way Dickinson's life accords with the standard biography of other women poets of the period.[15] It does not do so entirely, of course, but there are many parallels. Dickinson's father was the most important image of power and intellect in the household. Sometimes he is described as stern, even tyrannical. But he could just as easily be characterized by Lucy Larcom's description of her own father: "His reserved, abstracted manner—though his gravity concealed a fund of rare humor,—kept us children somewhat aloof from him" (*Girlhood*, p. 25). We must be careful with Dickinson's own characterizations of her parents, especially those written for T. W. Higginson, because they often represent stylized portraits carefully constructed for another's consumption. When she says, "My Mother does not care for thought–and Father, too busy with his Briefs –to notice what we do – He buys me many Books – but begs me not to read them – because he fears they joggle the Mind" (L. 261), we must remember that Cecilia Vaughan in *Kavanaugh,* one of the Dickinson children's favorite novels, is described in terms similar to the Higginson version of a motherless Emily, whose father is too busy with his law briefs to pay much attention to her. Dickinson often played with literary models. She also wrote: "I never had a mother. . . ." Of course, she did have a mother, one who was caring if not intellectual. Still, she is a shadowy figure who provided very little in the way of sensitive encouragement for her unusual daughter.[16] Her energies, when she was not incapacitated by illness, were directed toward domestic occupations. It was Dickinson's father who believed in women's education and who approved of Catherine Sedgwick, the famous novelist who was responsible for the biography of Lucretia Davidson.[17]

Like her poetic sisters, Dickinson sometimes chafed under the necessity to attend to household chores at the expense of her freedom. In a letter to Jane Humphrey she writes humorously but also revealingly:

> It is not easy to try just as we *are* at home – Vinnie away – and my hands but *two* – not four, or five as they ought to be – and so *many* wants – and me so *very* handy – and my time of so *little* account – and my writing so *very* needless – and really I came to the conclusion that I should be a villain unparalleled if I took but an inch of time for so unholy a purpose as writing a friendly letter. [L. 30]

Women's chores reinforce the feeling that their time is "of so *little* account,"[18] though Dickinson was well aware of the cult of true womanhood, which claimed to deny this. She was a woman of her time. At eighteen she writes archly to her brother of her training in manners at Mount Holyoke: "Are you not gratified that I am so rapidly gaining correct ideas of female propriety & sedate deportment?" (L. 22). To her friend Abiah Root she suggests a joint letter to a former preceptress about to be married: "I think that Abby – you & I had better write her a congratulatory letter after she arrives at her new home, telling her of our joy at her union with so worthy a man & giving her sundry bits of advice on the importance of her station & her household cares" (L. 15). Noticeable in all these extracts is the irony that Dickinson used to express her independence of spirit.[19] Although she never openly rebelled against the limitations of the female role, the only place where we see her waxing sentimental about domestic matters is in her references to her home.[20] And the home, for her, was not the same as a household. It was the space of her intellectual freedom. "God keep me from what they call *house-holds*," (L. 36) she exclaimed humorously at the age of twenty. Of course, her lifetime was spent in what seemed to many like the classical occupations of the unmarried daughter, keeping house, tending a garden, watching at bedsides, sending condolences. But Dickinson maintained her independence in spite of these outward shows of conformity. She could afford to compromise in what she considered minor areas of concern, since she remained uncompromising in the areas that were most important to her: poetry, perception, and private relations.

Like Lucy Larcom she never married. Like most of the women poets about whom we have information, she was ambivalent about sex and marriage. In one letter she called herself "by birth a bachelor." But her attitudes were more complex than that. At the age of twenty-two, before she had chosen to remove herself from society, she wrote to Susan Gilbert:

How dull our lives must seem to the bride, and the plighted maiden, whose days are fed with gold, and who gathers pearls every evening; but to the *wife*, Susie, sometimes the *wife forgotten*, our lives perhaps seem dearer than all others in the world; you have seen flowers at morning, *satisfied* with the dew, and those same sweet flowers at noon with their heads bowed in anguish before the mighty sun; think you these thirsty blossoms will *now* need naught but – *dew?* No, they will cry for sunlight, and pine for the burning noon, tho' it scorches them, scathes them; they have got through with peace – they know that the man of noon, is *mightier* than the morning and their life is henceforth to him. Oh, Susie, it is dangerous, and it is all too dear, these simple trusting spirits, and the spirits mightier, which we cannot resist! It does so rend me, Susie, the thought of it when it comes, that I tremble lest at sometime I, too, am yielded up. [L. 93]

We might dismiss this letter as being a momentary outburst from a young woman. However, a poem probably written around 1863, when the poet was thirty-three years old, expresses many of the same views:

> She rose to His Requirement – dropt
> The Playthings of Her Life
> To take the honorable Work
> Of Woman, and of Wife –
>
> If ought She missed in Her new Day,
> Of Amplitude, or Awe –
> Or first Prospective – Or the Gold
> In using, wear away,
>
> It lay unmentioned – as the Sea
> Develope Pearl, and Weed,
> But only to Himself – be known
> The Fathoms they abide –   [P. 732]

Secret sorrow, compensation, a shift of pronoun from "She," the wife, to "Himself," the sea—no longer ambivalence here but a palpable sense of disillusionment with the female role of wife, a sense of disillusionment Dickinson was able to share imaginatively.[21]

Dickinson used the exercise of her intellect to compensate for whatever she missed of the outside world. She had had a good education (Amherst Academy, one year of Mount Holyoke), but certainly it was no better than other women poets' of her time. Her distance from academic life made her, after a while, less "bookish" than some like Sarah Whitman or Elizabeth Oakes-Smith. Nevertheless, her intellectual and emotional heritage was certainly in line with theirs. She was a New England Puritan, born and bred.[22]

Sometimes in her letters we find her struggling with her own will. "Oh I struggled with great temptation, and it cost me much of denial, but in the end I conquered," (L. 36) she writes at one point. In a letter from 1883 she says: "Even my Puritan Spirit 'gangs' sometimes 'aglay –' " (L. 866). Although she resisted joining the Congregational Church and never became one of the "saved," she found something appealing in Puritanism. Like other women poets, she used it as a descriptive psychology.

Knowing that Dickinson ultimately renounced the world and became a recluse, we read with particular interest this letter written to Abiah Root at the age of sixteen. She is describing two Chinese people she has encountered in Boston. In China they were "Opium Eaters" but here, Dickinson says, "They have now entirely overcome the practice. There is something peculiarly interesting to me in their self *denial*" (L. 13). We are not surprised, therefore, to encounter several poems on the subject of martyrdom. Remembering Elizabeth Oakes-Smith's and Lucy Larcom's fascination with Foxe's *Book of Martyrs*, we recognize the sentiments in Dickinson's poem 260, originally titled "The Book of Martyrs" in the 1890 publication of the *Poems*. (Only a portion of the poem is given here.)

> Read – Sweet – how others – strove –
> Till we – are stouter –
> What they – renounced –
> Till we – are less afraid –   [P. 260][23]

Like the women mentioned above, Dickinson sometimes chose to see herself in the martyr role.

Like these others, too, she toyed with the image of the sanctuary. Home, for Dickinson, seems to have functioned as some form of sanctuary. But it was her room in particular that she considered the place of peace. Martha Dickinson Bianchi claims that Dickinson once took her upstairs, made as if to lock the door, and said, "Matty: here's freedom."[24] In a letter to Mrs. Holland of 1871, she writes ambiguously: "The Fence is the only Sanctuary. That no one invades because no one suspects it" (L. 359). One longs for a fuller rendering of this idea in the letter just as one wishes for more of this pencilled fragment, dated about 1870.

> Lest they should come – is all my fear
> When sweet incarcerated here.   [P. 1169]

These two lines certainly capture the essence of longing for sanctuary, the sense of vulnerability, and the preference for withdrawal. Dickinson rings innumerable changes on the sanctuary motif through her use of prison images. Like references to Chillon in the letters, these images abound in the poems.[25] The importance of Byron's prisoner of Chillon for Dickinson was that he "did not know Liberty when it came" (L. 1029). She once quoted Byron's character, "Even I regain my freedom with a Sigh" (L. 1042). Thus, the ambiguous nature of the prison, as both a symbol of inhibited freedom and a place of protection and peace, became part of her rhetorical exploration of sanctuaries. Incarceration, as she saw it, could be sweet because secure and familiar. "A Prison gets to be a friend –" (P. 652).

In fact, we know she felt vulnerable. For Dickinson and other women poets, one manifestation of this sense of vulnerability was the specter of mental breakdown. Considerable evidence in the poems and letters points to 1861 as a year of psychic crisis for the poet. She writes about herself in the third person to the Norcross cousins:

"Think Emily lost her wits – but she found 'em, likely. Don't part with wits long at a time in this neighborhood" (L. 234). In April of the next year, she writes to T. W. Higginson, "I had a terror since September – I could tell to none" (L. 261). Ten years later came another crisis, the death of her father. Again she confides to the Norcross cousins, "Though it is many nights, my mind never comes home" (L. 414). In 1882 more deaths led to this aphoristic statement: "Sorrow, benighted with Fathoms, cannot find its Mind" (L. 784). But it is not until after the completely unexpected death of her adored nephew, Gilbert Dickinson, in 1883 that we know she was treated for "nervous prostration." She never entirely recovered from this shock. It seems to have affected her both mentally and physically, and she died in 1886 at the age of 56.

As the composite biography in chapter 3 attempted to suggest, nineteenth-century women poets were often plagued by fears of instability. They, rather than male poets, are the first to develop a substantial body of American literary material on suicide and the death wish. As Emily Stipes Watts has also noted, Dickinson wrote a number of poems on these themes.[26]

Dickinson's only real refuge in times of trouble seems to have been her female friends. She once wrote coquettishly to Mrs. Holland, "I miss my little Sanctuary and her redeeming ways" (L. 521). One doesn't know what to make of her statement that the Reverend Charles Wadsworth was her "closest earthly friend," but if the extant letters are any indication, she rarely sought the kind of emotional support from men, from Bowles, Holland, Higginson or even from Judge Lord, that she routinely solicited from the Norcross cousins, Mrs. Holland, and numerous other female friends. However, probably the most important attachment she ever made outside of her family was made to a less comforting figure: Susan Gilbert, the friend who eventually became Emily's sister-in-law.

The issue of Susan deserves special attention. We now have Richard Sewall's fascinating story of the breakdown in relations between Susan's house and Emily's, which were next door to each other. Susan seems to be at the center of this drama, in her later years a threatening, conniving, sinister figure, tormented by jealousy at her husband's infidelity, disgusted at Emily for her Indian-summer affair with Judge Lord, yet still entertaining Amherst's elite in grand style and cloaking her bitterness with bravado.

After Martha Dickinson Bianchi's account of an unfaltering and sentimental devotion between Emily and Sue, it is refreshing to encounter Sewall's pungent version. However, neither seems to me entirely sufficient to deal with the tale told in poems and letters. Sewall emphasizes the story that between 1868 and 1883 Emily never visited her sister-in-law at the Evergreens, only a few feet away. This, he feels, is a sign of the deep disaffection between the two women. However, the relationship between them was so complex that one can hardly interpret it adequately in the light of any one fact, especially since Sue apparently made visits to Emily's house during this period.

In her early twenties Emily Dickinson had been passionately in love with Susan Gilbert. In 1852 she wrote:

> Thank you for loving me, darling, and *will* you "love me more if ever you came home"? – it is enough, dear Susie, I know I shall be satisfied. But what can I do towards you? – *dearer* you *cannot* be, for I love you so already, that it almost breaks my heart – perhaps I can love you *anew*, every day of my life, every morning and evening – Oh, if you will let me, how happy I shall be! [L. 74]

Sue became a kind of sanctuary for her. "And I do love to run fast – and hide away from them all; here in dear Susie's bosom, I know is love and rest" (L. 85). Sewall argues that after Susan's marriage to Emily's brother Austin in 1856, their relationship changed. However, in a letter dated September 1864, Emily writes: "Do not cease, Sister. Should I turn in my long night I should murmur 'Sue' –" (L. 294). One must remember that passionate letters between women were not unusual in the nineteenth century. However, Dickinson's are special because, as far as one can tell, Susan was not responding with the same degree of passion. The portrait of Susan that emerges even in Dickinson's own letters is one of an intensely feeling woman, yes, but one whose intensity was considerably controlled by natural aloofness and hauteur. She was not given to Emily's outbursts of affection.

Nevertheless, Susan Gilbert Dickinson seems to have served an important symbolic function for Emily. At first she may have been merely the confidante and intelligent correspondent that Cecilia Vaughan was to Alice Archer. However, over the years she became to Emily more than the typical nineteenth-century female friend, and thus the relationship developed in ways that make it unusual even in the annals of nineteenth-century sisterhood. "Only Woman in the World," Emily wrote about 1875, "Accept a Julep." Susan started out as a sentimental friend, but she became a representative of something which Dickinson needed much more. She became for Emily the embodiment of female power.

About 1877 Dickinson sent the following poem in a note to Sue.

> To own a Susan of my own
> Is of itself a Bliss –
> Whatever Realm I forfeit, Lord,
> Continue me in this!   [P. 1401]

The implication that devotion to Susan meant forfeiting salvation is worth noting. In a letter sent two years later, Emily comments, "Susan breaks many Commandments, but *one* she obeys – 'Whatsoever ye do, do it unto the Glory –'" (L. 626). Obviously, Susan never represented conventional mediocrity to Emily, and that was part of her attraction. She was dangerous, exciting, difficult, but worth the trouble, because she offered Emily vicarious experience. "With the exception of Shakespeare," Emily wrote, "you have told me of more knowledge than any one living – To say that seriously is strange praise" (L. 757).

In many places, both in the letters and in the poems, Emily associates Susan with power. "To see you unfits for staler meetings" (about 1870). "To miss you, Sue, is power" (September 1871). "Susan knows she is a Siren – and that at a word from her, Emily would forfeit Righteousness –" (mid-June 1878). "Cherish Power – dear – Remember that stands in the Bible between the Kingdom and the Glory, because it is wilder than either of them" (about 1878). "Thank her dear power for having come, an Avalanche of Sun!" (about 1882). "What depths of Domingo in that torrid Spirit!" (about 1883).

Thus, in spite of tensions between the households, especially after 1881, Emily continued to hold her sister-in-law in special regard. Lavinia, Emily's sister, supposedly said that Susan had such a powerful effect on Emily that Susan's cruelties would shorten her life (Sewall, p. 796). However, Emily seems to have assessed Susan's impact on her differently. The following poem, which was sent to Susan, captures the theme of this time.

> That she forgot me was the least
> I felt it second pain
> That I was worthy to forget
> Was most I thought upon
>
> Faithful was all that I could boast
> But Constancy became
> To her, by her innominate
> A something like a shame   [P. 1683][27]

The insight here, that Emily's own fidelity became a reproach to Susan, may well have some truth in it. If Mabel Loomis Todd can be trusted, Susan had betrayed Emily and thus had reason to feel guilty.

Then came a note from this mysterious Emily's housemate, her sister Lavinia, demanding that I call "at once, with my husband." She [Susan] said at that, "You will not allow your husband to go there, I hope!" "Why not?" I asked innocently. "Because they have not, either of them, any idea of morality," she replied, with a certain satisfaction in her tone. . . . She added, "I went in there one day, and in the drawing room I found Emily reclining in the arms of a man." [Sewall, p. 195]

This story certainly points to the extent of Susan's opposition to Emily's late passion for Judge Lord. It may also indicate a breakdown in family alliances. Still, even such a breakdown could not erase in Emily's mind the importance of Susan. During her lifetime she sent her sister-in-law 276 poems that we know of, far more than she sent to anyone else. This one is dated late in 1883, only three years before Emily's death.

> The Heart has many Doors –
> I can but knock –
> For any sweet "Come in"
> Impelled to hark –
> Not saddened by repulse,
> Repast to me
> That somewhere, there exists,
> Supremacy –   [P. 1567]

Susan was supremacy, or power, or dominion, to Emily Dickinson, and for this reason her image was treasured.

What this story of the relationship between the two women is meant to show, in addition to the common element of sisterhood, is that Emily Dickinson's poetry was inspirited in important ways by women. So much has been made over the identity of the "Master," Emily's supposed male lover, that this fact has until recently been overlooked.[28] Furthermore, Emily herself was capable of making misleading statements. According to T. W. Higginson, she once said, "Women talk: men are silent: that is why I dread women" (L. 342a). She may have dreaded the usual types of women she met, but she adored superior women who impressed her by their power and accomplishment.

One such woman was Elizabeth Barrett Browning. Emily felt a personal allegiance to Browning. She read her poems with special fervor and kept her picture in her room. We know from numerous quotations in her letters that she especially admired Browning's *Aurora Leigh.* Two copies were found in the Dickinson library, one belonging to Susan published in 1857 and a second one signed by Emily published in 1859. She probably read Sue's copy first and then obtained one of her own.

It is fascinating to observe the passages marked in the two copies. In Emily's book a faint pencil marking singles out this passage:

> By the way,
> The works of women are symbolical.
> We sew, sew, prick our fingers, dull our sight,
> Producing what? A pair of slippers, sir,
> To put on when you're weary—or a stool
> To stumble over and vex you. . . 'curse that stool!'
> Or else at best a cushion, where you lean
> And sleep, and dream of something we are not
> But would be for your sake. Alas, alas!
> This hurts most, this—that, after all, we are paid
> The worth of our work, perhaps.
>
> [*Aurora Leigh*, I, ll. 456–65]

This passage shows us Dickinson's sensitivity to the issues of male condescension and female mediocrity that were raised by the cult of true womanhood.

However, one quickly discovers passages, unmarked, that have as great or greater relevance to Dickinson's poetry. For instance, at one point Aurora muses over whether she can call herself a poet.

> Am I such indeed? The name
> Is royal, and to sign it like a queen
> Is what I dare not,—though some royal blood
> Would seem to tingle in me now and then,
> With sense of power and ache. [I, ll. 934–38]

Dickinson's many queen poems suggest among other interpretations her fierce desire for ascendancy as a woman poet. Certainly royalty is a constant resource for her when she wishes to use the imagery of power.

In *Aurora Leigh* Browning explores the difficulties of a woman who wants to be both powerful and feminine, both a poet and a fulfilled human being. Aurora chooses her career first and rejects her lover, but at the end she comes back to love and marries the man who has now been humanized by an appreciation for her art. Unsatisfactory as the plot may be, the poem is full of potent passages and prophetic feminist insights. Though unsympathetic critics have wondered how Dickinson could care so much for Browning's poem, the reasons are not hard to discover. What story could touch her more nearly than this one, the story of a woman poet? One of the passages marked in the 1857 copy is the one that describes the public's resistance to original talent: "You must not pump spring-water unawares / Upon a gracious public, full of nerves" (III, ll. 72–73). Dickinson echoes this thought in "Tell all the Truth but tell it slant" (P. 1129).

In addition to Browning's, quotations from other female writers come to mind.

> I looked, and had an acute pleasure in looking—a precious yet poignant pleasure; pure gold, with a steely point of agony: a pleasure like what the thirst-perishing man might feel who knows the well to which he has crept is poisoned, yet stoops and drinks divine draughts nevertheless.

Or:

> He stood between me and every thought of religion, as an eclipse intervenes between man and the broad sun. I could not, in those days, see God for His creature: of whom I had made an idol.[29]

Stylistically, of course, these sentiments are not Dickinson's, but ideologically they are precisely hers. Who is the speaker? Charlotte Brontë's Jane Eyre, another favorite of Dickinson's. Of course, Jane is a more hard-headed lover than Emily. She says: "It is madness in all women to let a secret love kindle within them, which, if unreturned and unknown, must devour the life that feeds it" (*Jane Eyre*, p. 190). But there is something of Emily in Jane, for she does let a secret love kindle in her heart despite her protestations. And there is something of Jane in Emily for both women make their own terms with the world and succeed in respect to them.

It is impossible to avoid the conclusion that Dickinson's sensibility was consistent in many important respects with the sensibility of other women writers of her time. For instance, like several poets we have looked at, she knew what it meant to be fearful of one's own power.

> We never know how high we are
> Till we are asked to rise
> And then if we are true to plan
> Our statures touch the skies –
>
> The Heroism we recite
> Would be a normal thing
> Did not ourselves the Cubits warp
> For fear to be a King –   [P. 1176]

In this poem one senses that the theological speculation is intentionally couched in ambiguous terms so that the issue of hiding one's true
power may be considered in a number of ways. Clearly the poet is
hesitant about recommending bold self-assertion which makes one
into a man, a "King." In a poem like "I took my Power in my Hand – /
And went against the World," (P. 540) she describes the results of one
such move:

> I aimed my Pebble – but Myself
> Was all the one that fell –
> Was it Goliah – was too large –
> Or was myself – too small?

Dickinson's letters are full of indications of the high respect she had
for power. She tells T. W. Higginson, "When a little Girl I remember
hearing that remarkable passage and preferring the 'Power,' not
knowing at the time that 'Kingdom' and 'Glory' were included"
(L. 330). However, we know that Dickinson restricted the range of
her own power by isolating herself in her Amherst home, and we
feel, I think, that she did this intentionally. "The power to fly is
sweet, though one defer the flying, as Liberty is Joy, though never
used" (L. 498).

Her ambivalence toward fame was so intense that we often find her
speaking out of both sides of her mouth about it, like Anne Bradstreet. In a letter she writes, "Success is dust, but an aim touched with
dew" (L. 898). Mostly, however, she seems to tell herself,

> Fame of Myself, to justify,
> All other Plaudit be
> Superfluous – An Incense
> Beyond Necessity –   [P. 713]

Of course, one of the difficulties of quoting a single Dickinson
poem to support any theory about her attitudes is that she used
poetry as a way of capturing in pure form all of her conflicting beliefs
and inclinations. She once wrote Higginson, "When I state myself, as
the Representative of the Verse – it does not mean – me – but a
supposed person" (L. 268). We suspect self-concealment here, for
Emily Dickinson is certainly a presence in her own poems. But it is
confusing sometimes to find her saying in one poem, " 'Tis thirsting
vitalizes wine," and in another that "for extatic need" the liquor that
is tasted "is superior – / I know for I have tried" (P. 1101). Nevertheless, the poetry does seem consistent with Dickinson's passionately held positions as we know them from the letters, and the fact
that it is sometimes contradictory does not argue for its treatment in

isolation from biography; rather it gives us material with which to expand our comprehension of her full range of feelings. Gilbert and Gubar conclude:

> Dickinson's life itself, in other words, became a kind of novel or narrative poem in which, through an extraordinarily complex series of maneuvers, aided by costumes that came inevitably to hand, this inventive poet enacted and eventually resolved both her anxieties about her art and her anger at female subordination. [*Madwoman*, p. 583]

One of these costumes "that came inevitably to hand" was that of the poetess. To a surprising degree, she shared the poetess sensibility. She was fearful, yet bold; diffident, yet brash; renunciatory, yet avid—in short, ambivalent, especially towards those dangerous shoals of fame which tempted her. However, though she once wrote that she preferred her "Barefoot-Rank" to fame, she also knew that "A Word that breathes distinctly / Has not the power to die" (P. 1651), and thus she was ready, as she says elsewhere, to "lay [her] Head / Upon this trusty Word –" (P. 1347).[30]

Finally, what distinguishes Emily Dickinson from other women poets is her skill with words, her use of language. She retained her compression despite pressure from her closest friends and critics, people like Samuel Bowles and T. W. Higginson, who would have made her more discursive. She introduced unusual vocabulary into women's poetry—vocabulary borrowed from various professions mainly closed to women, like law, medicine, the military, and merchandising. I agree with Adrienne Rich that she knew she was a genius.[31] Nothing else could explain her peculiar invulnerability to contemporary criticism of her work.

Dickinson wrote many poems about violation. The integrity of some poems was literally violated by editors who made unauthorized changes before printing them. But the poet triumphed in the end. She created a unique voice in American poetry and would not modulate it, even for Higginson who directed her to writers like Maria Lowell and Helen Hunt Jackson as models.

Like Lowell and Jackson, Dickinson did not look down on the female poetic subjects of her day. She used them; but she used them in what would come to be perceived as a poetic assault on the feminine conventions from which they sprung. She was not, for instance, taken in by the propaganda of "true womanhood." She saw behind the virtue of modesty the caricature of the double-bind.

A Charm invests a face
Imperfectly beheld –

> The Lady dare not lift her Vail
> For fear it be dispelled –
>
> But peers beyond her mesh –
> And wishes – and denies –
> Lest Interview – annul a want
> That Image – satisfies –   [P. 421]

Perhaps Dickinson's ambivalent relation to the world has more to do with this lady "who dare not lift her Vail" than has previously been perceived. What this poem captures is the feelings of a woman who must obtain what she wants through deception and manipulation. Thus it does not simply represent the familiar Dickinson wisdom that hunger tantalizes where satiety cloys. This woman's feelings become part of the substance of the poem. They are fear (of male rejection), curiosity, and desire. The lady must finally deny her desires, sublimate her will to power, and assume a passive role. "A Charm" might also serve as a commentary on a poem written three years earlier.

> Our lives are Swiss –
> So still – so Cool –
> Till some odd afternoon
> The Alps neglect their Curtains
> And we look farther on!
>
> *Italy* stands the other side!
> While like a guard between –
> The solemn Alps –
> The siren Alps
> Forever intervene!   [P. 80]

We recognize the theme of the unattained, so close to the hearts of women like Lucy Larcom and Elizabeth Oakes-Smith. Here, however, the barriers both forbid assault and invite it. They are both awesome and enticing. Like the lady who "peers beyond her mesh," this speaker hasn't accepted the limitations on her experience. Though undemonstrative, she remains unreconciled.

The insights made available by the comparison of these two poems can help us even when we examine the particular language that made Dickinson unique. Take, for example, the following poem written during her most creative period.

> I had not minded – Walls –
> Were Universe – one Rock –
> And far I heard his silver Call
> The other side the Block –

I'd tunnel – till my Groove
Pushed sudden thro' to his –
Then my face take her Recompense –
The looking in his Eyes –

But 'tis a single Hair –
A filament – a law –
A Cobweb – wove in Adamant –
A Battlement – of Straw –

A limit like the Vail
Unto the Lady's face –
But every Mesh – a Citadel –
And Dragons – in the Crease –   [P. 398]

This is a poem about the forbidden lover, and as such it reminds us of what Dickinson could do with conventional female subjects. Although this is not one of Dickinson's best poems, it exhibits many of her characteristic innovations and therefore makes an interesting focus for discussion. Does this poem have roots in real experience or was it merely an exercise?

In the second Master letter, probably composed about this time and intended for a recipient we can no longer identify,[32] the poet asked: "Couldn't Carlo [her dog], and you and I walk in the meadows an hour – and nobody care but the Bobolink – and *his* – a *silver* scruple? I used to think when I died – I could see you – so I died as fast as I could – but the 'Corporation' are going Heaven too so [Eternity] wont be sequestered – now [at all] –" (L. 233). Here we find the familiar impossible attachment forbidden by "the Corporation," the constituted powers. It is an attachment that can only be indulged in secret, in some "sequestered" place. This Master letter has too much unrefined feeling in it to be the product of a merely literary pose, and I suggest that the poem was also written out of felt experience, although the structural properties this experience assumed may well have been influenced by the vocabulary of secret sorrow.

Dickinson begins "I had not minded – Walls" in the subjunctive, one of her characteristic modes. Thus, she establishes the initial grounds of the poem as those of the non-real, the if. The first two stanzas posit a set of circumstances that would allow for fulfillment, the enticement of the view, as P. 80 says, when Alps neglect their curtains. The last two stanzas, in contrast, describe the limitations on fulfillment that forever intervene.

Typical of Dickinson's language, the poem contrasts short Anglo-Saxon words with longer Latinate ones. "Block," "eyes," "groove," "law," and "mesh," for example, are all Anglo-Saxon and convey even in their brevity a sense of abrupt limitation. "Recompense," "universe," "filament," "citadel," and "dragon," on the other hand, are Latinate words: softer and more excursive. They have feminine endings. Using the same short vowel sounds as the Anglo-Saxon words, they nevertheless convey an opposite sense of possibility. Although the words themselves do not always mean what their sounds convey ("citadel" being used to suggest an obstacle instead of a possibility), there is at the levels of both meaning and sound a sense of opposition: desire vs. frustration. Dickinson's language operates on the basis of paired antitheses. Other pairings include the concrete vs. the abstract (face/recompense), the material vs. the immaterial (rock/silver call), and the hard vs. the soft (adamant/cobweb). Her code is conflict.

Thus far we might compare her use of language to Shakespeare's, which also depends upon doublings, paradoxes, contrasts. However, Dickinson, though she loved Shakespeare, chose to be more obscure, and she did this largely by breaking linguistic rules out of a commitment to compression. The first stanza, for instance, might be paraphrased: I would not have minded walls. Were the universe to have been entirely made up of rock and were I to have heard his call from afar, it would have seemed to me merely a short distance, the other side of the block. This, of course, reduces the impact of Dickinson's compression. "Block" in her poem affects one like a pun, reminding us of "rock" earlier, as well as of the geographical meaning of "block," a city street division.

Dickinson was criticized in her day for this kind of compression. It flew in the face of most contemporary poetry, which aimed at comprehensiveness through discursive exposition. Emerson was probably her closest friend here, but even he did not break rules as flagrantly as she. Her editors also grumbled at her rhymes. "His" and "eyes" did not seem like rhyming words to them.

The structure of this poem represents a final contrast to the conventions of her time. In "Acquainted with Grief," Helen Hunt Jackson posits an unnatural occurrence by personifying grief. However, once this given is accepted, the poem never departs from its established world. Dickinson, however, reverses expectations everywhere. She begins in the realm of "if," making all the details of this realm concrete and existential: *walls, rock, block, tunnel, groove,* and *face* are part of her real world of experience. Nevertheless, when the tense shifts from the subjunctive to the present, suddenly we have paradoxes that do not belong to an experiential realm: a cobweb woven in adamant, a mesh that is a citadel, and finally, dragons, mythical beasts belonging to the world of imagination.

Furthermore, in the sequence filament/law, cobweb/adamant, and battlement/straw there is a reversal of terms in the final pair. The first two move from the insubstantial to the substantive, the last one from the substantive back to the insubstantial. "Adamant" is echoed in "battlement," but the "law" becomes "straw."

The structural progression from the real to the surreal is recognizably characteristic of Dickinson. And here the lines, "A limit like the Vail / Unto the Lady's face," become significant. Like the veil, the limitations Dickinson describes are restrictive in the real world. The seemingly insubstantial "hair" is tougher than rock, and like the veil of restrictions women must accept, to pass beyond these limitations forces one to encounter terrible dragons. However, a citadel, the *Oxford English Dictionary* tells us, is a "fortress commanding a city, which it serves both to protect and to keep in subjugation." Like the prison, this image reminds us of Dickinson's Houdini-like ability to wriggle out of confining spaces, to convert limitations into creative resources. Dragons are at least interesting to contemplate. The lady's veil—the symbol of Dickinson's sense of social, legal, and literary restrictions—provided her with a certain recompense. Thus the reversal in the third stanza, where limiting law becomes insubstantial straw, works.

Ultimately, Emily Dickinson transformed her closed world into a creative space. If there is a disappointment in this poem, it comes in the second stanza where "the looking in his eyes" seems a rather weak way of describing this triumph. But whatever its limitations, this poem shows us the way an artist like Dickinson could make interesting use of motifs such as the secret sorrow and the forbidden lover. Her vision was "slant," and therefore to us thoroughly refreshing.

Recently it has become fashionable to see Emily Dickinson as a woman who lived in the realm of transcendence, secure in the space she created for the exercise of her power. Although I am sympathetic with this view, I would like to add a word of caution. No one can read Dickinson's poems and letters in their entirety without a sense that the ground for security was forever shifting under her feet. She did not resort to references to fear only out of coyness. She felt it. She wrote: "In all the circumference of Expression, those guileless words of Adam and Eve never were surpassed, 'I was afraid and hid Myself'" (L. 946). And elsewhere: "Your bond to your brother reminds me of mine to my sister – early, earnest, indissoluble. Without her life were fear, and Paradise a cowardice, except for her inciting voice" (L. 827). To rejoice that she found ways of evading the subjugation of the spirit that her society enforced upon its women should not mean ignoring her sense of vulnerability, which was real, which was tragic.

In Dickinson's preoccupation with the imagery of royalty, we find her desire to exercise the full range of her talents; we find her will to power. In her preoccupation with falling, surrendering, confinement, and violation, we find her fears. Knowing what she had to give up, recognition within her lifetime, the chance to remain within the world she devoured information about through her friends and her newspaper, we can only be glad that at moments she had the perspective to write:

> The Heart is the Capital of the Mind –
> The Mind is a single State –
> The Heart and the Mind together make
> A single Continent –
>
> One is the Population –
> Numerous enough –
> This ecstatic Nation
> Seek – it is Yourself.   [P. 1354]

The puzzle of Emily Dickinson's work is finally not a question of the identity of the Master or the extent of her real experience, but one of tradition and the individual talent. Although the concern with intense feeling, the ambivalence toward power, the fascination with death, the forbidden lover and secret sorrow all belong to this women's tradition, Emily Dickinson's best work so far surpasses anything that a logical extension of that tradition's codes could have produced that the only way to explain it is by the single word, genius. She was "of the Druid." That a great many poems like "I tie my Hat – I crease my Shawl" are in places not much above the women's poetry of her time is only to be expected. What Emily Dickinson did for later women poets, like Amy Lowell who wanted to write her biography, was remarkable: she gave them dignity. No other aspect of her influence was so important. After Emily Dickinson's work became known, women poets in America could take their work seriously. She redeemed the poetess for them, and made her a genuine poet.

One Brief, Transitory Hour

Ella Wheeler Wilcox,
Lizette Woodworth Reese, and
Louise Imogen Guiney

5 By the time the first volume of Emily Dickinson's poems had gone through eleven editions, that is by the end of 1892, the "gentle lady" whose "dimity convictions" Dickinson had scorned no longer presided unopposed over the social scene. The theory of separate spheres was on the wane and the "new woman" had arrived, expressing herself with a new frankness and invading traditionally masculine enclaves. Genteel magazines were beginning to publish women in great numbers. Often the poems published in *Scribner's*, *Century*, and the *Atlantic* were unidentifiable as to gender. In this brief transitional period male and female poets were almost indistinguishable, which is why critics like George Santayana, Thomas Beer, and Fred Lewis Pattee were dissatisfied with the verse and called it effeminate, gutless, dainty.

One observer summarized the new situation in which women found themselves in the following way:

> Their volumes, bound in creamy vellum and daintily tinted cloth, began more and more to fill the book tables, until reviewers no longer could give separate notice to them, but must consider the poets of a month in groups of ten or twelve. The quality of the feminine product was high enough to find place in the most exclusive monthlies, and the quantity published was surprising. The *Atlantic Monthly*, for instance, during the decade from 1870 published 108 poems by Longfellow, Whittier, Holmes, Lowell, Aldrich, and 450 other poems, and of the latter 201 were by women.[1]

No longer were women praised for their effusiveness and men for their control of the language. In the introduction to his famous *American Anthology*, Edmund Clarence Stedman half-seriously called this period "the woman's age."[2] Unlike his predecessor, Rufus Griswold, Stedman did not relegate women poets to a separate volume. Women were still not the mainstay of American verse, he felt, but at least they were competing in the same league.

In spite of changing conditions, however, women's poems were

117

not substantially different in attitude from their predecessors'. Birds
winging their way into the ether still symbolically expressed missed
or rejected opportunities. The sanctuary motif remained a constant;
both Lizette Woodworth Reese and Louise Imogen Guiney—among
the most highly respected women poets of the day—wrote poems
titled "Sanctuary." Furthermore, women of the 1890s continued to
use poetry to create fantasies of power, only to end by rejecting their
implications. Martyrdom persisted as a haunting strain in their work.
To inhabit a purely spiritualized world seemed preferable than to bid
for this one.

Secret sorrow is present in the poetry also. Lizette Reese's "Reticence" and Margaret Deland's "Love's Wisdom" offer examples of
two different types. The Reese poem is of the older variety, similar to
Helen Hunt Jackson's, using a speaker who will hide her feelings
about her dead lover.

> They shall not know how stripped a thing am I,
> Unroofed, unharbored, clinging to a spar![3]

The Deland poem, however, is peculiarly modern in spite of its Renaissance language. Sara Teasdale, Elinor Wylie, Louise Bogan, and
Edna St. Vincent Millay would write many such poems. Secret sorrow here merges with Helen Hunt Jackson's theme of passionate
silence.

> So, though I worship at thy feet,
>   I'll be discreet—
> And all my love shall not be told,
>   Lest thou be cold,
> And, knowing I was always thine,
>   Scorn to be mine.
> So am I dumb, to rescue thee
>   From tyranny—
> And by my silence, I do prove
>   Wisdom and Love!   [Stedman]

Hardly for the first time but with a new boldness, women poets
took up the theme of passion. Ella Wheeler Wilcox's *Poems of Passion*
(1883) created a scandal and became a sensation. The burning kiss, so
offensive to some members of the Victorian world, grew to be a stock
feature in women's poems. However, more than ever before, sexuality and romantic love in general became hyphenated with an equally
old theme, death. Helen Hunt Jackson's ghostly lovers flit through
the poems of many *fin-de-siècle* females. Death itself is eroticized and

erotic love is made morbid. Emily Dickinson, with her "wild nights" and deflowering bees, could write provocatively, even frankly, about sex; one is sometimes unsure whether the experience a poem describes is love or death. But nowhere in her work does one find the morbid ecstasy of her niece, Martha Gilbert Dickinson, who wrote:

> Deep down in the dusk of passion-haunted ways,
> Lost in the dreaming alchemies of tone,—
> Drenched in the dew no other wings frequent,
>   —Our thirsting hearts drank in the breath
>   Of violets and love in death.—   [Stedman, "Her Music"]

The times seemed to inspire such poems, for men were writing them, too. Richard Hovey, for instance, put these fervent lines in a poem called "Laurana's Song: For 'A Lady of Venice' ":

> Let him come here, and kiss me on the mouth,
> And have his will!
> Love dead and dry as summer in the South
> When winds are still,
> And all the leafage shrivels in the heat!
> Let him come here and linger at my feet
> Till he grow weary with the over-sweet,
> And die, or kill.   [Stedman]

Perhaps some of this was due to the unacknowledged influence of poets like Swinburne, but more likely there was something in the late Victorians that coupled titillation with punishment. The pornography of the times attests to this, but at a more genteel level the poetry does, too. Death becomes at one and the same moment the final fillip in the decadents' demand for excitement and an escape from the intense psychic pressures this demand creates. Take, for instance, the opening lines of "Love's Kiss" by Helen Hay:

> Kiss me but once, and in that space supreme
> My whole dark life shall quiver to an end,
> Sweet Death shall see my heart and comprehend
> That Life is crowned, and in an endless gleam
> Will fix the color of the dying stream,
> That Life and Death will meet as friend with friend.
>
>   [Stedman]

The life that will "quiver to an end" vibrates with both pain and pleasure. Death, the climax to life, here comes as a "sweet" terminus.

Among male poets there were those, like Thomas Hornsby Ferril and Richard Hovey, who defied such tendencies in American poetry and wrote rugged nature poems, fierce accolades of Walt Whitman, or, like Hamlin Garland, stirring lyrics drawn from the American West. Among women, however, even a supposedly "virile" poet like Louise Imogen Guiney seems less hardy, less death-defying, than death-enamored.

In point of fact, women poets of this period were still more fully engaged in the drama of life's disappointments than were their male counterparts. Not completely at home with their recent past, they were still not quite attuned to their future. Femininity seemed too fragile, masculinity too alien to them. Their work dramatizes the development of preoccupations traditionally feminine into lyric expressions surprisingly modern. They were poets of the transition, wearing new fashions to do traditional work.

In an article entitled "The Transitional American Woman" published in the *Atlantic Monthly* in December 1880, Kate Gannett Wells describes the woman of the day in these terms:

> Women do not care for their home as they did; it is no longer the focus of *all* their endeavors; nor is the mother the involuntary nucleus of the adult children. Daughters must have art studios outside their home; authoresses must have a study near by; and aspirants to culture must attend classes or readings in some semi-public place. Professional women have found that, however dear the home is, they can exist without it.[4]

When we remember Emily Dickinson's feverish proclamations about her blessed home, when we recall Mary Hewitt's "Hearth of Home" and Lydia Sigourney's enthusiasm for the functions of housewife and mother, it seems we have come very far from them. Still, these new women could hardly be called liberated in the sense in which we understand the word today or even in the sense in which the 1920s might have used it. Poets and professional women may have been more self-sufficient than their mothers. They still lived in a world where many occupations were closed to them. Lizette Woodworth Reese had to support herself by being a schoolteacher for 48 years. Louise Guiney went from being postmistress of the Auburndale, Massachusetts, post office to becoming a cataloguer in the Boston Public Library. These were rather new jobs for women to hold but still low-paying and not nearly as glamorous as being a college professor or the editor of an important magazine, jobs held by her friends Oliver Wendell Holmes and Richard Watson Gilder. Furthermore, none of these women was sexually aggressive. They would have been horrified by Edna St. Vincent Millay. Ella Wheeler Wilcox was horrified by Amy Lowell. Although she was pro-suffrage, Louise Guiney was dismayed by America's overly eager "gynaecocracy." She preferred women who were sturdier and more reticent.

In this Guiney shared with a number of other successful women a profound suspicion about "the new woman" and the social changes inevitable in her wake. To Richard Watson Gilder she wrote in 1894: "I am not in the least given to any violent interest in womankind, such as has addled the country's brains of late. Give me a man-and-woman world: 'tis good enough!"[5]

Ella Wheeler Wilcox, for her part, took up "the woman question" with relish and published *Men, Women and Emotions* in 1893. In it she assaults the contemporary tendency to denigrate housekeeping as a woman's role. She says that the wife "should consider this work the sacrifice she offers on the altar of love, and compel herself to do it well, and cheerfully, if the necessity presents itself." However, Wilcox was also capable of writing, "I sometimes think that God is a woman—He is expected to forgive so much."[6] Wilcox did not wish to have the vote herself because she felt her domestic and professional activities left her too little time to inform herself adequately about politics. Although she castigated weak men who tried to belittle women's achievements, she was always very careful to present herself in public as a "man's woman," totally devoted to her husband. She wrote: "To be a gifted poet is a glory; to be a worth-while woman is a greater glory."[7]

The lives of Wilcox, Guiney, and Reese inform us in numerous ways that they were women of their generation. While the *Atlantic, Century,* and *North American Review* published articles like "Are Women to Blame?" "Our Foolish Virgins," "The Change in the Feminine Ideal," and "The Steel-Engraving Lady and the Gibson Girl," these women poets were themselves embodiments of the transition so interesting to the press.

Ella Wheeler Wilcox, the most shocking of the three to her generation, was probably the most deeply conventional. She would have agreed wholeheartedly with Lydia Sigourney that "the soul of woman lives in love." At an early age she became involved in the temperance movement and this gave her a taste for causes that lasted until the end of her life. She herself was her own greatest cause, but like many of her civic-minded female contemporaries, she extended her interests into other areas. During the first world war, Wilcox composed a famous poem as a reaction to the threat of venereal disease called "Soldiers, Come Back Clean." One cannot imagine Lydia Sigourney writing such a poem.

However, unlike many feminists of the time, Wilcox was not part of the Purity Crusade, intended in part to curb male passions in order to bring them more into line with women's supposedly moderate desires. Wilcox was a passionate woman. She wrote: "It is impossible for an absolutely passionless woman to be either just or generous in her judgments of humanity at large. It is a strange fact that she needs an admixture of the baser physical element, to broaden her spiritual vision, and quicken her sympathies" (*Men, Women and Emotions*, p. 298).

However, the accusations of immorality that greeted the publication of *Poems of Passion* in 1883 were entirely unfounded; Wilcox was not a libertine. A Chicago newspaper claimed that she had written poems that "out-Swinburned Swinburne and out-Whitmaned Whitman." She quickly sold 60,000 copies. Just as the book was coming out, however, she married Robert Wilcox, a 40-year-old gentleman of established respectability to whom she seems to have been utterly faithful and fiercely loyal all her life. That a thoroughly virtuous woman should produce remarks with the most startling implications was a phenomenon not uncharacteristic of the age. In an article called "Our Foolish Virgins" published in 1901, Eliot Gregory described what he called "bouyant hoidens" who offended Victorian ideas of decorum and yet were in fact girls "of spotless respectability."[8] This was a time of greater titillation than explicit sexuality. Ella Wheeler Wilcox enjoyed the shocked attention she received but she was firm with the men who wrote to her. One who sought her out was bought a ticket and put back on the train.

Although unusual in some ways, Wilcox was conventional to the extent that she wanted all her life to please the majority. She played to the masses and in doing so forfeited the respect of more critically sophisticated judges of her poetry like Edmund Clarence Stedman. Her career as a successful *woman*, in her terms, was more important to her than her art. For two years after her marriage she did not write, and when in her late fifties her husband died, she had a nervous breakdown. Ella Wheeler Wilcox died of cancer in 1919, having realized too late that instead of lifting the level of the general taste she had sunk to conforming to its dictates and thus reinforced mediocrity. However, her life was an inspiration to other women who saw her as an independent female who had managed marriage and a career without undue strain. As a matter of fact, from that point of view, she was quite unusual for her time, a professional woman who tried to play a conventional wifely role as well.

At the turn of the century America was producing a growing number of professional women. Between 1880 and 1900 women in the labor force doubled, and between 1890 and 1910 female enrollment in college tripled. In contrast to co-ed institutions, women's colleges in this period emphasized rigorous intellectual training for their female graduates, and a growing number of these did not marry.[9] In 1903 a sampling of Smith, Vassar, and Wellesley graduates between the ages of 26 and 37 showed that only 25% were married as opposed to the large majority of women married at similar ages in the rest of the population. In interviews women from this class of intellectuals admitted that they saw marriage and a career as mutually exclusive. Not always without regret, they accepted their role as outsiders to domestic culture.

Although neither Lizette Reese nor Louise Guiney attended college, they shared many of the same values as these professional women. Like them, neither Reese nor Guiney married. Theirs were lives of intellectual companionship with other women and with close male friends. Reese devoted her energies to reading and to teaching in the Baltimore school system. When one encounters her statement "that the pupils were in school to do their duty, and I was there to do mine," one is almost tempted to feel that the age of the "new woman" had passed her by. After all, Margaret Deland described one of the changes in the feminine ideal as the transformation of the nineteenth-century concept of duty into a new sense of duty to oneself. Yet, although Reese was still Victorian enough to assume she had a duty to others, she was hardly an old-fashioned "steel-engraving lady." From 1877 to 1881 she taught in a black high school in Baltimore, and she is said to have considered these some of the happiest years of her life. Furthermore, Reese was one of the founders of the Women's Literary Club in Baltimore. At a time when there was an enormous upsurge of women's clubs and societies, Reese became active in creating one devoted to literature. In 1931 she was named poet laureate of the state.

Lizette Reese's career spans a series of years in which great changes took place. She was born in 1856 and died in 1935. Her first book was *A Branch of May* published in 1887. The last book of her poems to be published during her lifetime was *Pastures* (1933). Throughout this period she maintained her own point of view with regard to literary fashions. During the heyday of the free verse movement, she wrote little. Later she commented: "The term free verse was untenable, for verse, like all Art, is under the law; its only liberty comes from that. But the movement, when it had spent its initial force, had succeeded in shaking up and revigorating the traditionalists; this was worth every blow struck in the battle."[10]

In the 1920s when women in great numbers were again publishing her kind of poetry, Reese began to re-emerge as a poet. Robert Hariss claims that both Teasdale and Millay were "deeply indebted" to her. It is curiously suggestive that there are prophetic echoes of Wylie, Teasdale, and Millay in the 1890s' poetry of all three of these women, Ella Wheeler Wilcox, Lizette Woodworth Reese, and Louise Imogen Guiney. Obviously, the 1920s' revolution in manners and morals that fostered the flapper poets had begun in the 1890s with the "bachelor woman" and "the Gibson Girl."

Caroline Ticknor, writing in 1901, characterized the Gibson Girl as wearing "a short skirt and heavy square toed shoes, a mannish collar, cravat, and vest, and a broad-brimmed felt hat tipped jauntily upon one side." She imagined her saying: "I can do everything my brothers do; and do it rather better, I fancy. I am an athlete and a college graduate, with a wide, universal outlook. My point of view is free from narrow influences, and quite outside of the home boundaries."[11]

Louise Guiney was not a Gibson Girl. None of the innocent impishness of this person could have been hers, and yet she was in her own way a rebel against Victorian prudery. Her contempt for Victoria was violent:

> That money-saving, gillie-adoring, etiquette-blinded, pudgy, plodding, unspiritual, unliterary, mercantile, dowdy, sparkless, befogged, continuous Teuton lady is not, in one's line of life, a Necessary. How could Van Dyke have posed her? What could Falkland have said to her which would have been comprehended? [*Letters*, I, pp. xiv–xv]

Fuming over Victoria's Diamond Jubilee, she wrote to a friend: "As the godly Mr. Wilfrid Meynell said in his pious paper . . . when reviewing a bookful of virtuous gentlewoman *circa* 1670, who were of a punless cast of mind—'O for an hour of Nell Gwynne!' " [*Letters*, I, p. 174].

Like the Gibson Girl, Guiney had a healthy taste for outdoor activities, particularly for brisk walking. She once remarked: "If ever I get to Paradise, I have a stipulation: that I shall play games in the open air, for ever and ever" (*Letters*, I, p. 140). In 1895 she took a walking tour of England and Wales with her friend Alice Brown. They were unchaperoned and they dressed unconventionally, in gaiters. She wrote: "Divided skirts are my horror. Gimme kilts to the knee, or trousers outright."[12] Most women were still wearing dresses that swept the ground. Encountering bewildered Englishmen, the strangely clad Guiney and Brown would inquire with perfectly straight faces if the gentleman had seen ten other women dressed just as they were.

In spite of her proclaimed lack of interest in womankind, Guiney spent a great deal of her time with women. Among her female literary friends were Louise Chandler Moulton, Sarah Orne Jewett, Annie Fields, and Alice Brown. She corresponded with Lizette Reese. Long before the advent of current interest in Katherine Phillips, she wrote a book about the "Matchless Orinda," which she published in 1904. Although her assessment of Phillips mixed praise and blame she was particularly sympathetic with the independence of this seventeenth-century woman poet. In essence, Guiney (and many others like her) did not wish to be lumped together with what Thomas Beer called "the Titaness," a stern, aggressive female reformer who abhorred strong passions and strong drink and whose power was clearly being felt in the 1890s. Nevertheless, Guiney favored women's suffrage and she admired other women poets. To Herbert E. Clarke she wrote enthusiastically in 1896: "There is a new volume coming from Miss Reese, Lizette Woodworth Reese, whom I have always 'ighly had-mired. The women over here are regular Atlantas in the poetic race" (*Letters*, I, p. 143). To her credit, she did not resent other women on their way up.

With all Guiney's adventurous spirit and hard-headedness, it comes as something of a shock to find her as deeply attracted to martyrs as her early nineteenth-century sister poets like Elizabeth Oakes-Smith. She once wrote: "Thwarted growths always have an attraction for me, and the might-have-beens are more interesting than Sarah Lynches" (*Letters*, II, pp. 44–45). Her elegy to Thomas Parsons could have been written by any nineteenth-century woman poet early or late.

> Look not on fame, but Peace; and in a bower
> Receive at last her fulness and her power:
> Not wholly, pure of heart!
> Forget thy few, who would be where thou art.[13]

The renunciation of ambition and worldly power in favor of peace, and ultimately death, is all too familiar among women of this tradition. Her sense of her own failure at the end of her life was intense. She wrote: "I am a rounded and perfect Failure, so far as getting on in this world is concerned" (*Letters*, I, p. 235). Two years before her death, she complained in a letter:

> I've been heading up against the wind very unnaturally for some six years now. Some sort of break-up is imminent, for I'm not getting any younger. I'm like a galvanized corpse kept alive by [others]; but in myself I have no weapon to fight the world with.

> And my mind is like the "walking-stick" insect, so infernally sensitive that if touched or breathed upon, it can only hang lifeless, instead of scuttling away. [*Letters*, II, pp. 243–44].

For a woman who had "hungered for a largeness like the sea, / For space, for freedom, scope, infinity,"[14] this is a sad confession, though a familiar one.

Although much had changed for women poets, underneath the bravado much had remained the same. This is particularly obvious if we analyze the poems of these women. They may have allowed themselves a new frankness in using the language of passion, but behind this bold display lay many of the same fears and hesitations we recognize earlier in the century.

One might look, for instance, at a poem by Ella Wheeler Wilcox entitled "The Tiger."

> In the still jungle of the senses lay
> A tiger soundly sleeping, till one day
> A bold young hunter chanced to come that way.
>
> "How calm," he said, "that splendid creature lies,
> I long to rouse him into swift surprise!"
> The well-aimed arrow shot from amorous eyes.
>
> And lo! the tiger rouses up and turns,
> A coal of fire his glowing eyeball burns,
> His mighty frame with savage hunger yearns.
>
> He crouches for a spring; his eyes dilate—
> Alas! bold hunter, what shall be thy fate?
> Thou canst not fly, it is too late, too late.
>
> Once having tasted human flesh, ah! then,
> Woe, woe unto the whole rash world of men,
> The wakened tiger will not sleep again.   [*Poems of Passion*]

At first glance this seems like a very modern-spirited poem for the 1880s. It can stand up to Santayana's attack on genteel American poetry as "simple, sweet, humane, Protestant literature, grandmotherly in that sedate spectacled wonder with which it gazed at this terrible world and said how beautiful and how interesting it all was."[15] Yet one immediately notices how fearfully sex is presented here. It is a "savage hunter" predicting the death of the hunter. Once awakened, sexual appetite becomes unappeasable (it "will not sleep again"), and it threatens more than the single hunter. One remembers Emily Dickinson's "In Winter in my Room" (P. 1670) in which a harmless worm ("pink, lank and warm") becomes a threatening snake from which the speaker flees in terror. Poems in which sex, or passion, appear threatening are rare among men, even in this relatively androgynous period. Women, on the other hand, have often written such poems. Christina Rossetti's "Goblin Market" stands as the paradigm.

In "As By Fire" Wilcox gives a more balanced view of the senses, without, however, allowing them a legitimate claim.

> Sometimes I feel so passionate a yearning
>   For spiritual perfection here below,
> This vigorous frame with healthful fervor burning,
>   Seems my determined foe.

The senses burn because the body is healthy not because it is diseased. But the speaker tells us she is striving for "a wholly spiritual existence." Her perspective on the struggle remains the traditionally feminine, quasi-religious one:

> Ah! when in the immortal ranks enlisted,
> I sometimes wonder if we shall not find
> That not by deeds, but by what we've resisted,
>   Our places are assigned.[16]

Although Wilcox was "intensely religious by temperament, she subscribed to no fixed religion" (Ballou, p. 23). Still we find here the Puritan echoes so typical of these women poets. Deeds, works, the world—all are rejected in favor of self-control, abnegation, the spiritual life. Or, as Dickinson wrote in poem 745:

> Renunciation – is the Choosing
> Against itself –
> Itself to justify

Nowhere does one find the pure sensual joy of dominating nature evident in many male poems of the period. Nor does one recognize in women's poems the optimistic bravado of Richard Hovey's "Unmanifest Destiny":

> I do not know beneath what sky
>   Nor on what seas shall be my fate,
> I only know it shall be high,
>   I only know it shall be great.   [Stedman]

Probably the most Dickinsonian poem Wilcox ever wrote is "The Voluptuary":

> Oh, blest is he who has some aim defeated,
>   Some mighty loss to balance all his gain.
> For him there is a hope not yet completed:
>   For him hath life yet draughts of joy and pain.
>
> But cursed is he who has no balked ambition,
>   No hopeless hope, no loss beyond repair
> But sick and sated with complete fruition,
>   Keeps not the pleasure even of despair.   [Ballou, p. 74]

For some reason the prospect of satisfaction and self-indulgence filled these women with horror, and this at a time when essayists in the magazines were writing about "the general idleness and self-centredness of the average American woman."[17] Quite possibly, at a subconscious level, guilt was still associated in their minds with ambition. The common wisdom of the day was that the past ethic of self-sacrifice had been replaced by women with a new ethic of self-fulfillment. "Formerly," wrote Kate Wells, "to be a good house-keeper, an anxious mother, an obedient wife, was the *ne plus ultra* of female endeavor,—to be all this *for others' sakes*. Now, it is to be more than one is, for *one's own sake*" (her emphasis; Wells, p. 821).

However, at a deeper level the ideal of renunciation and self-sacrifice did not lose its appeal for women so quickly. Much of the poignancy of Lizette Reese's poetry depends upon our recognition of woman's presumed need to serve. "Rachel" is a characteristic example in which we find not only "an anxious mother" but also the familiar notion that a woman's children are her wealth, her standard of success.

> No days that dawn can match for her
>   The days before her house was bare;
> Sweet was the whole year with the stir
>   Of small feet on the stair.
>
> Once was she wealthy with small cares,
>   And small hands clinging to her knees;
> Now is she poor, and, weeping, bears
>   Her strange, new hours of ease.   [*Selected Poems*]

In Reese's "Renunciation" a woman sends her lover away in order that he may be happy.

> Seek her and find her; I do grudge her naught.
> Love, after daylight, dark; so there is left
>   This season stripped of you; but yet I know,
>   Remembering the old, I cannot make

These new days bitter or myself bereft.
I know, O love, that I do love you so,
While peace is yours my true heart cannot break!

[*Selected Poems*]

This poem was published first in *A Handful of Lavender* in 1892, but its theme became a standard for women poets in the twenties, especially for Teasdale and Millay. Renouncing the lover seems somehow the only way of gaining control and attesting to one's own power.

For a good deal of this poetry one could use as a summary Mme. de Vionnet's comment to Lambert Strether in Henry James' novel *The Ambassadors:* "The wretched self is always there, always making us somehow a fresh anxiety. What it comes to is that it's not, that it's never, a happiness, any happiness at all, to *take.* The only safe thing is to give. It's what plays you least false."[18] James was sensitive enough to realize that this was in essence a woman's view, which is why Strether (and many another Jamesian hero) is more at home with women than with men.

Sometimes one can hear in the heart of this self-denial a hint of masochism, "the pleasure of despair" as Wilcox calls it. Elinor Wylie was to become an expert at it. Lizette Reese suggests it in "To Life":

Unpetal the flower of me,
And cast it to the gust;
Betray me if you will;
Trample me to dust.

But that I should go bare,
But that I should go free
Of any hurt at all—
Do not this thing to me!   [*Selected Poems*]

Obviously this conjunction of pain and pleasure has something to do with the ecstatic rendering of love as an image of death or of death as love. "Cruel and sweet," Louise Guiney's pairing, make up the quintessential 1890s' expression of deathly lust or lustful death. Guiney is probably the most interesting of the turn-of-the-century poets, less of a hack than Wilcox and more vibrant than Reese, but even she is not immune to the love/death union, as we can see by this poem called "Borderlands":

Through all the evening,
All the virginal long evening,
Down the blossomed aisle of April it is dread to walk alone;
For there the intangible is nigh, the lost is ever-during;

And who would suffer again beneath a too divine alluring,
Keen as the ancient drift of sleep on dying faces blown?

Yet in the valley,
At a turn of the orchard alley,
When a wild aroma touched me in the moist and moveless air,
Like a breath indeed from out Thee, or as airy vesture round Thee,
Then was it I went faintly, for fear I had nearly found Thee,
O Hidden, O Perfect, O Desired! O first and final Fair!

[Happy Ending]

This poem seems to me intentionally ambiguous. Are we meant to conclude that the terrifying yet longed-for figure is God? Whoever the "Thee" is, the "too divine alluring" is a threat to the "virginal long evening." We recognize the diction of sexual desire here but it is a passion "keen as the ancient drift of sleep on dying faces blown." Is the valley, the valley of the shadow of death? Fear and desire combine to make this "first and final Fair" a haunting presence seemingly amoral, certainly not traditionally Christian. Yet even when Guiney is at her most vibrant and militaristic, as in "The Knight Errant," death is presented invitingly:

The passion for perfection
Redeem my failing way!
The arrows of the upper slope
From sudden ambush cast,
Rain quick and true, with one to ope
My Paradise at last!   *[Happy Ending]*

Although she did not reprint it in later editions, Guiney wrote one extraordinary ballad that must be of interest to those concerned with women's poetry as female expression. "Tarpeia" has unfortunately been omitted from women's anthologies. Though its subject is overtly classical, and part of the revival of classicism in which Guiney participated with male poets like Trumbull Stickney and William Vaughn Moody, the handling of the theme is characteristically feminine.

Woe: lightly to part with one's soul as the sea with its foam!
Woe to Tarpeia, Tarpeia, daughter of Rome!

Lo, now it was night, with the moon looking chill as she went:
It was morn when the innocent stranger strayed into the tent.

The hostile Sabini were pleased, as one meshing a bird;
She sang for them there in the ambush: they smiled as they heard.

Her sombre hair purpled in gleams, as she leaned to the light;
All day she had idled and feasted, and now it was night.

The chief sat apart, heavy-browed, brooding elbow on knee;
The armlets he wore were thrice royal, and wondrous to see:

Exquisite artifice, whorls of barbaric design,
Frost's fixèd mimicry; orbic imaginings fine

In sevenfold coils: and in orient glimmer from them,
The variform voluble swinging of gem upon gem.

And the glory thereof sent fever and fire to her eye.
'I had never such trinkets!' she sighed,—like a lute was her sigh.

'Were they mine at the plea, were they mine for the token, all told,
Now the citadel sleeps, now my father the keeper is old,   ·

'If I go by the way that I know, and thou followest hard,
If yet at the touch of Tarpeia the gates be unbarred?'

The chief trembled sharply for joy, then drew rein on his soul:
'Of all this arm beareth I swear I will cede thee the whole,'

And up from the nooks of the camp, with hoarse plaudit outdealt,
The bearded Sabini glanced hotly, and vowed as they knelt,

Bare-stretching the wrists that bore also the glowing great boon:
'Yea! surely as over us shineth the lurid low moon,

'Not alone of our lord, but of each of us take what he hath!
Too poor is the guerdon, if thou wilt but show us the path.'

Her nostril upraised, like a fawn's on the arrowy air,
She sped; in a serpentine gleam to the precipice stair,

They climbed in her traces, they closed on their evil swift star:
She bent to the latches, and swung the huge portal ajar.

Repulsed where they passed her, half-tearful for wounded belief,
'The bracelets!' she pleaded. Then faced her the leonine chief,

And answered her: 'Even as I promised, maid-merchant, I do.'
Down from his dark shoulder the baubles he sullenly drew.

'This left arm shall nothing begrudge thee. Accept. Find it sweet.
Give, too, O my brothers!' The jewels he flung at her feet,

The jewels hard, heavy; she stooped to them, flushing with dread,
But the shield he flung after: it clanged on her beautiful head.

Like the Apennine bells when the villagers' warnings begin,
Athwart the first lull broke the ominous din upon din;

With a 'Hail, benefactress!' upon her they heaped in their zeal
Death: agate and iron; death: chrysoprase, beryl and steel.

'Neath the outcry of scorn, 'neath the sinewy tension and hurl,
The moaning died slowly, and still they massed over the girl

A mountain of shields! and the gemmy bright tangle in links,
A torrent-like gush, pouring out on the grass from the chinks,

Pyramidical gold! the sumptuous monument won
By the deed they had loved her for, doing, and loathed her for, done.

Such was the wage that they paid her, such the acclaim:
All Rome was aroused with the thunder that buried her shame.

On surged the Sabini to battle. O you that aspire!
Tarpeia the traitor had fill of her woman's desire.

Woe: lightly to part with one's soul as the sea with its foam!
Woe to Tarpeia, Tarpeia, daughter of Rome![19]

At the heart of this poem, so thrilling and yet so disturbing, is an unresolved tension between the judgment expressed against Tarpeia and the injustice at a human level of her fate. If we assume, for a moment, that the poem is about what it claims to be about, that is, the betrayal of a great city, then Tarpeia is a villain deserving of her fate. Yet the poem refuses to consider the assault of the city seriously. It leaves off where the battle begins, and the refrain informs us that the real issue is lightly parting with one's soul. Of primary importance is not the betrayal of the city but the betrayal of the self. To make us despise Tarpeia, the poet need only have dwelt on the havoc she created or the defects of her character. Clues in terms of the imagery associated with her might have convinced us. However, her mercenary desires seem utterly childish rather than deeply wicked. She is characterized at the beginning of the poem as "innocent." She strays into the tent like a young animal who has lost her way. The Sabini are "pleased, as one meshing a bird." In the actual accomplishment of her traitorous act, the only description given is of her "nostril upraised, like a fawn's on the arrowy air." Why did the poet choose such a simile? The fawn is a young animal, relatively helpless, concerned merely with self-preservation in a dangerous environment, "the arrowy air." What's more, Guiney intensifies the description of Tarpeia's death to make the Sabine warriors seem far more barbaric than she. Theirs is a vengeful, adult destructiveness; hers merely a short-sighted, puerile selfishness. If we take her "woman's desire" to be one of mercenary self-interest, we might consider Guiney's warning in light of the endless reprimands of women for marrying for money which were published in the magazines, usually by women themselves. Commentators often described such marriages as a betrayal of the citadel, the home, resulting from women's immature and selfish desires. In suggesting such an interpretation, we have already stepped outside the intentional boundaries of the poem, but to deal adequately with it, it seems we must do so.

At a deeper level the poem is not about treason but prostitution; it is about sexual rather than national politics. It is useful to remember that prostitution was a live issue in this period, and one over which women were divided between feeling that prostitutes were utterly degraded and that they were innocent victims of male lust. Some of this conflict of attitudes is evoked in us by the poem's handling of Tarpeia. How are we to see her as a sexual figure?

To begin with, the image of a lone maiden in a campful of soldiers immediately suggests sexual danger. The structure of the bargain is further suggestive: the girl agrees to sell her favors for a material reward. The moon is "lurid," the men glance "hotly." However, the unmistakable clue that we are concerned with lust comes at the point where the Sabini take revenge on Tarpeia for "the deed they had loved her for, doing, and loathed her for, done." At this point her betrayal seems secondary to the betrayal of human trust that she suffers. Furthermore, the city is roused to action by the noise of her murder. Guiney's final words are deeply ambiguous: "O you that aspire! / Tarpeia the traitor had fill of her woman's desire."

It is probable that Louise Imogen Guiney was not fully aware of the issues she was raising. Consciously she seems to have had a healthy appreciation for sexual life. In the Tudor Exposition she found herself dissatisfied because the paintings so completely avoided what she called "the mystery of sex." However, at a deeper level she was as unnerved by woman's sexual vulnerability in a patriarchal society as her less liberated, earlier nineteenth-century sisters. The clear message is that what men will love you for doing at the moment, they will hate you for afterward. (One might compare Emily Dickinson's poems 213 and 1339.) In "Tarpeia" passion and death merge, with the gravest implications. Aspiration itself is guilty and must be punished. The traitor Tarpeia becomes through a curious inversion one of Guiney's martyrs.

Perhaps the unresolved tension in this poem was what led Guiney not to reprint it. Among serious women poets at the turn of the century, it is hard to find a poem that celebrates a woman for her aggressiveness or her success at doing "unwomanly" things. One mourns the fact that the feminist Charlotte Perkins Gilman did not give more time to her poetry for she was a talented writer, and her refusal to accept the terms of the patriarchy, particularly her refusal to find renunciation a virtue, makes refreshing reading. Ironically, a male poet—William Vaughn Moody—could celebrate feminine defiance more readily than a Louise Guiney. In "I am the Woman" he created a female speaker who is defiant and yet admirable. In "The Death of Eve" Moody made Eve, the breaker of the covenant, into the instrument of human redemption. She returns to God at the end of her life, seeking reconciliation but unrepentant:

> Thine ample, tameless creature,—
> Against thy will and word, behold, Lord, this is She![20]

Women were not absent from male poems. Edwin Arlington Robinson wrote beautifully in "Eros Turannos" of a wealthy spinster whose love for a heartless opportunist destroys her. She is aware of his faults,

> But what she meets and what she fears
> Are less than are the downward years,
> Drawn slowly to the foamless weirs
> Of age, were she to lose him.[21]

What women's poetry of the period shows, however, is a growing female interest in women's sexual role. As with Guiney, one senses a certain ambivalence in the portrayals of women assuming non-traditional roles. In "The Death Potion" Lizette Reese makes her speaker contrive the death of her rival. She is openly unrepentant about her sexual liaison with her lover: "Though we had shame, yet had we bliss." And all that is provided in the way of a negative judgment of her is the refrain, "(Hear, Lord Jesus!)" as though Jesus were being made aware that here was a woman who certainly did not subscribe to his ethic of forgiving one's enemies. Nevertheless, this speaker is obviously not intended as a positive model. What Agnes Repplier described as "the repeal of reticence" was only beginning to occur in the 1890s. "Sex o'clock in America," as William Marion Reedy would call it in 1913, had not yet chimed.[22]

In general, women poets at the turn of the century sounded a mournful note, as non-controversial as Ina Coolbrith's "Fruitionless":

> Ah, little flower, upspringing, azure-eyed,
> . . . .
> Living and blooming thy brief summer-day:
> So, wiser far than I,
> That only dream and sigh,
> And, sighing, dream my listless life away.   [Stedman]

The mournful note might have been sounded for the passing away of a world in which women at least had well-defined roles. Yet, beneath the listlessness of the 1890s was a restless hunger which surfaced at moments only to be subsumed under a philosophy of renunciation. As Louise Guiney wrote of Pascal in *Happy Ending:*

> Spirit so abstinent, in thy deeps lay
> What passion of possession?

Ambivalence continued to be for women poets their primary attitude toward engaging in the struggle for power—sexual, literary, or political.

When Reese's authoritarian father died, her mother became the autocrat of the neighborhood. Reese, musing upon the transformation, wondered in *A Victorian Village* if her mother had not always desired power. The question of the legitimacy of women's self-interested demands—for the vote, for jobs, for time away from the children—was endlessly debated in magazines like the *Atlantic*, with women often attacking each other for what they considered feminine selfishness.[23] In order to circumvent the opposition of the patriarchy and those who supported its claims, many educated, intellectual women did not marry. Yet this was not enough. What the poetry of women like Guiney and Reese shows is that aspiration and success still made them uneasy. Even the feminists suffered from doubts; Christopher Lasch refers to "the suspicion that obsessed the feminist imagination: that in pursuing a masculine ideal she had betrayed her own femininity."[24] Despite her bravado, the Gibson Girl's self-confidence was only skin-deep.

In "Astraea" Louise Guiney's speaker asks of the men she is leaving behind:

> Are ye unwise, who would not let me love you?
> Or must too bold desires be quieted?
> Only to ease you, never to reprove you,
> I will go back to heaven with heart unfed:
> Yet sisterly I turn, I bend above you,
> To kiss (ah, with what sorrow!) all my dead.   [*Happy Ending*]

In 1900 the question still hung in the air: Must too bold desires be quieted? Those like Victoria Woodhull, advocate of free love, who answered "no" were outcasts. Most tried in the best way they could to negotiate their own peace. In this atmosphere of compromise and self-denial, it is no wonder that the most highly respected women poets like Guiney and Reese were attracted to an aesthetic of self-restraint. In "Planting the Poplar" Guiney describes her sense of her own craft.

> In loneliness, in quaint
> Perpetual constraint,
> In gallant poverty,
> A girt and hooded tree,
> See if against the gale
> Our leafage can avail.   [*Happy Ending*]

Reese, for her part, added:

> If you dig a well,
> If you sing a song,
> By what you do without,
> You make it strong.   ["Scarcity"]

Both poets shared an eerie sense of martyrdom about their professions. "Bargain," from Reese's last book *Pastures*, expresses it most directly:

> A rose will cost you more
> Than its gathering;
> A song be such a price
> You dare not sing.
>
> What must you pay for each,
> Else loveliness fare amiss?
> Yourself nailed to a Tree—
> This.[25]

Wilcox, Reese, and Guiney all shared a high degree of popularity in their time, although they are mostly forgotten today. Wilcox remained a poet of fireside sentiment, the author of "Laugh, and the world laughs with you; / Weep, and you weep alone." William Randolph Hearst was her champion. H. L. Mencken thought Reese had written some of the greatest sonnets in the language and he continued to praise her work after her death. Willa Cather remarked that during her time at *McClure's Magazine* no verse "passed from hand to hand with so much excitement" as Guiney's (Fairbanks, p. ix).

Still, these women ended their lives feeling unfulfilled. Wilcox and Guiney both had nervous breakdowns in their last years. Reese's poem is eloquent concerning the "bargain" she felt she had made. They had gained a certain degree of recognition and independence but at a great price. Wilcox's comments in "An Open Letter to Literary Aspirants" may serve as a characteristically ambivalent summary for them all:

> Seen from a distance, fame may seem to a woman like a sea bathed in tropical suns, where in she longs to sail. Let fame once be hers, she finds it a prairie fire consuming or scorching all that is dearest in life to her. Be careful before you light these fires with your own hands. [*Men, Women and Emotions,* p. 291]

Conclusion

The Mythical Nineteenth Century and Its Heritage

6

In 1900 few commentators would have suggested that the women of the day were as little prepared for worldly success as their grandmothers. Enormous changes had taken place since Caroline Gilman had cried herself to sleep at the thought that one of her poems would be published in a Boston paper. Women wrote without Gilman's fear of being "detected in man's apparel." There were far more females in college and in the work force than ever before. Furthermore, the decline in fidelity to the notion of "woman's sphere" made Julia Ward Howe's "Woman"—a "vestal priestess, proudly pure, / But of a meek and quiet spirit; / With soul all dauntless to endure"—seem like a nearly mythical creature, someone's great-aunt who smelled of camphor and mothballs.

People forgot that to Julia Ward Howe she had also been a fantasy but one that came readily to mind because of a shared female acceptance of woman's circumscribed role in the world of male power. Few serious steps had been taken toward transforming this world by the turn of the century. To the extent that women had drawn alongside their male counterparts—in literature, in scholarship, in the professions—they had made great strides. Yet they had done so without seriously threatening the patriarchal structure. Separate but equal was the best that could be hoped for in 1895: women professors in women's colleges. If one were trying to compete in a male-dominated field, one must do so at the expense of placing undue emphasis on one's sex. So we find Louise Imogen Guiney writing to Richard Watson Gilder, "I am not in the least given to any violent interest in womankind, such as has addled the country's brains of late. Give me a manandwoman world: 'tis good enough!"

With the appearance of greater prospects at the turn of the century, the lifting of veils as Dickinson's Alps seemed now to "neglect their curtains," a peculiar reaction set in, something which might almost be called a cultural surrender to the unconscious. The whole nineteenth century began to assume the proportions of a mythical creation, useful principally as a highly colored background against which to measure the superiority of contemporary progress and fidelity to the Real. The generation maturing in the 1890s, among them Amy Lowell, identified their position as incompatible with even the nineteenth-century moderns of that era. Nothing less than a complete break with the past was insisted upon. In her description of the emerging leaders of the "new poetry" movement, Lowell emphasized discontinuity with the nineteenth century in a way that marked her as one of the new breed. She wrote:

> This little handful of disconnected souls, all unobtrusively born into that America which sighed with Richard Watson Gilder, wept with Ella Wheeler Wilcox, permitted itself to dance delicately with Celia Thaxter, and occasionally to blow a graceful blast on the beribboned trumpet of Louise Imogen Guiney, was destined to startle its progenitors.[1]

(Later, in an ironic turnabout, Ella Wheeler Wilcox would attack Amy Lowell's poetry on the grounds of obscenity, the grounds upon which she herself had once been attacked.)

It must have seemed to those beginning to assess their position in 1900 that growth demanded the effective burial of the prudish and submissive past. In fact, however, the cost of mythologizing the nineteenth century, and thus obscuring the struggles of real women with its various creeds and credos, was great. As women looked back and estimated how much freer and more modern they were, compared with their grandmothers, they tended to overlook the evidence of dissatisfaction that was part of their grandmothers' lives as well. Articles like Carolyn Ticknor's "The Steel-Engraving Lady and the Gibson Girl" (1901) emphasized the lady's accommodation to the mythic ideal of female self-sacrifice and the new woman's rejection of it. However, any such breezy dissociation of the present from the past ignored the function of myth—for the 1850s as well as the 1890s—as a psycho-social tool for embodying certain deep-lying aspects of human existence.

The myth of the vestal priestess against which the woman of the 1850s measured herself engendered the same emotions of fear and desire that motivated the woman of 1900 to try effectively to bury her grandmother's conflicts. The central issue was still one of power but the "new woman" at the turn of the century hoped to establish her claim to it by carefully dissociating herself from the sighs and tears, the delicate dancing and graceful blasts on beribboned trumpets, that symbolized her mother's and grandmother's failure.

Yet, despite all the social and political changes that had occurred over the past one hundred years, these women were as deeply hampered in some ways as those grandmothers they wished to disclaim. They were hampered by a patriarchal system still firmly in place, hampered by a set of conventions that could be circumvented but not yet changed. Most of all they were inhibited by their own need to see the past as irrelevant. Thus, they were unable to read the lesson buried in the poetic tradition exemplified by women like Louise Imogen Guiney.

If they had read this lesson, they might have seen that despite substantial external changes, the deeper truth was that women were still appetitive yet renunciatory, fearful of aspiration, laudatory of martyrdom. They remained ambivalent about worldly power, ill-equipped because inexperienced at taking it into their own hands. Even the imposing Amy Lowell would come to sound like one of these nineteenth-century women poets in her later years. Edna St. Vincent Millay, ensnared in a net of appetite and idealism, would turn to renunciation at last.

At the beginning of the nineteenth century no one suspected that women's poetry would continue to express such a deep and ineradicable strain of female pessimism. When Elizabeth Oakes-Smith wrote: "no lofty flight be mine, / I would not soar like thee, in loneliness to pine," it is doubtful that she thought of herself as creating an archetypal expression of female renunciation. More likely she saw the problem as one of peculiar personal interest to herself. Nevertheless, the same structure that underlies "An Incident," the same ambivalence that permeates what I have called the "free bird" poem, brings Louise Imogen Guiney to warn: "O you that aspire! / Tarpeia the traitor had fill of her woman's desire." The subtext of this message suggests women's continuing fears of openly opposing the patriarchy. The "power fantasy" is a fantasy precisely because its message cannot be expressed without dissimulation.

In 1900 there were several writers who had given this perplexing female condition a piercing look. In that year Kate Chopin was recovering from the abusive criticism she had received in the reviews of *The Awakening,* a novel about a woman who refuses to answer "yes" to the question: "Must too bold desires be quieted?" Edna Pontellier, the novel's heroine, follows the *ignis fatuus* of self-realization, "the light which, showing the way, forbids it," and ends up a suicide. Having tried to imitate the free bird, she must acknowledge her impotence against the constituted powers of patriarchal authority. "A bird with a broken wing was beating the air above, reeling, fluttering, circling disabled down, down to the water."[2] The only freedom left to her comes through death.

In 1901 Edith Wharton was playing with the image of Lily Bart, the heroine whose life was also to end in suicide in *The House of Mirth* (1905). Lily too hopes to find a way of exercising her power without compromising her values. At a climactic point early in the novel, Wharton says:

> There were in her at the moment two beings, one drawing deep breaths of freedom and exhilaration, the other gasping for air in a little black prisonhouse of fears. But gradually the captive's gasps grew fainter, or the other paid less heed to them: the horizon expanded, the air grew stronger, and the free spirit quivered for flight.[3]

Lily tries to ignore her captive status, but her success is dependent upon her willing subjugation and when she attempts independence, "the fetter 'neath the flowers" tears her to pieces. At a critical juncture just before her downfall, Sim Rosedale—one of the men who wants to own her—tells her the story of Tarpeia.

> "There was a girl in some history book who wanted gold shields, or something, and the fellows threw 'em at her, and she was crushed under 'em: they killed her. Well, that's true enough: some women look buried under their jewelry. What I want is a woman who'll hold her head higher the more diamonds I put on it."[4]

In other words, what he wants is a woman who will play her role as an object of conspicuous display without drawing attention to her victimization. Like Tarpeia, Lily seeks selfish gratification. And like Guiney's Tarpeia, she dies in the end more sinned against than sinning. She is destroyed by the system she hoped to manipulate to her advantage.

The implications are disturbing ones, consistent with nineteenth-century poetic pessimism about woman's destiny. What these references to Chopin and Wharton are meant to suggest is that the tradition of women's poetry we have been examining shares its preoccupation with disillusionment, ambivalence, and renunciation with a broad community of women writers. This community extends beyond boundaries of genre, time period, and even nation.

What is useful about regarding this tradition from the perspective of 1900 is that we can see it whole at a moment when its burden of dark and sometimes secret truths was about to be massively ignored. Yet for the first half of the twentieth century, at least, women poets would harken back to these feelings of anger, frustration, and denial without much sense that in doing so they were repeating women's wisdom of the past. What were the elements of this tradition that would survive in the poetry of twentieth-century female poets?

To begin with, a deep current of Puritan psychology would continue to flow in some of the most prominent women poets of the twentieth century. The most striking example is Elinor Wylie, who would write of "the Puritan marrow of my bones," but the refinements of this strain appear in many other poets as well. The triumph over self we witness in the work of Anne Bradstreet, the attitude toward power that appears in Emily Dickinson's "Power is only Pain – / Stranded, thro' Discipline," show up in new mutations where women poets insist on the value of stifling parts of the self. Thus, Louise Bogan writes:

> Henceforth, from the mind,
> For your whole joy, must spring
> Such joy as you may find
> In any earthly thing.[5]

Self-discipline, long a heroic triumph in the minds and works of earlier women poets, develops particularly in terms of the theme of silence. Sara Teasdale works in this vein, writing verse after verse about smothering her heart's words, and Edna St. Vincent Millay, in a different mood, longs for silence as for a "frigid bosom" upon which, "unquestioned, uncaressed," she can lie down "out of the urgent heat." Millay's "Ode to Silence" exalts the pleasures of conventual tranquility and in so doing allies itself with this whole female poetic tradition. Even Sylvia Plath moves obsessively toward the nun as a preferred image of the self.

Anne Bradstreet, of course, was a Puritan of a very different order from these women who merely share some of her desires to stifle their insistent longings. Both they and she, however, can be seen in moments of ambivalence, seeking rebelliously to revise the patriarchal text and then turning their anger inward in a strange capitulation to guilt. Thus, the revisionist moment we examined in Bradstreet's treatment of David's lament occurs in Teasdale's "Guenevere" and in H. D.'s *Helen in Egypt,* among other places.

No longer do women poets pore admiringly over the lives of the martyrs and yet a curious sense of martyrdom persists. Sometimes it is expressed in words of self-pity like those of Amy Lowell:

> My soul is blunted against dullard wits,
> Smeared with sick juices,
> Nicked impotent for other than low uses.[6]

Like Lowell and Lizette Reese, H. D. writes about "the cold splendor of song / and its bleak sacrifice."[7] Martyred by public outrage against her romantic escapades, Elinor Wylie turns again and again to poetic heroes whom the world victimizes:

> One man stands as free men stand,
> As if his soul might be
> Brave, unbroken; see his hand
> Nailed to an oaken tree.[8]

More disturbing than these poems, however, are those that further develop this preoccupation with self-denial and martyrdom—masochistic poems, usually addressed to a lover, in which the speaker seeks pain. Lowell's "Granadilla" is one example:

> I touch the blade of you and cling upon it,
> And only when the blood runs out across my fingers
> Am I at all satisfied.

Wylie's "Malediction Upon Myself" revels in an ecstasy of fantasized self-destruction:

> Stop up my nostils in default of breath
> With graveyard powder and compacted death,
> And stuff my mouth with ruin for a gag,
> And break my ankles of a running stag:
> Let the long legs of which I am so proud
> Be bended, and the lifted throat be bowed.

In these poems there is rarely a hint of the spiritual uplift that sustained the martyr fantasies of earlier women poets.

If Anne Bradstreet's Puritan sensibility continues to operate at the core of this tradition of women's poetry, it does so by assuming a number of new guises. The poetic categories we established by examining the works of early nineteenth-century women poets do not remain fixed either. And yet they too have their counterparts in the twentieth century. The sensibility poem, for instance, in which a woman defines herself in terms of her immoderate and often agonized sensitivities, would not have been acceptable had it appeared in the twentieth century in the form given it by Frances Osgood. Yet many women poets of the 1920s, following Edna St. Vincent Millay, trembled under the burden of beauty. These revised sensibility poems came to be so common that Beth Atkins referred to a whole generation of women poets as the "Oh-God,-the-pain,-

girls" set. H. D.'s Grecian images were not what Atkins had in mind,
and yet "Orchard" belongs to this group of poems, too.

> I saw the first pear
> as it fell—
> the honey-seeking, golden-banded,
> the yellow swarm,
> was not more fleet than I,
> (spare us from loveliness)
> and I fell prostrate,
> crying:
> you have flayed us
> with your blossoms,
> spare us the beauty
> of fruit-trees.[9]

Often these poems have a tinge of hysteria about them as though
the speaker is incapable of filtering out any of the effects of these
sensual stimuli and is therefore abnormally vulnerable to them.
Madness may be the central premise, as it is with Wylie's prose poem
"Heart's Desire," a fragment of which is quoted here.

> . . . faces best known and most remembered estranged and a mil-
> lion miles away, and strange greasy faces passing in the dust of
> evening and now returning illuminated into godhead, cruelty
> where it cannot be, kindness where hatred is as inevitable as the
> white rising of a morning where morning may after all never more
> rise, disintegrate yet exquisite destruction of the heart at the mo-
> ment of waking, desire for death like the vagueness of a thirst for
> thin extra-vagant wine, unredeemed by fear, mortal and importu-
> nate screams of why, why, why, in the extreme desolation of re-
> gained consciousness. . . .

If not the central premise, madness may be seen lurking at the
edges of a poem about overly acute sensitivities. Two examples are
Louise Bogan's "I Saw Eternity" and Sylvia Plath's "Tulips." In the
former poem the speaker addresses herself to an abstraction, "O
beautiful Forever!" The beauty and intensity of the experience that
corresponds to this abstraction seem to have undone her:

> O brilliant, O languishing
> Cycle of weeping light!
> The mice and birds will eat you,
> And you will spoil their stomachs
> As you have spoiled my mind.

In "Tulips" the very strength of the speaker's attraction to the blood-red flowers threatens her stability and fills her with resentment.

> The tulips are too red in the first place, they hurt me.
> Even through the gift paper I could hear them breathe
> Lightly, through their white swaddlings, like an awful baby.
> Their redness talks to my wound, it corresponds.
> They are subtle: they seem to float, though they weigh me down,
> Upsetting me with their sudden tongues and their colour,
> A dozen red lead sinkers around my neck.[10]

In fact, in the sensibility poem it is always the strength of the speaker's response to the scene around her that creates the threat. Thus, Bogan ends her poem "Women" by commenting critically on female vulnerability, implying that women make themselves too accessible to demands from others:

> They hear in every whisper that speaks to them
> A shout and a cry.
> As like as not, when they take life over their door-sills
> They should let it go by.

The sanctuary poem emerges out of just such a set of feelings, and after Dickinson's development of it one wonders what there is left to say. Yet, at least among the principal twentieth-century figures of this tradition—Lowell, Teasdale, Wylie, Millay, H. D., Bogan, and Plath—there are plenty of examples of further attempts. Sara Teasdale and Elinor Wylie actually wrote poems titled "Sanctuary." Like Dickinson's, Wylie's captures the ambiguity of the sanctuary's benefits. The enclosure, promising invulnerability, is first sought in order to escape from a threatening environment. The speaker addresses the bricklayer:

> Make my marvellous wall so thick
> Dead nor living may shake its strength.

However, her final ironic twist exposes the danger implicit in this escape:

> Full as a crystal cup with drink
> Is my cell with dreams, and quiet, and cool. . . .
> Stop, old man! You must leave a chink;
> How can I breathe? *You can't, you fool!*

Writing of tortured sensitivities and the need for sanctuaries, no matter how ambiguous their offer of protection, women of the nineteenth and twentieth centuries have confessed their sense of helplessness. If we wish to mark the position of these poems, we would do so most accurately along the fear axis of ambivalence. However, there are other poems that more closely parallel the desire axis, and some of these we have labelled power fantasies. The power fantasy persists as a vigorous expression of twentieth-century women poets right down to Margaret Atwood in the present.

For our purposes the poems most intricately bound up with this tradition are those that present no simple identification with power but rather retain their ambivalent suggestions, like A. R. St. John's "Medusa" and Dickinson's "Loaded Gun." Such poems are easily found among the works of twentieth-century poets, from Amy Lowell's tantalizing "Which, Being Interpreted, Is As May Be, Or Otherwise" to Plath's "Ariel." The desire to see the self (a self) as larger than life, appetitive and potent, is often in the poems darkened by the suggestion that such potency is fragile, limited, or self-destructive. Emily Dickinson's gun-self has the power to kill but not the power to die and be redeemed. Louise Bogan's "Dragonfly" is certainly appetitive and potent but it is all the other adjectives as well—fragile, limited, its life-force devouring the self.

> Twice-born, predator,
> You split into the heat.
> Swift beyond calculation or capture
> You dart into the shadow
> Which consumes you.

Bogan's wish for the poet—that she be blessed "by a spirit loud as a houseful of alien voices ever tortured and divided with itself"[11]— makes a virtue of the ambivalence characteristic of the poets of this tradition. Their handling of the power fantasy is a reliable measure with which to gauge the connection between these women's attitudes toward power and that mixture of fear and desire which characterizes their deepest beliefs about their relation to the world. Women's wisdom in these poems tells us that life breaks the spirit. Aspiration is certain to meet with bitter disappointment. Sara Teasdale's "Wisdom" is not less pessimistic in this respect than Bogan's "Kept." Both identify maturity with banked fires. Teasdale writes:

> When I have ceased to break my wings
> Against the faultiness of things,
> And learned that compromises wait

> Behind each hardly opened gate,
> When I can look life in the eyes,
> Grown calm and very coldly wise,
> Life will have given me the Truth,
> And taken in exchange—my youth.

Nothing could be more consistent with the expectations about woman's destiny of nineteenth-century women poets. Elizabeth Oakes-Smith's "Duty" envisioned the calm, pale face of the mature and dutiful woman replacing the ardent spirit of her youth. What is missing in Teasdale's poem is the concept of duty; the attitude toward acceptance is identical.

In some twentieth-century poems a narrowing of horizons is presented as the inevitable consequence of participating in the struggle of existence. Thus, Bogan ends "Kept" by saying:

> The playthings of the young
> Get broken in the play,
> Get broken, as they should.

Life is the culprit; we are powerless to oppose it with our hungers, our resentment. We would do well to learn our lesson early. In other poems, however, the argument of the free bird poem can be discerned. We reject freedom, because of the burden of loneliness it forces us to carry or because of our own incapacities. A classic example of this kind of poem is Millay's "On the Wide Heath" in which the protagonist returns to an incompatible household:

> Home to the worn reproach, the disagreeing,
>   The shelter, the stale air; content to be
> Pecked at, confined, encroached upon,—it being
>   Too lonely, to be free.[12]

Though it is highly doubtful that Millay knew of Elizabeth Oakes-Smith's work, we hear the echo of the earlier poet's decision here: "I would not soar like thee, in loneliness to pine."

In general, Millay would be the last one to recommend such a choice. Yet, at moments she understood and shared the attitude of her friend Elinor Wylie that, rather than seek freedom and fulfillment in the open air, one was better off going underground. In Wylie's "The Eagle and the Mole" the free bird—who is isolated and stoic on his inviolable cliff—becomes a rejected guide, much the way Philomel becomes a rejected guide for the speaker in Anne Bradstreet's "Contemplations":

> If in the eagle's track
> Your sinews cannot leap,

says Wylie's speaker, you have another choice.

> Live like the velvet mole;
> Go burrow underground.

> And there hold intercourse
> With roots of trees and stones,
> With rivers at their source,
> And disembodied bones.

If you must have company, let it be uncontaminating. Only the elemental spirits will "keep your soul / From spotted sight or sound." In this poem the sanctuary urge is combined with the desire to preserve the self from contaminating influences, which we saw in the early development of the sensibility poem. Wylie could never see herself as an eagle. She tells us in "Let No Charitable Hope" that no one should try to confuse her mind with images of eagle and antelope, since she is "in nature none of these." Yet the fact that such images should be allied with a "charitable hope" in her mind suggests the deeper truth, everywhere evident in her work, that she fervently wished to be a grand, fearless, powerful creature like the eagle. I pause over Wylie here only because she presents so well the conflicting emotions of these women. As Margaret Atwood writes: "They who say they want nothing / want everything."[13] The renunciatory gesture we so often encounter is a signal, not of the weakness of their desires, but of their strength.

As the twentieth century progresses, sexual appetite comes more and more often into the limelight as a focus for these conflicts, yet it is by no means true—as we might first suspect—that fear of sex or sexual disgust dies out. For many women this is the battleground upon which their opposition to male domination manifests itself most strongly, and in their poetry defiance of sexual codes (Millay) and denial of sexual feelings (Wylie) are often simply two modes of the same basic need to resist. In many poems by twentieth-century women, sexual power is presented as a peculiarly potent female strength. Yet there remains an undercurrent of suspicion and fear that men will pervert this power for their own uses. Such is the case in the poetry of Amy Lowell, of Elinor Wylie, of Sylvia Plath. Love and death—the great erotic combination of the 1890s—retains its dualistic potency in these later women's poems. H. D. ends *Helen of*

Egypt with the mysterious message that "the dart of Love / is the dart of Death."[14] Though by this she means to inspire in us no despair, nevertheless the message fills us with mixed emotions and is meant to.

What happens to the forbidden lover and the secret sorrow? In the nineteen twenties and thirties these archetypal concerns had their greatest twentieth-century vogue.[15] Wylie, Teasdale, Millay, and Bogan drew upon the subject of illicit attachments to explore a whole range of issues, including some of those we have looked at earlier, like self-discipline, martyrdom, power, freedom, and the love/death combination. If it is true, as I have suggested before, that the real forbidden lover is the world or worldly power, this poem by Louise Bogan takes on an added significance. Though it occurs at the end of her final collection, *Blue Estuaries,* it was written many years earlier when the forbidden-love motif was still in vogue. Its title—"Masked Woman's Song"—suggests a mythical female figure, perhaps Justice.

> Before I saw the tall man
> Few women should see,
> Beautiful and imposing
> Was marble to me.
>
> And virtue had its place
> And evil its alarms,
> But not for that worn face,
> And not in those roped arms.

Although the language is quite different, there is something peculiarly Dickinsonian about this poem. Bogan left it ambiguous intentionally, but if we read it as an expression in the forbidden-lover tradition, we might interpret it as suggesting the deeply revolutionary consequences of indulging one's desire for power. Read this way, the line "Few women should see" becomes the viewpoint of the patriarchy, and virtue and evil its categorical distinctions. Obviously, this forbidden lover has the capability of overturning the speaker's previously safe and neat categories, including those usually used to keep woman in her place.

Whether or not we interpret this poem in light of words by Maria Brooks and Emily Dickinson—both of whom Bogan read and wrote about—we should acknowledge that this poem belongs not to our time but to an earlier one. After World War II the whole women's poetry scene changed dramatically. Suddenly the tradition we have been examining was no longer much regarded by either women or men.[16] A variety of female voices could be heard—Elizabeth Bishop's, Denise Levertov's, the early Adrienne Rich's. Secret sorrow and the forbidden lover became obsolete at a time when women were no longer presenting themselves poetically as creatures who lived mainly out of the world—in domesticity, in love relationships, in nature. These new women poets did not want themselves seen as part of a long line of women poets to whom they owed attention and respect. Their acknowledged models were male. They played down their sex and women's traditional belief that their gender entitled them to special knowledge. However, one can find echoes of an earlier era. In Adrienne Rich's first book, *A Change of World* (1951), "An Unsaid Word" belongs with the silence poems of other women. "Aunt Jennifer's Tigers," however, operates as a critique of this tradition's timorousness. The voice in the poems establishes superiority over Aunt who will die "still ringed with ordeals she was mastered by."[17]

All of this was possible because, despite the fifties' dogma of domesticity, women were assuming multiple roles much more readily than they had ever done before. Of course, this situation did not mean true liberation by any means. We might also look at the dissociation of sensibility from gender in this generation's early work as suggesting another form of subjugation in the belief that in order to succeed they had to seem as masculine as the men. A slightly later generation of writers, which would include Anne Sexton and Sylvia Plath, would turn once again to female personal experience to nourish their poems, and in so doing would link themselves with the nightingale tradition in ways that neither of them probably fully understood.[18]

Looking at the war and its aftermath, we must conclude that social, political, and economic realities have exerted an important influence on the direction this poetic tradition has taken. As women's lives have changed, their "wisdom," their shared expression of the way things are, has changed as well. Now that we have such diversity among women poets, now that there are women surrealists, women conceptualists, women in every school and literary movement, expressing every kind of poetic truth, it only becomes more significant that most women poets continued to demonstrate a shared poetic sensibility for such a long time.

There are, of course, aspects of the nineteenth-century picture that do not reappear to any great extent in the twentieth century. The most extreme expressions of limitation, the agonized apostrophes to "the unattained" and the images of prisons, fetters, and the like disappeared. This is not to say that women no longer felt their aims inhibited. Rather, their presentation of inhibitions seems at one and the same time more subtle and more direct. As economic opportunities for self-support became realities, women no longer seemed quite so cabin'd, cribbed, confined. Their images became those of a more public existence. Of course, the subtler dissuaders in our experience can be just as limiting, and these are often given primary consideration by twentieth-century women poets. Though the nightingale tradition is no longer predominant, there are echoes of it in many contemporary women poets' work.

"Captivity is Consciousness – / So's Liberty," wrote Emily Dickinson a hundred years ago. We have hardly gone further than that today. As twentieth-century women, we can learn much, and see much that we have learned powerfully expressed, by reading Dickinson. It is no use ignoring the fact that she is the only great woman poet nineteenth-century America produced. If the poetic tradition we have examined here is interesting, it is not because we find ourselves compelled to re-evaluate the little-known women poets who gave it life, elevating them to positions of artistic centrality. We must rather find this tradition interesting because knowledge of it helps us to read better. We then encounter nineteenth-century poets with a richer, more sharpened sense of the way their gender was involved in their art. And we can read the women poets of our own century with a new sense of their work's continuity or discontinuity with the past.

It should also be remembered that nineteenth-century America produced only one great male poet, Walt Whitman. One can argue that the middle range of male poets was stronger than the middle range of women poets. Yet, considering the enormous disadvantages women poets faced, they did not do so badly themselves. We must consider that the publishing world expected mediocrity from women poets and encouraged "the slight themes" Lydia Sigourney ruefully agreed to produce. Any who, like Emily Dickinson, was too innovative or startling could find no ready access to the world of established letters. Furthermore, women often wrote to support themselves or their families and had to combine domestic labors with literary ones. The drawback of not having a wife must have been evident to them when they compared their lives with those of Emerson, Bryant, and Lowell. Even Poe amid his manic labors could leave the preparation of meals and the running of the household to his wife and mother. With little direct experience of the world to draw upon, women's compositions were also naturally limited in scope. They could not hope to present the panorama of American life found in a Melville, a Bryant, or a Whitman.

Yet women, partly because they were denied access to what was thought of as the male sphere, drew upon the resources of their own internal experiences and wrote poems that are still worth reading for the glimpses of inner life they provide. It is rare to read a poem by a nineteenth-century American male poet and come away feeling that one knows the poet's sensibility intimately. With many of the women, however—with Maria Brooks, Lucy Larcom, Frances Osgood, Emily Dickinson, and Louise Guiney—one does feel this vibrant surge of personality. Their truths are marked with their fingerprints, and the effect is stimulating in what can be a peculiarly satisfying way. Louise Bogan noticed this and commented in her literary history, *Achievement in American Poetry:*

> It is clear that Robinson, in spite of his central contribution to poetic truth, did little to reconstitute any revivifying warmth of feeling in the poetry of his time. This task, it is now evident, was accomplished almost entirely by women poets through methods which proved to be as strong as they seemed to be delicate. . . . The line of poetic intensity which wavers and fades out and often completely fails in poetry written by men, on the feminine side moves on unbroken.[19]

The line of intensity Bogan speaks of vibrates in the songs of the nightingale poets. The nightingale's theme, or burden, is contrapuntal, fraught with ambivalence. Though it is antique to the degree that it approves accommodation, it is modern in the sense in which it betrays a divided mind. The nightingale is in earnest; her burden preoccupies her. Her song is the moment of her freedom even as that moment hovers between babble and silence, between time and timelessness.

If we could say for certain that there was a time in America when women did not write these poems, long ago or today, we could speak of the meaning of that time more explicitly. The fact that there have been eras in which the nightingale's theme has predominanted and others in which it has been heard only faintly but none in which it has not been heard at all suggests that the conditions of this freedom, like the conditions of its limitation, are never wholly absent.

Thus poetry attains a special ontological status for women. The "Word made Flesh" Emily Dickinson describes in poem 1651 redeems objectification, the flesh made word. And a word "that breathes distinctly" breathes time into eternity. Poetry (this "loved Philology") is the essential condition for that freedom to be a powerful self in the world, to become a creator, not just a creation in someone else's universe. For women, who have always suffered from objectification, this freedom has a pungent flavor.

In spite of adverse conditions, the nightingale poets tasted "with ecstasies of stealth / the very food" they needed to sustain the image of their selfhood in American culture; and I speak here not of their personal selfhood but of their dark, unruffled, fierce, hypothetical selves. What they have said in their nightingale poems is not what we might have wanted them to say, perhaps. Their expressions are too often warped toward melancholy or self-destruction. But the anger and the hunger are there as well. It is this deeper self—a fledgling eagle rather than a nightingale—who refused to be silenced, who may have written of renunciation but who refused it to the extent that she kept on writing, it is this self who appears gradually in the twilight of literary scholarship. She is not the historical woman but the lost woman poet whom the real woman harbored and occasionally nourished. Dark, unruffled, and fierce, she rises like a free bird aloft in our dismal past.

Notes

Preface

1. Here is a partial list of anthologies that have come out since I began my work in early 1972. Ann Stanford, ed., *The Women Poets in English* (New York: McGraw-Hill, 1972); Florence Howe and Ellen Bass, eds., *No More Masks!* (New York: Anchor Press, 1973), Laura Chester and Sharon Barba, eds., *Rising Tides* (New York: Washington Square Press, 1973); Barbara Segnitz and Carol Rainey, eds., *Psyche: The Feminine Poetic Consciousness* (New York: Dell Publishing Company, 1973); Louise Bernikow, ed., *The World Split Open* (New York: Vintage, 1974); Cora Kaplan, ed., *Salt and Bitter and Good* (New York: Paddington Press Ltd., 1975); Elly Bulkin and Joan Larkin, eds., *Amazon Poetry* (Brooklyn, New York: Out and Out Books, 1975); Carol Konek and Dorothy Walters, eds., *I Hear My Sisters Saying* (New York: Thomas Y. Crowell Company, 1976); Carol Cosman, Joan Keefe, and Kathleen Weaver, eds., *The Penguin Book of Women Poets* (New York: Penguin Books, 1978); Aliki Barnstone and Willis Barnstone, eds., *A Book of Women Poets from Antiquity to Now* (New York: Schocken Books, 1980); Pattie Cowell, ed., *Women Poets in Pre-Revolutionary America 1650–1775* (Troy, N.Y.: Whitston Publishing Company, 1980); Erlene Stetson, ed., *Black Sister: Poetry by Black American Women Poets 1746–1980* (Bloomington: Indiana University Press, 1981). The following critical works about women poets have been particularly helpful. Emily Stipes Watts, *The Poetry of American Women from 1632 to 1945* (Austin: University of Texas Press, 1977); Suzanne Juhasz, *Naked and Fiery Forms, Modern American Poetry by Women: A New Tradition* (New York: Harper Colophon Books, 1976); Sandra M. Gilbert and Susan Gubar, *The Madwoman in the Attic: The Woman Writer and the Nineteenth-Century Imagination* (New Haven: Yale University Press, 1979); Sandra M. Gilbert and Susan Gubar, *Shakespeare's Sisters: Feminist Essays on Women Poets* (Bloomington: Indiana University Press, 1979); and Margaret Homans, *Women Writers and Poetic Identity* (Princeton: Princeton University Press, 1980).

2. For instance, in Watts's treatment of the Childhood section of Bradstreet's "Of the Four Ages of Man," she comments: "Bradstreet's 'Childhood' is a description of a child—cantankerous and spoiled, perhaps a reflection of one of Anne's own children, but nevertheless a generalized portrait (linked, however, to reality by the 'realistic' details)" (p. 14). The view of children as willful and cantankerous was a completely conventional seventeenth-century view (see Edmund S. Morgan, *The Puritan Family*). This treatment of childhood cannot be used to show that Bradstreet was interested in real children rather than stylized portraits of children as subjects for serious adult poetry, as Watts says. Furthermore, in trying to argue that the children described by

women poets in the nineteenth century appear more "real" than those conjured up by Wordsworth, Emerson, Longfellow, etc., I think she makes a less than convincing case.

3. Sarah Helen Whitman was briefly engaged to Edgar Allan Poe and has survived in critics' minds because of this. However, as Watts says, her poetry is generally impersonal and highly derivative of Bryant and Poe. She was a scholar, read German, and seems to have chosen to avoid the subjects of women's magazine verse intentionally. As recently as 1979 a book quoting extensively from her letters about Poe was published by the University Press of Virginia, Charlottesville (*Poe's Helen Remembers*, ed. John Carl Miller).

4. See Gilbert and Gubar, *Madwoman in the Attic*, ch. 1.

5. For discussions of types of poems I do not consider, see especially Watts, Cowell, and Gilbert and Gubar.

1. Methodology and Mystery: Anne Bradstreet

1. Roy Harvey Pearce's *Continuity of American Poetry* (Princeton: Princeton University Press, 1961), for instance, is a standard critical text. It is nearly 450 pages long, and Pearce treats many minor poets at length, yet the only women poets who are given more than a mention are Marianne Moore and Emily Dickinson. Edna St. Vincent Millay is merely listed as one of the poets published by Harriet Monroe. Amy Lowell and H. D. never appear at all, although James Russell Lowell and Conrad Aiken are treated at length. But all of this should not surprise us since Pearce (p. 54) lets us know "what it means to be a poet—a man speaking of men to man"!

2. Lyle Koehler classifies Lucy Downing as a manipulator, a woman who could think for herself but phrased her judgments of the patriarchy in a submissive way (see Lyle Koehler, *A Search for Power: The "Weaker Sex" in Seventeenth-Century New England*. Urbana: University of Illinois Press, 1980, pp. 183–84). Koehler's book and Mary Beth Norton's *Liberty's Daughters* (Boston: Little, Brown, 1980) have increased our knowledge of the colonial period. However, these authors have also found the lack of materials frustrating.

3. We actually know very little about Anne Bradstreet herself. She had smallpox as an adolescent but whether her face was scarred is a matter of debate that cannot be resolved. During her residence in town, Bradstreet lived near Anne Hutchinson. Her father served as a magistrate at Hutchinson's trial. But whether the two Annes were friends, as John Berryman speculates, is not known. There are civil documents that Bradstreet, along with her husband, signed. But whether she attended public meetings and was involved in the political life of the colony cannot be stated with certainty. All that remains to us is her poetry, extracts from her journal, comments made about her in formal, literary settings like the verses appended to her first book, and the vital statistics of her life: birth, death, number of children, places of residence, etc. The rest is mostly conjecture.

4. David J. Latt, "Praising Virtuous Ladies: The Literary Image and Historical Reality of Women in Seventeenth-Century England" in *What Manner of Woman*, Marlene Springer, ed. (New York: New York University Press, 1977), pp. 39–64.

5. Quoted in Eugenie Andress Leonard, *The Dear-Bought Heritage* (Philadelphia: University of Pennsylvania, 1965), p. 239.

6. It is also true that husbands were punished for abusing their wives.

Husbands, in accordance with the teachings of St. Paul, were to love their wives like their own bodies, and in Massachusetts it was unlawful for a husband to strike his wife. However, women were punished for refusing to submit to their husbands. Although they might be counselled to be gentler, men were never punished for refusing to submit to the authority of their wives.

7. Quoted in Carl Holliday, *Woman's Life in Colonial Days* (1922; rpt. New York: Frederick Ungar Publishing Company, 1960), p. 35.

8. John Winthrop, *The History of New England*, James Savage, ed. (Boston, 1853), vol. 2, p. 216.

9. Thomas Parker, *The Coppy of a Letter Written . . . to his Sister* (London, 1650), p. 13.

10. Lyle Koehler, *A Search for Power*, p. 52.

11. All quotations from Anne Bradstreet are taken from *Poems of Anne Bradstreet*, Robert Hutchinson, ed. (New York: Dover, 1969).

12. Kenneth Requa's "Anne Bradstreet's Poetic Voices," published in *Early American Literature* 9 (1974): 3–18, argues that Bradstreet reveals her lack of comfort when she is writing in "masculine" modes, that is, when she is imitating forms used by men like her father and Du Bartas. Requa claims that she is most comfortable and therefore writes with the greatest ease when she is dealing with more personal topics and not attempting to imitate these masculine modes. However, I do not find this argument entirely convincing. The poet sometimes confesses great anguish ("Ah, and Ah, again, my imbecility!") in a poem otherwise meeting Requa's criteria for ease and comfort like "Contemplations." And her personal poems to her husband, one of which Requa quotes as an example of Bradstreet's control of her material, seem to me highly conventionalized and least characteristic of Bradstreet's personal voice.

13. Pattie Cowell, ed., *Women Poets in Pre-Revolutionary America, 1650–1775* (Troy, N.Y.: Whitston Publishing Company, 1980). One of the poets Cowell treats, Jane Colman Turell, confesses she is unaware of other American women poets and even Cowell admits that the extent to which colonial American women poets read one another is unclear. Lyle Koehler asserts that Bradstreet's book was the only book of verse published by an American woman in New England during the seventeenth century.

14. Pattie Cowell also notes that the conflict between a desire for personal recognition and the modesty enjoined by female conventions is a recurring motif in colonial women poets. Margaret Homans discusses the difficulty of women poets asserting subjectivity in *Women Writers and Poetic Identity* (Princeton: Princeton University Press, 1980).

15. See also Wendy Martin's discussion of the Puritan wife's position in "Anne Bradstreet's Poetry: A Study in Subversive Piety," in *Shakespeare's Sisters: Feminist Essays on Women Poets*, Sandra M. Gilbert and Susan Gubar, eds. (Bloomington: Indiana University Press, 1979), pp. 25–26. For an interesting comparison of the conventions differentiating elegies for women and elegies for men, see Lonna M. Malmsheimer, "Daughters of Zion: New England Roots of American Feminism," *New England Quarterly* 50 (September 1977), pp. 484–504.

16. Emily Stipes Watts, *The Poetry of American Women*, p. 26.

17. Adrienne Rich reads the last two lines of this stanza as a bitter jest. However, I do not hear Bradstreet sounding bitter when she calls her lines

"lowly" and when she modestly declines the bay wreath. These statements are too much like others Bradstreet made confessing her lack of ability. Furthermore, such disclaimers were conventional in Renaissance literature. Even Ralegh's *History of the World* (which Bradstreet knew) is full of elaborate apologies for the writer's flaws. Thus, it is not irony we are dealing with here but camouflage.

18. The chronology of works by Anne Bradstreet that Ann Stanford provides in *The Worldly Puritan* dates the formal elegies that praise earthly fame in the early 1640s. During the 1650s the poet wrote mostly religious meditations. The real turning point, as Stanford points out, came in 1647–48, the year of the composition of "Of the Vanity of All Worldly Creatures." Of the poems written after 1660 only "The Flesh and the Spirit" conveys any sense of unresolved longing for a worldly existence, and it, like the "Contemplations," seems to have been written partly in order to quiet such longings.

19. Emily Stipes Watts, *The Poetry of American Women*, pp. 18 and 19. My argument, though formulated earlier, agrees in substance with that of Karl Keller, *The Only Kangaroo Among the Beauty* (Baltimore: Johns Hopkins, 1979), pp. 16ff.

20. Elizabeth Singer Rowe, the British poet, was much admired by an eighteenth-century American poet, Jane Turell. Her father, Benjamin Colman, nurtured his daughter's literary aspirations. Yet in one of his own poems, addressed to "Philomela," he implies a criticism of Rowe in his satirical suggestion that women poets leave men out of their poems. Eden becomes Eve's domain alone. "Only there wants an Adam on the Green, / Or else all Paradise might here be seen" (see Harrison T. Meserole, ed., *Seventeenth-Century American Poetry*). Pattie Cowell discusses the relationship between Colman and his daughter as well as Turell's admiration for Rowe.

22. All quotations from Emily Dickinson are taken from Thomas Johnson's *The Poems of Emily Dickinson* (Cambridge: Harvard University Press, 1955). Johnson's numbering system is used to refer to Dickinson's poems throughout this book. This poem is #252.

21. For another interpretation of these lines and their gloss in the Geneva Bible, see Robert D. Richardson, "The Puritan Poetry of Anne Bradstreet," in *The American Puritan Imagination: Essays in Revaluation*, Sacvan Bercovitch, ed. (New York: Cambridge University Press, 1974).

23. Louise Bogan, *A Poet's Alphabet: Reflections on the Literary Art and Vocation*, Robert Phelps and Ruth Limmer, eds. (New York: McGraw-Hill, 1970), p. 429.

24. Evert A. and George L. Duyckinck, *Cyclopaedia of American Literature* (New York: Scribner's, 1855).

25. Adrienne Rich, *On Lies, Secrets, and Silence: Selected Prose 1966–1978* (New York: Norton, 1979), p. 21.

2. Founding the Tradition: The Poetess at Large

1. Geoffrey Hartman, *Beyond Formalism* (New Haven: Yale University Press, 1970), p. 353.

2. Gilbert and Gubar, *Madwoman in the Attic*, p. 43. Hereafter cited in the text as *Madwoman*.

3. Edith Hamilton, *Mythology* (New York: New American Library—Mentor Books, 1942), p. 270.

4. Sir Philip Sidney's poem "The Nightingale" provides a chilling example of the way the image of Philomela affects a male poet. Since he cannot identify with her, she becomes the Other to whom the poet compares himself. The persona passes off rape here as though it were a mere nothing compared to his sense of sterility and shame.

> Alas, she hath no other cause of anguish
>> But Tereus' love, on her by strong hand wroken,
> Wherein she suffering, all her spirits languish;
>> Full womanlike complains her will was broken.
>> But I, who daily craving,
> Cannot have to content me,
> Have more cause to lament me,
>> Since wanting is more woe than too much having,
> O Philomela fair, O take some gladness,
> That here is juster cause of plaintful sadness:
> Thine earth now springs, mine fadeth;
> Thy thorn without, my thorn my heart invadeth.

[Leonard Dean, ed. *Renaissance Poetry* (Englewood Cliffs, N.J.: Prentice-Hall, 1961), p. 50.]

5. Cowell, *Women Poets in Pre-Revolutionary America*, p. 12.

6. Terence Collins, "Phillis Wheatley: The Dark Side of the Poetry," *Phylon* 36 (1975): 78–88.

7. Mark Twain, *Adventures of Huckleberry Finn*, Norton Critical Edition, 2nd ed. (New York: Norton, 1977), pp. 85–86.

8. *The Memorial: Written by Friends of the Late Mrs. Osgood*, Mary E. Hewitt, ed. (New York: George Putnam, 1851), hereafter cited in the text as *The Memorial*.

9. *The Works of Mrs. Hemans*, with an Essay on Her Genius by Mrs. Sigourney, 7 vols. (Philadelphia: Lea and Blanchard, 1840), p. xv. I have not attempted to affix specific dates to the prevalence of the attitudes mentioned as characteristic of the nineteenth century. This is because these attitudes persist throughout the period I am describing (1820–1870) and can be found even earlier, as well as later.

10. Ann Douglas, *The Feminization of American Culture* (New York: Knopf, 1977), p. 8.

11. For examples see Frances Osgood's poem to Amelia Welby, Lucy Hooper's "Last Hours of a Young Poetess," Elizabeth Eames's poems to Elizabeth Oakes-Smith, the numerous poems to Frances Osgood in *The Memorial*.

12. Carroll Smith-Rosenberg, "The Female World of Love and Ritual: Relations between Women in Nineteenth-Century America," *Signs* 1 (1975):14.

13. *The Autobiography of Elizabeth Oakes-Smith*, Mary Alice Wyman, ed. (Lewiston, Me.: Lewiston Journal Company, 1924), p. 91, hereafter cited as *Autobiography*. For a firsthand look at the unpleasant side of female competition, one might look at the widely available letters of Sarah Helen Whitman in *Poe's Helen Remembers*, John Carl Miller, ed. (Charlottesville: University Press of Virginia, 1979).

14. Rufus Griswold, ed., *The Sacred Poets of England and America* (New York: D. Appleton, 1849), p. 461.

15. "Biographical memoir of the Late Mrs. Hemans" in *The Poetical Works of Mrs. Felicia Hemans* (Philadelphia: Grigg and Eliot, 1836), p. xiii. All poetry by Hemans used here is quoted from this text unless otherwise indicated. This text is not to be confused with the 1840 edition published by Lea and Blanchard which includes Sigourney's tribute.

16. For a discussion of the relationship between American women poets and Sappho, see Emily Stipes Watts, *The Poetry of American Women*, pp. 76–78.

17. Throughout, when poems appear in Rufus Griswold's *The Female Poets of America* (1848, new ed. 1873; rpt. New York: Garrett Press, 1969), they will be referenced by a G following the poem; when they come from Caroline May's *The American Female Poets* (Philadelphia: Lindsay and Blakiston, 1856) they will be followed by an M. If a poem appears in both texts, G will be cited, for the Griswold is more easily obtained than the May.

18. See especially Barbara Welter, *Dimity Convictions: The American Woman in the Nineteenth Century* (Athens: Ohio University Press, 1976), hereafter cited as Welter, and Nancy Cott, *The Bonds of Womanhood: "Women's Sphere" in New England, 1780–1835* (New Haven: Yale University Press, 1977), hereafter cited as Cott.

19. Frances Osgood, *Poems* (Philadelphia: Carey and Hart, 1850), hereafter cited as *Poems*.

20. Margaret Homans, *Women Writers and Poetic Identity*, p. 216.

21. John Evangelist Walsh, *Plumes in the Dust: The Love Affair of Edgar Allan Poe and Fanny Osgood* (Chicago: Nelson-Hall, 1980), p. 11.

22. Ibid., p. 10.

23. *The Autobiography of Elizabeth Oakes Smith*, Mary Alice Wyman, ed. (Lewiston, Me.: Lewiston Journal Co., 1924), p. 100.

24. Catharine Beecher, *An Essay on Slavery and Abolition With Reference to the Duty of American Females* (Philadelphia: Henry Perkins, 1837), p. 101.

25. An interesting example of this phenomenon is Anna Peyre Dinnies' poem "Wedded Love." Here the wife is attempting to rouse her husband from depression, but in the process she presents her own role in the language of power.

> Full well I know the generous soul
>   Which warms thee into life—
> Each spring which can its powers control,
>   Familiar to thy wife;
> For deemst thou she had stooped to bind
> Her fate unto a common mind?
> The eagle-like ambition, nursed
> From childhood in her heart, had first
> Consumed, with its Promethean flame,
> The shrine—then sunk her soul to shame.   [G]

26. *Notable American Women*, Edward T. James et al., eds. (Cambridge, Mass.: Belknap Press of Harvard University Press, 1971), p. 38.

27. *Ladies Magazine* 2 (1829):142.

28. Lucy Larcom, *A New England Girlhood* (1889; rpt. Gloucester, Massachusetts: Peter Smith, 1973), p. 222, hereafter cited as *New England Girlhood*.

29. Quoted in Ann Douglas (Wood), "Mrs. Sigourney and the Sensibility of the Inner Space," *New England Quarterly* 45 (June 1972): 166.

30. These quotations come from a statement made by Nathaniel P. Willis quoted in Ann Douglas, *The Feminization of American Culture*, p. 103.

31. Rufus Griswold, ed., *The Poets and Poetry of America* (Philadelphia: Parry and McMillan, 1856), hereafter cited as G, *Poets and Poetry*.

32. For other poems expressing this vision of the poet, see Elizabeth Oakes-Smith's "The Poet," Lydia Pierson's "To an Aolian Harp," Emma Embury's "The Aolian Harp," Lucy Hooper's "Last Hours of a Young Poetess," Lydia Sigourney's "Monody on Mrs. Hemans," Lavinia Stoddard's "Song," and Emily Judson's "The Weaver." Obviously, American women poets did not originate the idea of conjoining poetry with suffering, but their adherence to this point of view is nevertheless significant for what it reveals about them and the American cultural scene. The relationship between women poets' conception of poetry and the secret sorrow will be developed more fully in the chapter on Emily Dickinson.

33. *Godey's Lady's Book* 44 (1852): 147.

34. Justin Kaplan, *Walt Whitman: A Life* (New York: Simon and Schuster, 1980), p. 225. Fanny Fern (Sara Parton) was one of the most popular and prolific prose writers of her day. She had once been interested in Whitman and flattered his vanity but the relationship went sour as this quotation shows.

35. One version of this guilt is manifested by the heroine of Elizabeth Barrett Browning's poem *Aurora Leigh* who marries in order to avoid the stigma of self-centered ambition (see *The Poetical Works of Elizabeth Barrett Browning* [Boston: Houghton Mifflin, 1974]). Josiah Holland in his novel *Miss Gilbert's Career* (1860) elucidates the way contemporary American writers continually reinforced this concept of guilt in women. Fanny Gilbert, the heroine, is interested in a literary career. She avoids becoming entangled in love in order to pursue her literary ambitions. But she becomes more feminine, according to Holland, when she gives up her aspirations in exchange for marriage and self-sacrifice. "She had lost her habitual self-seeking—lost her imperious will—gladly laid down her proud self-reliance and found her womanhood." And again: "She learned that a woman's truest career is lived in love's serene retirement—lived in feeding the native forces of her other self—lived in the career of her husband." Josiah Holland, *Miss Gilbert's Career* (New York: Scribner's, 1860), p. 466.

36. Kathryn Kish Sklar, *Catharine Beecher: A Study in American Domesticity* (New York: Norton, 1973), p. 271.

37. In the Theodore S. Fay poem given later in this chapter the male persona also escapes confinement by pressing through a hole, but the image carries none of the implications it gathers here. Emily Stipes Watts also discusses this poem in *The Poetry of American Women*, pp. 118–19. I agree with Watts's choices of Osgood, Oakes-Smith, and Sigourney as the most interesting of the early nineteenth-century women poets. However, Watts sometimes exaggerates her judgments as when she says, "Not only by talent but also by poetic interest, Osgood is separated from her male and female contemporaries nearly as much as Dickinson is separated from hers," p. 105.

38. Quoted in Don Hausdorff, ed., *Literature in America: A Century of Expansion* (New York: Macmillan, 1971), pp. 254–55.

39. The sexual threat posed by men is a major factor in Margaret Fuller's argument in favor of women's marital rights. One can feel the horror of enforced cohabitation with a drunkard or a brute in Fuller's *Woman in the*

Nineteenth Century. Oakes-Smith comes as close as decorum permitted to saying in her memoirs that the sexual side of marriage was horrifying to her at the age of 16 when she first confronted it. She says, "I had vast ideas of immaculate purity, consecration to God, living in the spirit." She warns men against marrying such naive young girls, since they must be completely made over and fitted "for common life" (*Autobiography*, p. 44).

40. Walsh, *Plumes in the Dust*, p. 11.

41. Margaret Fuller, *Memoirs of Margaret Fuller Ossoli* (Boston: Phillips, Sampson, 1852), vol. 2, p. 98.

42. Lucy Larcom, *The Poetical Works of Lucy Larcom* (Boston: Houghton Mifflin, 1884), hereafter cited as *Poems*.

43. Elizabeth Oakes-Smith, *The Poetical Writings of Elizabeth Oakes Smith*, 2nd ed. (New York: J. S. Redfield, 1846), hereafter cited as *Poems*.

44. See Welter, *Dimity Convictions*, pp. 15 and 59; Sklar, *Catharine Beecher*, p. 211, e.g.

45. William H. Chafe, *Women and Equality: Changing Patterns in American Culture* (New York: Oxford, 1977), p. 66. In *A Social History of the American Family* (Cleveland: Arthur M. Clark, 1918), Arthur Calhoun quotes Emily Collins, a nineteenth-century woman: "In those early days a husband's supremacy was often enforced in rural districts by corporeal chastisement and it was considered by most people as quite right and proper—as much so as the correction of refractory children in like manner" (vol. 2, p. 92). The idea that this only occurred "in those early days" is, of course, a false one. Recent revelations have shown that battered wives are part of every class and every kind of community. It is still true that, in many mountain and rural communities, beating a wife or lover is looked upon as an acceptable way for males to express hostility.

46. Ellen Moers in *Literary Women* (New York: Doubleday, 1976), hereafter cited as *Literary Women*, has also noticed the prevalence of bird images in women's writing. Her discussion of them, broader and more general than mine, can be found in chapter 11.

47. See Barbara Welter's excellent discussion of this, "Coming of Age in America: The American Girl in the Nineteenth Century," in *Dimity Convictions*.

48. This poem is quoted in Lydia Sigourney's *Letters of Life* (New York: D. Appleton, 1867).

49. *Poetical Remains of the Late Lucretia Maria Davidson* (Philadelphia: Lea and Blanchard, 1847), hereafter cited as *Poetical Works*.

50. L. H. Butterfield, Marc Friedlaender, and Mary-Jo Kline, eds., *The Book of Abigail and John: Selected Letters of the Adams Family 1762–1784* (Cambridge, Mass.: Harvard University Press, 1975), p. 159. Some time after I formulated the concept of the "sanctuary poem," I read Elaine Showalter's *A Literature of Their Own* in which she discusses at great length the way the sanctuary motif operates in the novels of British women. Her discussion and mine seem to me to complement each other.

51. Ann Douglas in *The Feminization of American Culture* provides an illuminating account of nineteenth-century cemeteries as sanctuaries. See p. 211.

52. For further consideration of the issue of renunciation in women's literature, see Gilbert and Gubar's "The Aesthetics of Renunciation," *Madwoman*, pp. 539ff.

53. See Welter, *Dimity Convictions*, p. 77.
54. Quoted in Grace Lathrop Collin, "Lydia Huntley Sigourney," *New England Magazine*, September 1902, p. 23.
55. *Adrienne Rich's Poetry*, Barbara Gelpi and Albert Gelpi, eds. (New York: Norton, 1975).

3. A Composite Biography: Nineteenth-Century Women Poets

1. Seamus Heaney, "Current Unstated Assumptions about Poetry," *Critical Inquiry* 7 (Summer 1981): 650.
2. Ralph Waldo Emerson, *Selections from Ralph Waldo Emerson*, Stephen Whicher, ed. (Boston: Houghton, Mifflin, 1957), p. 271. This quotation is from the "Experience" essay.
3. Alicia Ostriker, "The Nerves of a Midwife: Contemporary American Women's Poetry," *Parnassus: Poetry in Review* 6 (Fall/Winter 1977): 69–87.
4. The following works are not widely available but can still be found. I have used them extensively in this chapter and will hereafter refer to them in the text by abbreviations: Mrs. Zadel Barnes Gustafson's introduction to Maria Brooks, *Zophiël, or the Bride of Seven* (Boston: Lea and Blanchard, 1879), hereafter cited as Gustafson; Ruth Shepard Grannis, *An American Friend of Southey* (privately printed in New York: The De Vinne Press, 1913), hereafter cited as Grannis; the biographical introduction by Catherine Sedgwick in Lucretia Davidson, *Poetical Remains of the Late Lucretia Davidson* (Philadelphia: Lea and Blanchard, 1847), hereafter cited as Sedgwick; William Still, *The Underground Rail Road* (Philadelphia: Porter and Coates, 1872), hereafter cited as Still; Lucy Larcom, *A New England Girlhood* (1889; rpt. Gloucester, Massachusetts: Peter Smith, 1973), hereafter cited as *Girlhood*; Daniel Dulany Addison, *Lucy Larcom: Life, Letters, and Diary* (Boston: Houghton, Mifflin, 1894), hereafter cited as Addison; Mary Alice Wyman, *The American Pioneers: Seba Smith and Elizabeth Oakes-Smith* (New York: Columbia University Press, 1927), hereafter cited as Wyman; Elizabeth Oakes-Smith, *The Autobiography of Elizabeth Oakes-Smith*, Mary Alice Wyman, ed. (Lewiston, Me.: Lewiston Journal Company, 1924), hereafter cited as *Autobiography*; Elizabeth Oakes-Smith, *Woman and Her Needs* (New York: Fowlers and Wells, 1851), hereafter cited as *Woman and Her Needs*; Gordon Haight, *Mrs. Sigourney: Sweet Singer of Hartford* (New Haven: Yale University Press, 1930), hereafter cited as Haight; Lydia Sigourney, *Letters of Life* (New York: Harper & Brothers, 1837), hereafter cited as *Letters of Life*; Grace Lathrop Collin, "Lydia Huntley Sigourney," *New England Magazine* (September 1902): 15–30, hereafter cited as Collin; Lydia Sigourney, *Letters to Young Ladies* (New York: Harper & Brothers, 1837), hereafter cited as *Letters to Young Ladies*.
5. Even Maria Brooks, who lived for many years in Cuba, was raised in Medford, Massachusetts, in the company of her father's friends, many of whom were Harvard professors. She married a Boston merchant and her son went to Dartmouth. During his college years, she returned to New England and worked in the library in Hanover, New Hampshire.
6. Quoted in Genevieve Taggard's *The Life and Mind of Emily Dickinson* (New York: Knopf, 1930), pp. 209–10.
7. The story of Davidson's relationships with her father and Moss Kent exposes some bizarre and tantalizing facts. The story is told in a seemingly innocent and unselfconscious way by Catherine Sedgwick. Moss Kent, although supposedly an old family friend, did not meet Lucretia until she was

fifteen. At that time he was reportedly overwhelmed by her beauty and creative promise, and he asked the family if he could adopt her. Although no reason is given in support of this scheme, Sedgwick says if Lucretia had lived, Kent would have been given permission to adopt her. In the interim, he was allowed to oversee her education, and she was sent away to school where he visited her periodically. Lucretia returned very ill from Emma Willard's seminary at Troy, New York. However, the doctor recommended a change of scene and she returned to another school, this time at Albany. Here a severe illness set in. At each danger point, however, her father reacted in a strangely unfeeling manner. Her mother wanted once again to withdraw her from school, but as Sedgwick tells us, her father's "colder judgment" advised that if Lucretia were truly ill, her friends would have written them about her. Finally, Lucretia's mother, who was herself ill, set out and brought her home. Once again her father was ready to pronounce her healthy, but her mother had seen the tell-tale crimson spot of consumption, and Lucretia died relatively soon thereafter. At the time of her death, she was reportedly asking for Moss Kent, to whom she had written a poem, calling him "my father and my friend." If, as this strange story seems to suggest, Kent was her real father (or perhaps Mrs. Davidson's later lover), Mr. Davidson's coldness toward her, and even toward his wife's feelings, is explained. Even if Kent was regarded only as a friend, however, he clearly fulfilled Lucretia's need to have a supportive male parent.

For a discussion of the importance of fathers to British women novelists, a discussion that complements mine, see Elaine Showalter, *A Literature of Their Own*, p. 61.

8. Catherine Sedgwick cannot be considered an unbiased biographer. She was a successful writer in her own right although she mainly concentrated on novels. Sedgwick publicly espoused the view that it was more important for a woman to be successful in the domestic sphere than in the literary one. Her attack on Mr. Davidson, however, implies covert hostility against the "colder judgment" of the patriarchy.

9. Gerda Lerner, *The Female Experience: An American Documentary* (Indianapolis: Bobbs-Merrill, 1977), p. 224.

10. Larcom's poetry is very uneven. However, she wrote several dramatic monologues that use Browning's techniques with great success. One of these—"Getting Along"—conveys the lack of fulfillment a woman experiences in her marriage. The whole poem, spoken by the wife, does a nice job of capturing both the reality of the situation and the woman's attempt to deny her own feelings about it. Here is a sample:

> He seems not to know what I eat, drink, or wear;
> He's trim and he's hearty, so why should I care?
> No harsh word from him my poor soul ever shocks:
> I wouldn't mind scolding,—so seldom he talks.
>
> Ah, well! 't is too much that we women expect:
> He only has promised to love and protect.
> See, I lean on my husband, so silent and strong;
> I'm sure there's no trouble;—we're getting along.

Another poem, "Unwedded," describes the nobility of a single woman's life and criticizes those who make fun of spinsters.

> Would she have walked more nobly, think,
> With a man beside her, to point the way,
> Hand joining hand in the marriage-link?
> Possibly, Yes: it is likelier, Nay.

11. *American Women Writers*, Lina Mainiero, ed. (New York: Frederick Ungar Publishing Company, 1979), hereafter cited in the text as A.W.W.

12. Ann Douglas (Wood), "Mrs. Sigourney and the Sensibility of Inner Space," p. 166.

13. *Notable American Women, 1607–1950*. Edward T. James et al., eds. (Cambridge, Mass.: Belknap Press of Harvard University Press, 1971), hereafter cited as N.A.W.

14. A quotation from Elizabeth Gaskell highlights a difference between literary women and literary men in this period. Gaskell says:

> When a man becomes an author, it is probably merely a change of employment to him. He takes a portion of that time which has hitherto been devoted to some other study or pursuit; . . . and another merchant or lawyer, or doctor, steps into his vacant place, and probably does as well as he. But no other can take up the quiet, regular duties of the daughter, the wife, or the mother. . . ; a woman's principal work in life is hardly left to her own choice; nor can she drop the domestic charges devolving on her as an individual, for the exercise of the most splendid talents that were ever bestowed. (*Literary Women*, 22)

15. Southey may have been some help to Maria Brooks and, belatedly, to Lucretia Davidson, but he may also be regarded as a discouraging example of the way even supportive men could reverse themselves on occasion. To Charlotte Brontë he wrote: "Literature cannot be the business of a woman's life and it ought not to be."

16. Smith-Rosenberg, "The Female World of Love and Ritual," p. 10. Lillian Faderman, *Surpassing the Love of Men: Romantic Friendship and Love Between Women from the Renaissance to the Present* (New York: William Morrow, 1981). In "Love and 'Women Who Live by Their Brains' " Faderman discusses specifically literary friendships.

17. For this sample study, I used the following list of poets, whose probable age at the time of death is given here: Anne Lynch (Botta), 76; Elizabeth Ellet, 65; Caroline Gilman, 94; Julia Ward Howe, 91; Caroline Sawyer, 82; Anna Peyre Dinnies, 81; Elizabeth Kinney, 79; Maria Brooks, 50; Lydia Sigourney, 74; Katharine Ware, 46; Cynthia Taggart, 48; Francesca Canfield, 19; Emma Embury, 57; Elizabeth Chandler, 27; Lucretia Davidson, 16; Margaret Davidson, 15; Elizabeth Oakes-Smith, 87; Julia Scott, 33; Sarah Smith, 21; Laura Thurston, 30; Emily Judson, 36; Margaret Fuller, 40; Anna Ritchie, 50; Frances Osgood, 38; Lucy Hooper, 25; Sarah Mayo, 30; Amelia Welby, 31; Alice Haven, 33; Lucy Larcom, 67; Alice Carey, 51; Phoebe Carey, 46; Maria Lowell, 32; Frances Harper, 86; Sarah Whitman, 75. Canfield, the Davidsons, Scott, Osgood, and Hooper all died of consumption. Fuller's case is moot because she drowned in a storm off Long Island.

18. Susan Sontag's articles on disease as metaphor all appeared in the *New York Review of Books* (January 26, 1978; February 9, 1978; and February 23,

1978). They have now been published as a book entitled *Illness as Metaphor* (New York: Farrar, Straus & Giroux, 1978).

19. There are provocative and interesting discussions of this relationship in Lyle Koehler's *A Search for Power* and Gilbert and Gubar's *Madwoman in the Attic*. Emily Stipes Watts says: "In American women's poetry, the theme [of suicide] extends from Brooks' *Zophiël; or, The Bride of Seven* to the verse of Sylvia Plath. I have found no such self-destructive tendencies expressed by male American poets in their verse until the twentieth century" (p. 133).

20. Gloria Hull's essay "Afro-American Women Poets: A Bio-Critical Survey," published in *Shakespeare's Sisters*, suggests that black women poets have their own tradition. Anne Spencer, a twentieth-century woman poet, was to follow Harper's lead. In her own poem "Shushan" she draws on the same material as "Vashti." Only Angelina Grimké and Georgia Douglas Johnson seem to fall back on the nightingale tradition and then only in some poems. See Hull, *Shakespeare's Sisters*, Gilbert and Gubar, eds., pp. 165–182.

4. Tradition and the Individual Talent: Helen Hunt Jackson and Emily Dickinson

1. It is likely that Dickinson knew these poets because Samuel Bowles had sent Susan and Austin Dickinson *The Household Book of Poetry*, edited by Charles Dana and published in 1860. Books like this were usually shared between the households. This one contained works by Maria Brooks, Caroline Gilman, Maria Lowell, and Amelia Welby. (It also included poems by Elizabeth Barrett Browning and Felicia Hemans.) *The Sacred Poets of England and America* (1849), edited by Rufus Griswold, was found in the Dickinson library. It included works by Felicia Hemans and Lydia Sigourney. T. W. Higginson apparently recommended Maria Lowell to Dickinson (see L. 352). She asks him in a letter where she can find Lowell's poems, published in 1855. Longfellow also quotes Maria Brooks's *Zophiël* in *Kavanaugh* ("descends and sips the nearest draft").

2. Throughout this study, references to Johnson and Ward's *The Letters of Emily Dickinson* (Cambridge, Massachusetts: Harvard University Press, 1958) and *The Poems of Emily Dickinson* (Cambridge, Massachusetts: Harvard University Press, 1955), three volumes each, will be made according to the particular number assigned to the document. Thus, here L. 8 refers to letter 8 in Johnson's edition. The same system is used for the poems; P. 121 is poem 121.

3. Gilbert and Gubar have a very useful discussion of the white dress in *Madwoman*, pp. 613–622. For a further exploration of parallels between Rossetti and Dickinson, see a very interesting essay by Joan Feit Diehl which says that Emily Dickinson, Elizabeth Barrett Browning, and Christina Rossetti all show an awareness of tradition and a distinctly similar structure of dealing with it. Diehl is talking mainly about the problems of a woman poet facing a male tradition but she also talks about the sanctuary, the fears Dickinson faced, and her ambivalence. She says, "Dickinson wavers between feeling that she must wait to receive her Master/muse and radical rejection of his presence" (p. 578). According to Diehl, Rossetti knew Dickinson's work. See Joanne Feit Diehl, " 'Come slowly – Eden': An Exploration of Women Poets and Their Muse," *Signs* 3 (Spring 1978): 572–87.

4. George Frisbie Whicher, *This Was a Poet: A Critical Biography of Emily Dickinson* (New York: Scribner's, 1938), p. 136.

5. Quoted in Richard B. Sewall, *The Life of Emily Dickinson*, 2 vols. (New York: Farrar, Straus, 1974), p. 203, hereafter cited as Sewall.

6. Henry Wadsworth Longfellow, *Kavanaugh* in *The Works of Henry Wadsworth Longfellow*, vol. 8 (Boston: Houghton, Mifflin, 1886), p. 313.

7. Helen Hunt Jackson (pseud. Saxe Holm), "Esther Wynn's Love Letters," *Scribner's Magazine* 3 (December 1871): 168.

8. Helen Hunt Jackson, *Mercy Philbrick's Choice*, No Name Series (Boston: Roberts, 1876), pp. 285–86.

9. Both George Whicher *(This Was a Poet)* and John Evangelist Walsh *(The Hidden Life of Emily Dickinson*. New York: Simon and Schuster, 1971) have suggested that Jackson used Dickinson's life as a source for these works.

10. In "My Life had stood – a Loaded Gun" (P. 754) Dickinson changes the word "art" in the last line to "power"—which suggests in some way she saw the two terms as interchangeable.

11. Vivian R. Pollak, "Thirst and Starvation in Emily Dickinson's Poetry," *American Literature* 51 (March 1979): 39. See also the discussion of Emersonian compensation in Karl Keller, *The Only Kangaroo Among the Beauty* (Baltimore: Johns Hopkins University Press, 1979).

12. Evelyn L. Banning, *Helen Hunt Jackson* (New York: Vanguard Press, 1973), p. 48, hereafter cited as Banning.

13. For a discussion of the importance of female figures as subjects for women poets, see Emily Stipes Watts, *The Poetry of American Women*, pp. 74–78.

14. Allen Tate, "Emily Dickinson," in *Emily Dickinson: A Collection of Critical Essays*, Richard B. Sewall, ed. (Englewood Cliffs, New Jersey: Prentice-Hall, 1963), pp. 16–27.

15. Albert Gelpi is one of the few critics before the feminists who made biographical comparisons between Dickinson's life and the lives of other women poets. In *Emily Dickinson: The Mind of the Poet* (Cambridge, Massachusetts: Harvard University Press, 1965), he wrote:

> There are interesting biographical parallels between Margaret Fuller and Emily Dickinson; the awesome and possessive father; the sense of difference, the sensitivity and superiority; the inherited New England temperament at odds with the insurgent Romantic spirit; the craving for love (which became with Margaret a kind of psychological assault on her intellectual associates); the resistance to a reciprocal human relationship. [pp. 184–85]

16. For further discussions of Emily Dickinson's mother, see John Cody, *After Great Pain: The Inner Life of Emily Dickinson* (Cambridge, Mass.: Harvard University Press, 1971) and the commentary on Cody in Sewall, *The Life of Emily Dickinson*. Also Jean McClure Mudge, *Emily Dickinson and the Image of Home* (Amherst: University of Massachusetts Press, 1975).

17. Although Edward Dickinson could hardly be called a feminist sympathizer, he was committed to the idea of female education. He once wrote: "Females, also, have a sphere of action, which, tho' different entirely in its kind from that of the other sex, is no less important." He had clearly felt the influence of the theory of separate spheres. In a letter of August 3, 1826 he wrote to his future wife about an evening spent with Catherine Sedgwick: "I feel happy at having an opportunity of seeing a female who had done so

much to give our works of taste so pure and delicate a character—and a conscious pride that women of our own country & our own state, too, are emulating not only the females but the men of England & France & Germany & Italy in works of literature—" (Sewall, pp. 48–49).

18. For an excellent set of examples of this phenomenon, see Mary Beth Norton's selection of letters and diary entries in *Liberty's Daughters*.

19. Although my work on Dickinson was completed before I read Gilbert and Gubar's "A Woman—White: Emily Dickinson's Yarn of Pearl" in *Madwoman in the Attic*, our arguments converge in many places. They analyze "She rose to His Requirement" (pp. 588ff.), as I will do in the following pages, and they also conclude:

> The fact that in some poems Dickinson analyzes this female double life of surface requirements and sea-deep pearl with surgical calm does not mean she is unsympathetic to the women who endure the psychic splits she describes. Nor does it mean that she supposed herself exempt from such problems because she never officially undertook the work of wife. On the contrary, both her irony and her objectivity were intensified by her sense that she herself was trapped in the Requirements by which all women were surrounded, a tangled set of implicit laws." [p. 590]

20. For a book-length discussion of Emily Dickinson's relation to the phenomenon of the nineteenth-century home, see Jean McClure Mudge, *Emily Dickinson and the Image of Home*.

21. When Emily, late in her life, became involved with Judge Otis P. Lord, she seems to have considered marriage from a more positive perspective. Letter 780 has her writing to Lord, "Emily 'Jumbo'! Sweetest name, but I know a sweeter – Emily Jumbo Lord. Have I your approval?" We don't know what precisely this was meant to convey but Dickinson throughout the courtship seems to have enjoyed coquetting with Lord. About 1878 she wrote him: "Dont you know you are happiest while I withhold and not confer – dont you know that 'No' is the wildest word we consign to Language?" (L. 562) A little further on in the same letter she reflects more ambivalence: "It is Anguish I long conceal from you to let you leave me, hungry, but you ask the divine Crust and that would doom the Bread." That the two never married was probably due in part to Dickinson's preference for tantalizing her lover. But there may have been fears as well. Part of the following poem is reproduced in the fragmented letter to Lord quoted above.

> Oh, honey of an hour
> I never knew thy power,
> Prohibit me
> Till my minutest dower,
> My unfrequented flower
> Deserving be.   [P. 1734]

Karl Keller in *The Only Kangaroo Among the Beauty* rightly reminds us of Dickinson's discomfort with political feminism as represented by women like Elizabeth Stuart Phelps. Yet the very ritual of confinement and escape that Keller examines as proof of "her yearning for power *within a controlled life*"

(p. 244) is part of her pre-feminist not her anti-feminist sympathies. That Keller says he finds it not hard to imagine her "as a hooker" seems to me a gross misunderstanding of her nature. We have now gone the full gamut in Dickinson criticism from the virgin/spinster/child to the whore.

22. For a lengthy discussion of this issue, see Sewall's chapter, "The New England Dickinsons and the Puritan Heritage," and Keller.

23. For other examples see poems 295 and 544.

24. Adrienne Rich comments on Dickinson's attachment to her home in "Vesuvius at Home: The Power of Emily Dickinson," *Parnassus: Poetry in Review* (Fall/Winter 1976): 49.

25. The following is a partial listing of poems that use prison imagery: 77, 80, 119, 277, 384, 532, 613, 652, 661, 725, 728, 947, 1166, 1334, 1532, 1594, 1601. These poems, it should be recognized, belong to the general category of limitation poems examined in chapter 2.

26. Emily Stipes Watts, *The Poetry of American Women from 1632 to 1945*, p. 133. Maria Brooks's "Song" was included in *The Household Book of Poetry* which Dickinson probably saw and *Zophiël* is quoted by Longfellow in *Kavanaugh*. "Song"—which Louise Bogan called a lyric "of surprising fervor"—ends:

> Absent still! Ah! Come and bless me!
> Let these eyes again caress thee;
> Once, in caution, I could fly thee;
> Now, I nothing could deny thee;
> In a look if death there be,
> Come, and I will gaze on thee!   [G]

Brooks actually attempted suicide twice according to her biographer in *American Women Writers*.

27. Although this poem remains undated in Johnson's edition, if one compares #1560 (dated about 1883) the similarities immediately become apparent, suggesting an approximate date for this poem also.

28. Rebecca Patterson has argued that the key to Emily Dickinson's secrecy was lesbianism. However, Patterson's *The Riddle of Emily Dickinson* (Boston: Houghton, Mifflin, 1951) is unconvincing to me. The letters to Judge Lord are both passionate and sensual. Of course, Dickinson loved women. But the references to kissing and hugging that appear in the letters to Kate Anthon and Susan Dickinson seem so unselfconscious that it is hard to regard them as evidence of an affectional preference that the nineteenth century would have regarded with horror. The most important thing to remember is that women were deeply important to Dickinson, more consistently important as objects of affection than the men about whom we have evidence at this point. A much better discussion than Patterson's, and one that emphasizes Dickinson's homoerotic relations with women, is Lillian Faderman's "Emily Dickinson's Letters to Sue Gilbert," *Massachusetts Review* 18 (Summer 1977): 197–225. Faderman expands this argument in *Surpassing the Love of Men: Romantic Friendship and Love Between Women from the Renaissance to the Present* (New York: William Morrow, 1981).

29. Charlotte Brontë, *Jane Eyre* (1847; rpt. Baltimore: Penguin, 1966), pp. 203 and 302 respectively, hereafter cited in the text as *Jane Eyre*. For a more

extended discussion of *Jane Eyre*'s relevance to Dickinson, see Gilbert and Gubar, *Madwoman in the Attic.*

30. The wordplay that produces "trusty word" instead of the more familiar "trusty sword" implies that Dickinson saw language as a potentially destructive force. This point of view is reflected in numerous poems, probably the most famous of which is "My Life had stood – a Loaded Gun" (P. 754), which is examined by Adrienne Rich ("Vesuvius at Home") and Albert Gelpi ("Emily Dickinson and the Deerslayer: The Dilemma of the Woman Poet in America") in *Shakespeare's Sisters.* The statement that "A Word that breathes distinctly / Has not the power to die" provides a useful commentary on the loaded gun poem. The "I" in the poem may be read as "language," the "He" as the poet. See also Joan Feit Diehl and Gilbert and Gubar. The latter state categorically that "This Gun clearly is a Poet" (*Madwoman,* p. 609).

31. See Adrienne Rich, "Vesuvius at Home." For some poems that may be read as interesting commentaries on Dickinson's sense of herself, see 789, 822, 1427, 1465, 1475 and 1510.

32. The three letters to an unknown recipient known as the Master letters were found among Dickinson's possessions after her death. Although she had asked her sister Lavinia to burn all her correspondence and Lavinia had complied to the best of her abilities, these letters survived. Whether these are copies of letters actually sent or letters she wrote but did not send, we do not know. Albert Gelpi argues in *The Tenth Muse* that these letters represent Dickinson's encounter with the animus. Although the letter to Beethoven from Margaret Fuller (also quoted by Gilbert and Gubar) makes a fascinating comparison, I am not convinced that the Master letters were simply imaginative projections of a mind in dialogue with itself. Nevertheless, Gelpi's discussion of the animus deserves serious consideration as does the discussion of Dickinson's need for a Master in *Madwoman in the Attic.* See Albert Gelpi, *The Tenth Muse: The Psyche of the American Poet* (Cambridge, Massachusetts: Harvard University Press, 1975), pp. 255ff.

5. One Brief, Transitory Hour: Ella Wheeler Wilcox, Lizette Woodworth Reese, and Louise Guiney

1. Fred Lewis Pattee, *A History of American Literature Since 1870* (New York: Century Company, 1915), p. 335.

2. Edmund Clarence Stedman, ed., *American Anthology 1787–1900* (Boston: Houghton Mifflin, 1900). Poems taken from this text will hereafter be cited as Stedman.

3. Lizette Woodworth Reese, *The Selected Poems of Lizette Woodworth Reese* (New York: Doran, 1926), hereafter cited as *Selected Poems.*

4. Kate Gannett Wells, "The Transitional American Woman," *Atlantic Monthly* 46 (December 1880): 819, hereafter cited as Wells.

5. Louise Imogen Guiney, *Letters of Louise Imogen Guiney,* Grace Guiney, ed., 2 volumes (New York: Harper & Brothers, 1926). Hereafter cited as *Letters* with the volume number and page. This quotation comes from volume 1, p. 60.

6. Ella Wheeler Wilcox, *Men, Women and Emotions* (Chicago: Morrill, Higgins, 1893), p. 302, hereafter cited as *Men, Women and Emotions.*

7. Jenny Ballou, *Period Piece: Ella Wheeler Wilcox and Her Times,* (Boston: Houghton Mifflin, 1940), p. 149, hereafter cited as Ballou.

8. Eliot Gregory, "Our Foolish Virgins," *Century Magazine*, 63 (November 1901): 3–15.

9. These statistics are widely available. For one account, see Mary P. Ryan, *Womanhood in America*. For a discussion of coed schools vs. women's colleges, see "The End of the Victorian Era: 1890–1919," *Him/Her/Self: Sex Roles in Modern America* by Peter Filene (New York: Harcourt, Brace, 1974), especially pp. 24ff.

10. Lizette Woodworth Reese, *A Victorian Village* (New York: Farrar and Rinehart, 1933), p. 262.

11. Caroline Ticknor, "The Steel-Engraving Lady and the Gibson Girl," *Atlantic Monthly* 88 (July 1901): 106.

12. Henry G. Fairbanks, *Louise Imogen Guiney: Laureate of the Lost* (Albany: Magi, 1972), p. 69, hereafter cited as Fairbanks.

13. Louise Imogen Guiney, *Happy Ending* (Boston: Houghton, Mifflin, 1909). All poems from this, Guiney's collected poems, will be cited as *Happy Ending*.

14. A poem from *The Crucible* (September 20, 1905), quoted in Fairbanks, p. 13.

15. George Santayana, *The Genteel Tradition: Nine Essays by George Santayana*, Douglas L. Wilson, ed. (Cambridge, Mass.: Harvard University Press, 1967), p. 73. Emily Stipes Watts also mentions "The Tiger" and refers us to another Wilcox poem published in *Poems of Pleasure* (1892) where Wilcox admits that, for her, sex is "all the tiger in my blood" (*The Poetry of American Women*, p. 145).

16. Ella Wheeler Wilcox, *Poems of Passion* (Chicago: W. B. Conkey, 1883).

17. Anna A. Rogers, "Why American Marriages Fail," *Atlantic Monthly* 100 (September 1907): 293. This was reputed to be one of the most widely read articles of the decade.

18. Henry James, *The Ambassadors* (New York: New American Library, 1960), p. 349.

19. Louise Imogen Guiney, *The White Sail* (Boston: Ticknor & Company, 1887).

20. William Vaughn Moody, *The Poems and Plays of William Vaughn Moody*, 2 volumes (Boston: Houghton, Mifflin, 1912). Watts makes a useful distinction between male and female traditions by reminding us of "the American Adam" in male poetry and the unavailability of Eve as a comparable ego-model for women. She says: "While the men turned their attention to utopian and 'cosmic' concerns (i.e., the creation of that masculine, nationalistic image, the American Adam), the women looked at themselves and their situations and found many other things to say" (p. 66). Eve represented a tainted symbol because of her connection to the fall in Puritan theology. Still, Watts does not say why women did not revise the Eve tradition, as Moody has done here. I suggest that female ambivalence toward power is in part responsible for this refusal to take up that task.

21. Edwin Arlington Robinson, *Selected Poems of Edwin Arlington Robinson*, Morton Dauwen Zabel, ed. (New York: Macmillan-Collier Books, 1966).

22. See Agnes Repplier, "The Repeal of Reticence," *Atlantic Monthly* 113 (March 1914): 297–304. For a discussion of this period, including Reedy's famous phrase, see James R. McGovern, "The American Woman's Pre-World War I Freedom in Manners and Morals," in *Our American Sisters: Women in American Life and Thought*, Jean E. Friedman and William G. Shade, eds. (Boston: Allyn and Bacon, 1973), pp. 237–59.

23. Examples of such articles include Anna Rogers's (mentioned above) "Are Women to Blame?" (a symposium including responses by Rebecca Harding Davis and others) in *North American Review* 148 (April 1889): 622–42; and Margaret Deland, "The Change in the Feminine Ideal," *Atlantic Monthly* 105 (March 1910): 289–302.

24. Christopher Lasch, "Woman as Alien," in *Our American Sisters*, p. 181.

25. "Scarcity" is from *White April* (New York: Farrar and Rinehart, 1930); "Bargain" is from *Pastures* (New York: Farrar and Rinehart, 1933). It is impossible to tell to what degree Reese is echoing in her later books the sentiments expressed by Amy Lowell, H. D., and Elinor Wylie. For convenience's sake, I have dealt with her work as though it belongs to the 1890s. The tone becomes more vibrant after the poetry renaissance of the 1910s and '20s, but the sentiments are relatively consistent throughout her work.

6. Conclusion: The Mythical Nineteenth Century and Its Heritage

1. Amy Lowell, *Poetry and Poets* (Boston: Houghton, Mifflin, 1930), p. 111.

2. Kate Chopin, *The Awakening*, Margaret Culley, ed. (New York: W. W. Norton, 1976), pp. 14 and 113 respectively.

3. Edith Wharton, *The House of Mirth* (New York: Charles Scribner's, 1905), p. 64.

4. Ibid., p. 176.

5. Louise Bogan, *The Blue Estuaries: Poems 1923–1968* (New York: Farrar, Straus & Giroux, 1968). All poems by Louise Bogan hereafter cited in the text will be from this edition.

6. Amy Lowell, *The Complete Poetical Works of Amy Lowell* (Boston: Houghton, Mifflin, 1955). This poem, "La Vie de Boheme," is from "Pictures of the Floating World" contained in *The Complete Poetical Works*. All other Lowell poems quoted in this chapter are also from *The Complete Poetical Works*.

7. H. D., "The Islands" in *Selected Poems of H. D.* (New York: Grove Press, 1957).

8. Elinor Wylie, *Collected Poems of Elinor Wylie* (New York: Alfred Knopf, 1971). All poems by Wylie quoted in this chapter are taken from this edition.

9. H. D., "Orchard" in *Selected Poems of H. D.*

10. Sylvia Plath, *Ariel* (New York: Harper & Row, 1966).

11. Louise Bogan, "The Springs of Poetry," *The New Republic*, Supplement, 37 (December 5, 1923): 8.

12. Edna St. Vincent Millay, *Collected Poems* (New York: Harper & Row, 1956). All poems by Millay quoted in this chapter are from this edition. It is interesting to compare this with W. H. Auden's poem "A Household," which deals with the same situation. In it a lonely man returns to a "miserable runt" and a "slatternly hag," but his justification for the return is very different:

> Besides, (which might explain why he has neither
> Altered his will nor called the doctor in)
> He half believes, call it a superstition,
>
> It is for his sake that they hate and fear him:
> Should they unmask and show themselves worth loving,
> Loving and sane and manly, he would die.

See W. H. Auden, *Selected Poetry of W. H. Auden* (New York: Random House, Vintage, 1971).

13. Margaret Atwood, *Selected Poems* (New York: Simon and Schuster, 1976), p. 201.

14. H. D., *Helen in Egypt* (New York: New Directions, 1961).

15. Although I characterize the 1930s as a time when this motif was particularly prevalent in the writers who belong to this tradition of women's poetry, I am well aware that there were other women poets writing during this period who departed from the thrust of this tradition and directed their poetry to social and political concerns. Millay did this at times, and yet she remains fundamentally in the mainstream I am considering. Poets who belong to the alternative tradition include Lola Ridge, Muriel Rukeyser, and the later Genevieve Taggard.

16. A good example of the way the mainstream of women's poetry had altered its course can be found in the reaction of Bette Richart to Edna St. Vincent Millay after World War II. (See "Poet of Our Youth," *Commonweal*, 10 May 1957, p. 150). In this article Richart castigates herself for having admired Millay when she was young. Now Richart finds Millay's poetry neurotic, sentimental, lacking in intellectual substance. Her response shows that women readers were looking for something very different by this time from women poets.

17. Adrienne Rich, *Poems: Selected and New, 1950–1974* (New York: Norton, 1974). Since I place Adrienne Rich in the new generation of poets after World War II who played down their sex in their early poems, I feel it necessary to add that neither she nor Denise Levertov can be dealt with adequately in these terms. Rich has become the most articulate and powerful spokesperson we have for the relation between gender and art. In recent years Levertov has reduced the distance between personal self and poem. *The Freeing of the Dust* marks the beginning of the change.

18. In "Armored Women, Naked Men," Terence Diggory argues that men have actually been the confessional poets whereas women belong primarily to an anti-confessional tradition. Although Diggory's article makes interesting reading, I think Diggory misses the central nuance of nakedness for women. What women shy away from in nakedness is not self-revelation but vulnerability. Their communications may be complicated by efforts at self-concealment, but self-exposure is a primary impetus in their work as well. I agree with Diggory's conclusion that "women have sought means to suggest what they did not want to say" (*Shakespeare's Sisters*, p. 150).

19. Louise Bogan, *Achievement in American Poetry* (Chicago: Gateway Editions, 1951), p. 19.

Selected Bibliography

This bibliography includes *only* those works of particular interest to this study. It does not contain all the background sources used, nor does the appearance of a work in this bibliography mean that I agree with its conclusions. These works concentrate on the position of women in American culture, women poets in particular, or literary culture in specific time periods. The bibliography is arranged according to the separate time periods covered in the book.

Anne Bradstreet and the Colonial Period

Books

Altbach, Edith Hoshino. *Women in America*. Lexington, Mass.: D. C. Heath, 1974.

Bercovitch, Sacvan, ed. *The American Puritan Imagination: Essays in Revaluation*. New York: Cambridge University Press, 1974.

Berryman, John. *Homage to Mistress Bradstreet and Other Poems*. New York: Noonday Press, 1968.

Boynton, Percy H., ed. *American Poetry*. New York: Scribner's, 1919.

———. *Literature and American Life*. New York: Ginn & Company, 1936.

Cairns, William B., ed. *Early American Writers: 1607–1800*. New York: Macmillan, 1924.

Caldwell, Colonel Luther. *An Account of Anne Bradstreet the Puritan Poetess and Kindred Topics*. Boston: Damrell & Upham, 1898.

Cowell, Pattie, ed. *Women Poets in Pre-Revolutionary America 1650–1775*. Troy, New York: Whitston Publishing Company, 1980.

Daly, Robert. *God's Altar: The World and the Flesh in Puritan Poetry*. Los Angeles: University of California Press, 1978.

Dexter, Elisabeth. *Colonial Women of Affairs*. New York: Houghton Mifflin, 1931.

Dorson, Richard, ed. *America Begins: Early American Writing*. Bloomington: Indiana University Press, 1950.

Duyckinck, Evert A. and George L. *Cyclopaedia of American Literature*, vol. 1. New York: Scribner's, 1855.

Earle, Alice Morse. *Colonial Dames and Good Wives*. New York: Macmillan, 1924.

Ellis, John Harvard. *The Works of Anne Bradstreet*. 2nd ed., 1867; rpt. New York: Peter Smith, 1932.

Hensley, Jeanine, ed. *The Works of Anne Bradstreet*. (Introduction by Adrienne Rich.) Cambridge, Mass.: Belknap Press of Harvard University Press, 1967.

Holliday, Carl. *Women's Life in Colonial Days.* 2nd ed., 1922; rpt. New York: Frederick Ungar, 1960.

Hutchinson, Robert, ed. *Poems of Anne Bradstreet.* New York: Dover. 1969.

Jantz, Harold S. *The First Century of New England Verse.* New York: Russell and Russell, 1962.

Koehler, Lyle S. *A Search for Power: The "Weaker Sex" in Seventeenth-Century New England.* Urbana: University of Illinois Press, 1980.

Leonard, Eugenie, et al. *The American Woman in Colonial and Revolutionary Times.* Philadelphia: University of Pennsylvania, 1962.

Leonard, Eugenie Andress. *The Dear-Bought Heritage.* Philadelphia: University of Pennsylvania Press, 1965.

Mather, Cotton. *Ornaments for the Daughters of Zion: Or the Character and Happiness of a Vertuous Woman.* Boston: Phillips, 1692.

Meserole, Harrison T., ed. *Seventeenth-Century American Poetry.* New York: W. W. Norton, 1968.

Morgan, Edmund S. *The Puritan Family: Religion and Domestic Relations in Seventeenth-Century New England.* Rev. ed. New York: Harper & Row, 1966.

Murdock, Kenneth B., ed. *Handkerchiefs from Paul.* Cambridge, Mass.: Harvard University Press, 1927.

———. *Literature and Theology in Colonial New England.* Cambridge, Mass.: Harvard University Press, 1949.

Norton, Mary Beth. *Liberty's Daughters.* Boston: Little, Brown, 1980.

Pearce, Roy Harvey, ed. *Colonial American Writing.* 2nd ed. New York: Holt, Rinehart, 1969.

———. *The Continuity of American Poetry.* Princeton: Princeton University Press, 1961.

Piercy, Josephine K. *Anne Bradstreet.* New York: Twayne, 1965.

Silverman, Kenneth, ed. *Colonial American Poetry.* New York: Harper Publishing Company, 1968.

Smith, Page. *Daughters of the Promised Land.* Boston: Little, Brown, 1970.

Springer, Marlene, ed. *What Manner of Woman: Essays on English and American Life and Literature.* New York: New York University Press, 1977.

Stanford, Ann. *Anne Bradstreet: The Worldly Puritan.* New York: Burt Franklin, 1974.

Tyler, Moses Coit. *A History of American Literature 1607–1775.* 1878; rpt. Ithaca: Cornell University Press, 1949.

White, Elizabeth Wade. *Anne Bradstreet: "The Tenth Muse."* New York: Oxford University Press, 1971.

Wright, Thomas Goddard. *Literary Culture in Early New England 1620–1730.* New Haven: Yale University Press, 1920.

Articles and Shorter Works

Barker-Benfield, Ben. "Anne Hutchinson and the Puritan Attitude Toward Women." *Feminist Studies* 1 (Fall 1972): 65–96.

Cowell, Pattie. "Jane Colman Turell: 'A Double Birth.'" *13th Moon* 4 (1978): 59–70.

Eberwein, Jane Donohue. "The 'Unrefined Ore' of Anne Bradstreet's Quaternions." *Early American Literature* 9 (1974): 19–26.

Faragher, John. "Old Women and Old Men in Seventeenth-Century Weathersfield, Connecticut." *Women's Studies* 4 (1976): 11–31.

Hildebrand, Anne. "Anne Bradstreet's Quaternions and 'Contemplations.'" *Early American Literature* 8 (1973): 117–25.

Irwin, William J. "Allegory and Typology 'Embrace and Greet': Anne Bradstreet's Contemplations." *Early American Literature* 10 (1975): 30–45.

Laughlin, Rosemary. "Anne Bradstreet: Poet in Search of Form." *American Literature* 42 (1970): 1–17.

Malmsheimer, Lonna. "Daughters of Zion: New England Roots of American Feminism." *New England Quarterly* 50 (1977): 484–504.

Martin, Wendy. "Anne Bradstreet's Poetry: A Study of Subversive Piety." In *Shakespeare's Sisters: Feminist Essays on Women Poets,* edited by Sandra M. Gilbert and Susan Gubar. Bloomington: Indiana University Press, 1979, pp. 19–31.

Masson, Margaret W. "The Typology of the Female as a Model for the Regenerate: Puritan Preaching 1690–1730." *Signs* 2 (1976): 304–15.

Requa, Kenneth. "Anne Bradstreet's Poetic Voices." *Early American Literature* 9 (1974): 3–18.

Rosenfield, Alvin H. "Anne Bradstreet's 'Contemplations': Patterns of Form and Meaning." *New England Quarterly* 43 (1970): 79–96.

Rosenmeier, Rosamond R. "Hidden Manna: Truth and Method in the Art of Anne Bradstreet," an unpublished paper in the archives of Harvard University, Pusey Library, 1970.

Stanford, Ann. "Anne Bradstreet: Dogmatist and Rebel." *New England Quarterly* 39 (1966): 373–89.

Ulrich, Laurel Thatcher. "Vertuous Women Found: New England Ministerial Literature, 1668–1735." *American Quarterly* 28 (1976): 19–40.

Walker, Cheryl. "Anne Bradstreet." *American Writers.* Supplement. Edited by Leonard Unger. New York: Scribner's, 1979, pp. 95–123.

The Poetess and Her Nineteenth-Century Milieu

Books

Addison, Daniel Dulany. *Lucy Larcom: Life, Letters, and Diary.* Boston: Houghton Mifflin, 1894.

American Women Writers. Edited by Lina Mainiero. 3 vols. New York: Frederick Ungar Publishing Company, 1979, 1980, 1981.

Beecher, Catharine. *An Essay on Slavery and Abolitionism with Reference to the Duty of American Females.* Philadelphia: Henry Perkins, 1837.

———. *Treatise on Domestic Economy for the Use of Young Ladies at Home and at School.* Boston: T. H. Webb, 1843.

Benson, Mary Sumner. *Women in Eighteenth-Century America.* 1938; rpt. Port Washington, New York: Kennikat Press, 1966.

Berg, Barbara J. *The Remembered Gate: Origins of American Feminism.* New York: Oxford University Press, 1978.

Brooks, Maria Gowen. *Judith, Esther, and Other Poems.* Boston: Cummings and Hilliard, 1820.

———. *Zophiël, or The Bride of Seven.* With a Biography by Mrs. Zadel Barnes Gustafson. Boston: Lea and Blanchard, 1879.

Bryant, William Cullen. *A New Library of Poetry and Song.* 2 vols. New York: Fords, Howard, and Hulbert (no date).

Calhoun, Arthur W. *A Social History of the American Family.* 3 vols. Cleveland: Arthur H. Clark, 1918.

Chafe, William H. *Women and Equality: Changing Patterns in American Culture.* New York: Oxford, 1977.

Conrad, Susan P. *Perish the Thought: Intellectual Women in America, 1830–1860.* New York: Oxford, 1976.

Cott, Nancy F. *The Bonds of Womanhood: "Woman's Sphere" in New England, 1780–1835.* New Haven: Yale University Press, 1977.

Davidson, Lucretia. *Poetical Remains of the Late Lucretia Davidson,* with a Biography by Miss [Catherine] Sedgwick. Philadelphia: Lea and Blanchard, 1847.

Douglas, Ann. *The Feminization of American Culture.* New York: Knopf, 1977.

Fuller, Margaret. *Memoirs of Margaret Fuller Ossoli.* 2 vols. Boston: Phillips, Sampson, 1856.

Gilbert, Sandra M., and Gubar, Susan. *The Madwoman in the Attic: The Woman Writer and the Nineteenth-Century Literary Imagination.* New Haven: Yale University Press, 1979.

———, eds. *Shakespeare's Sisters: Feminist Essays on Women Poets.* Bloomington: Indiana University Press, 1979.

Grannis, Ruth Sheperd. *An American Friend of Southey.* Privately printed. New York: The De Vinne Press, 1913.

Griswold, Rufus, ed. *The Female Poets of America.* Rev. ed. 1873; rpt. New York: Garrett Press, 1969.

———, ed. *The Poets and Poetry of America.* Philadelphia: Perry and McMillan, 1856.

Groves, Ernest R. *The American Woman.* New York: Emerson, 1944.

Haight, Gordon. *Mrs. Sigourney: Sweet Singer of Hartford.* New York: Yale University Press, 1930.

Hale, Sara Josepha. *Woman's Record: or Sketches of Distinguished Women, from "The Beginning" till A.D. 1850.* New York: Harper and Brothers, 1853.

Harper, Frances Watkins. *Poems.* Philadelphia: Merrihew & Son, 1871.

Hausdorff, Don, ed. *Literature in America: A Century of Expansion.* New York: Macmillan-Free Press, 1971.

Hemans, Felicia. *The Poetical Works of Mrs. Felicia Hemans.* Philadelphia: Grigg & Eliot, 1836.

———. *The Works of Mrs. Hemans.* With an Essay on Her Genius by Mrs. Sigourney. 7 vols. Philadelphia: Lea and Blanchard, 1840.

Hewitt, Mary E., ed. *The Memorial: Written by Friends of the Late Mrs. Osgood.* New York: George Putnam, 1851.

Holland, Josiah Gilbert. *Miss Gilbert's Career.* New York: Scribner's, 1860.

Homans, Margaret. *Women Writers and Poetic Identity.* Princeton: Princeton University Press, 1980.

Larcom, Lucy. *A New England Girlhood.* 1889; rpt. Gloucester, Massachusetts: Peter Smith, 1973.

———. *The Poetical Works of Lucy Larcom.* Boston: Houghton Mifflin, 1884.

May, Caroline, ed. *The American Female Poets.* Philadelphia: Lindsay & Blakiston, 1856.

Miller, John Carl, ed. *Poe's Helen Remembers.* Charlottesville: University Press of Virginia, 1979.

Miller, Perry, ed. *Margaret Fuller, American Romantic.* Garden City, New York: Doubleday, 1963.

Moers, Ellen. *Literary Women.* New York: Doubleday, 1976.

Notable American Women, 1607–1950. Edited by Edward T. James et al. Cambridge, Massachusetts: Belknap Press of Harvard University Press, 1971.

Oakes-Smith, Elizabeth. The Autobiography of Elizabeth Oakes Smith. Edited by Mary Alice Wyman. Lewiston, Maryland: Lewiston Journal Company, 1924.

———. The Poetical Writings of Elizabeth Oakes Smith. 2nd ed. New York: J. S. Redfield, 1846.

———. Woman and Her Needs. New York: Fowler and Wells, 1851.

Osgood, Frances Sargent. Poems. Philadelphia: Carey & Hart, 1850.

Parker, Gail, ed. The Oven Birds: American Women on Womanhood, 1820–1920. Garden City, New York: Doubleday, 1972.

Pattee, Fred Lewis. The Feminine Fifties. New York: Appleton-Century, 1940.

Poe, Edgar Allan. The Literati—Minor Contemporaries, Etc. in The Works of Edgar Allan Poe, vol. 8. Edited by Edmund Clarence Stedman and George Edward Woodberry. New York: Scribner's, 1895.

Richmond, M. A. Bid the Vassal Soar. Washington: Howard University Press, 1974.

Ross, Ishbel. Ladies of the Press: The Story of Women in Journalism by an Insider. New York: Harper, 1936.

Ryan, Mary P. Womanhood in America. New York: Franklin Watts-New Viewpoints, 1979.

Showalter, Elaine. A Literature of Their Own: Women Novelists from Brontë to Lessing. Princeton: Princeton University Press, 1977.

Sigourney, Lydia Huntley. Letters of Life. New York: D. Appleton, 1867.

———. Letters to Young Ladies. New York: Harper & Brothers, 1837.

———. Pocahontas, and Other Poems. New York: Harper & Brothers, 1841.

———. Select Poems. 8th ed. Philadelphia: Carey & Hart, 1849.

Sklar, Kathryn Kish. Catharine Beecher: A Study in American Domesticity. New York: Norton, 1973.

Still, William. The Underground Rail Road. Philadelphia: Porter and Coates, 1872.

Walsh, John Evangelist. Plumes in the Dust: The Love Affair of Edgar Allan Poe and Fanny Osgood. Chicago: Nelson-Hall, 1980.

Welter, Barbara. Dimity Convictions: The American Woman in the Nineteenth Century. Athens, Ohio: Ohio University Press, 1976.

Wheatley, Phillis. The Poems of Phillis Wheatley. Edited by Julian D. Mason, Jr. Chapel Hill: University of North Carolina Press, 1966.

Wyman, Mary Alice. Two American Pioneers: Seba Smith and Elizabeth Oakes Smith. New York: Columbia University Press, 1927.

Articles and Shorter Works:

Arvin, Newton. "Lydia Huntley Sigourney." American Pantheon. Edited by Daniel Aaron and Sylvan Schindler. New York: Delacorte Press, 1966.

Bogan, Louise. "Poetesses in the Parlour." New Yorker, 5 December 1936, p. 42ff.

Clark, John L. "The Rights of Women." Godey's Magazine and Lady's Book 47 (December 1853): 544.

Collin, Grace Lathrop. "Lydia Huntley Sigourney." New England Magazine 27 (September 1902): 15–30.

Collins, Terence. "Phillis Wheatley: The Dark Side of her Poetry." *Phylon* 36 (1975): 78–88.

Fuller, Margaret. "Woman in the Nineteenth Century." *Margaret Fuller: American Romantic.* Edited by Perry Miller. Garden Grove, New York: Doubleday, 1963, pp. 135–90.

Haight, Gordon S. "Longfellow and Mrs. Sigourney." *New England Quarterly* 3 (Fall 1930): 532–37.

Hale, Sara Josepha. "Editor's Corner." *Ladies Magazine* 2 (1829): 142.

Hull, Gloria T. "Afro-American Women Poets: A Bio-Critical Survey." In *Shakespeare's Sisters,* edited by Sandra M. Gilbert and Susan Gubar. Bloomington: Indiana University Press, 1979.

Neal, Alice B. "American Female Authorship." *Godey's Lady's Book* 44 (1852): 147.

Smith-Rosenberg, Carroll. "The Female World of Love and Ritual: Relations between Women in Nineteenth-Century America." *Signs* 1 (Autumn 1975): 1–30.

Taylor, William R., and Lasch, Christopher. "Two 'Kindred Spirits': Sorority and Family in New England, 1839–1846." *The New England Quarterly* 36 (1963): 23–41.

Wood, Ann Douglas. "Mrs. Sigourney and the Sensibility of the Inner Space." *New England Quarterly* 45 (June 1972): 163–81.

Emily Dickinson and Helen Hunt Jackson and Their Times

Books

Banning, Evelyn I. *Helen Hunt Jackson.* New York: Vanguard, 1973.

Bianchi, Martha Dickinson. *Emily Dickinson, Face to Face.* New York: Archon Books, 1970.

———. *The Life and Letters of Emily Dickinson.* Boston: Houghton Mifflin, 1924.

Bingham, Millicent Todd. *Ancestor's Brocades: The Literary Debut of Emily Dickinson.* New York: Harper and Brothers, 1945.

Blake, Caesar R., and Carlton F. Wells, eds. *The Recognition of Emily Dickinson.* Ann Arbor: University of Michigan Press, 1964.

Browning, Elizabeth Barrett. *Aurora Leigh.* New York: Francis, 1859; Emily Dickinson's copy.

———. *The Poetical Works of Elizabeth Barrett Browning.* Boston: Houghton Mifflin, 1974.

Capps, Jack L. *Emily Dickinson's Reading, 1836–1886.* Cambridge, Mass.: Harvard University Press, 1966.

Cody, John. *After Great Pain: The Inner Life of Emily Dickinson.* Cambridge, Mass.: Harvard University Press, 1971.

Dana, Charles A., ed. *The Household Book of Poetry.* New York: D. Appleton, 1860.

Dickinson, Emily. *The Letters of Emily Dickinson.* 3 vols. Edited by Thomas H. Johnson and Theodora Ward. Cambridge, Mass.: Harvard University Press, 1958.

———. *The Poems of Emily Dickinson.* 3 vols. Edited by Thomas H. Johnson. Cambridge, Mass.: Harvard University Press, 1955.

Faderman, Lillian. *Surpassing the Love of Men: Romantic Friendship and Love Between Women from the Renaissance to the Present.* New York: William Morrow, 1981.

Gelpi, Albert. *Emily Dickinson: The Mind of the Poet.* Cambridge, Mass.: Harvard University Press, 1966.

————. *The Tenth Muse: The Psyche of the American Poet.* Cambridge, Mass.: Harvard University Press, 1975.

Griffith, Clark. *The Long Shadow: Emily Dickinson's Tragic Poetry.* Princeton: Princeton University Press, 1964.

Griswold, Rufus, ed. *The Sacred Poets of England and America.* New York: D. Appleton, 1849.

Higgins, David. *Portrait of Emily Dickinson: The Poet and Her Prose.* New Brunswick, New Jersey: Rutgers University Press, 1967.

Jackson, Helen Hunt. *Mercy Philbrick's Choice.* No Name Series. Boston: Roberts, 1876.

————. *Poems.* Boston: Roberts, 1892.

————. [Saxe Holm, pseud.] *Saxe Holm's Stories.* New York: Scribner's, 1890.

Johnson, Thomas. *Emily Dickinson: An Interpretive Biography.* Cambridge, Mass.: Harvard University Press, 1955.

Leyda, Jay. *The Years and Hours of Emily Dickinson.* 2 vols. New Haven: Yale University Press, 1960.

Longfellow, Henry Wadsworth. *Kavanaugh* in *The Works of Henry Wadsworth Longfellow,* vol. 8. Boston: Houghton Mifflin, 1886.

MacLeish, Archibald; Bogan, Louise; and Wilbur, Richard. *Emily Dickinson: Three Views.* Amherst: Amherst College Press, 1960.

Miller, Ruth. *The Poetry of Emily Dickinson.* Middletown: Wesleyan University Press, 1968.

Mudge, Jean McClure. *Emily Dickinson and the Image of Home.* Amherst: University of Massachusetts Press, 1975.

Patterson, Rebecca. *The Riddle of Emily Dickinson.* Boston: Houghton Mifflin, 1951.

Rosenbaum, S. P. *A Concordance to the Poems of Emily Dickinson.* Ithaca: Cornell University Press, 1964.

Sewall, Richard B. *The Life of Emily Dickinson.* 2 vols. New York: Farrar, Straus & Giroux, 1974.

————, ed. *Emily Dickinson: A Collection of Critical Essays.* Twentieth Century Views Series. Englewood Cliffs, New Jersey: Prentice-Hall, 1963.

Sherwood, William R. *Circumference and Circumstance: Stages in the Mind and Art of Emily Dickinson.* New York: Columbia University Press, 1968.

Taggard, Genevieve. *The Life and Mind of Emily Dickinson.* New York: Knopf, 1930.

Walsh, John Evangelist. *The Hidden Life of Emily Dickinson.* New York: Simon and Schuster, 1971.

Whicher, George. *This Was A Poet.* New York: Scribner's, 1938.

Shorter Works

Cameron, Sharon. "Naming as History: Dickinson's Poems of Definition." *Critical Inquiry* 5: 223–52.

Cunningham, J. V. "Sorting Out: The Case of Dickinson." *Southern Review* 5 (New Series): 436–56.

Diehl, Joanne Feit. " 'Come Slowly – Eden': An Exploration of Women Poets and Their Muse." *Signs: A Journal of Women in Culture and Society* 3: 572–87.

Diggory, Terence. "Armored Women, Naked Men: Dickinson, Whitman, and

Their Successors." In *Shakespeare's Sisters*, edited by Gilbert and Gubar, pp. 135–50.

Donoghue, Denis. "Emily Dickinson." In *American Writers: A Collection of Literary Biographies*, edited by Leonard Unger. New York: Scribner's, 1974, pp. 451–73.

"Elizabeth Barrett Browning." *Atlantic Monthly* 13 (September 1861): 368–76.

Faderman, Lillian. "Emily Dickinson's Letters to Sue Gilbert." *Massachusetts Review* 18 (1977): 197–225.

Gelpi, Albert. "Emily Dickinson and the Deerslayer: The Dilemma of the Woman Poet in America." In *Shakespeare's Sisters*, edited by Gilbert and Gubar, pp. 122–134.

Gilbert, Sandra M., and Gubar, Susan. "A Woman—White: Emily Dickinson's Yarn of Pearl." In *The Madwoman in the Attic*, pp. 581–650.

Greene, Elsa. "Emily Dickinson was a Poetess." *College English* 34 (October 1972): 63–70.

Higginson, Thomas Wentworth. "Helen Hunt Jackson." In *Contemporaries*. Boston: Houghton Mifflin, 1899, pp. 108–67.

Homans, Margaret. "Emily Dickinson." In *Women Writers and Poetic Identity*, pp. 162–214.

Johnson, Finley. "Poetry." *Godey's Lady's Book* 63 (1861): 48.

Juhasz, Suzanne. " 'A Privilege So Awful': The Poetry of Emily Dickinson." In *Naked and Fiery Forms: Modern American Poetry by Women—A New Tradition*. New York: Harper & Row, 1976, pp. 7–32.

Kaufman, Jule S. "Emily Dickinson and the Involvement of Retreat." *Tulane Studies in English* 21 (1974): 77–90.

Patterson, Rebecca. "Emily Dickinson's 'Double' Tim: Masculine Identification." *American Imago* 28 (1971): 330–62.

Pollak, Vivian R. "Thirst and Starvation in Emily Dickinson's Poetry." *American Literature* 51 (1979): 33–49.

Rich, Adrienne. "Vesuvius at Home: The Power of Emily Dickinson." In *Shakespeare's Sisters*, edited by Gilbert and Gubar, pp. 99–121.

Wilcox, Reese, and Guiney: The New Women of the 1890s

Books

Ballou, Jenny. *Period Piece: Ella Wheeler Wilcox and Her Times*. Boston: Houghton Mifflin, 1940.

Beer, Thomas. *The Mauve Decade*. Garden City, New York: Garden City Publishing Company, 1926.

Fairbanks, Henry G. *Louise Imogen Guiney: Laureate of the Lost*. Albany: Magi, 1972.

Filene, Peter Gabriel. *Him/Her/Self: Sex Roles in Modern America*. New York: Harcourt Brace, 1974.

Friedman, Jean E., and Shade, William G., eds. *Our American Sisters: Women in American Life and Thought*. Boston: Allyn and Bacon, 1973.

Guiney, Louise Imogen. *Happy Ending*. Boston: Houghton Mifflin, 1909.

———. *Letters of Louise Imogen Guiney*. 2 vols. Edited by Grace Guiney. New York: Harper & Brothers, 1926.

———. *The Martyr's Idyl*. Boston: Houghton Mifflin, 1899.

———. *Patrins*. Boston: Copeland and Day, 1897.

———. *Songs at the Start*. Boston: Cupples, Upham, 1884.

————. *The White Sail*. Boston: Ticknor & Company 1887.

Jones, Howard Mumford. *The Bright Medusa*. Urbana: University of Illinois Press, 1952.

May, Henry F. *The End of American Innocence*. Chicago: Quadrangle Books, 1964.

Millett, Fred B. *Contemporary American Authors*. New York: Harcourt, Brace, 1940.

Moody, William Vaughn. *The Poems and Plays of William Vaughn Moody*. 2 vols. Boston: Houghton Mifflin, 1912.

Pattee, Fred Lewis. *A History of American Literature Since 1870*. New York: Century Company, 1915.

Pizer, Donald, ed. *American Thought and Writing: The 1890s*. Boston: Houghton Mifflin, 1972.

Reese, Lizette Woodworth. *A Branch of May*. Portland, Maryland: Mosher, 1887, 1909.

————. *A Handful of Lavender*. Portland, Maryland: Mosher, 1891, 1919.

————. *A Quiet Road*. Boston: Houghton Mifflin, 1896.

————. *Pastures*. New York: Farrar and Rinehart, 1933.

————. *The Selected Poems of Lizette Woodworth Reese*. New York: Doran, 1926.

————. *The Old House in the Country*. New York: Farrar and Rinehart, 1936.

————. *A Victorian Village*. New York: Farrar and Rinehart, 1929.

————. *White April*. New York: Farrar and Rinehart, 1930.

————. *Wild Cherry*. Baltimore: Norman, Remington, 1923.

Rittenhouse, Jessie B., ed. *The Little Book of American Poets*. Boston: Houghton Mifflin, 1917.

Robinson, Edwin Arlington. *Selected Poems of Edwin Arlington Robinson*. Edited by Morton Dauwen Zabel. New York: Macmillan-Collier Books, 1966.

Santayana, George. *The Genteel Tradition: Nine Essays by George Santayana*. Edited by Douglas L. Wilson. Cambridge, Mass.: Harvard University Press, 1967.

Stedman, Edmund Clarence, ed. *American Anthology 1787–1900*. Boston: Houghton Mifflin, 1900.

Tenison, E. M. *Louise Imogen Guiney: Her Life and Works*. London: Macmillan, 1923.

Wasserstrom, William. *Heiress of All Ages: Sex and Sentiment in The Genteel Tradition*. Minneapolis: University of Minnesota, 1959.

Wilcox, Ella Wheeler. *Men, Women, and Emotions*. Chicago: Morrill, Higgins, 1893.

————. *Poems of Passion*. Chicago: W. B. Conkey, 1883.

————. *Poems of Pleasure*. Chicago: Morill, Higgins and Company, 1892.

————. *Three Women*. Chicago: W. B. Conkey, 1897.

Wirth, Alexander C. *Complete Bibliography of Lizette Woodworth Reese*. Baltimore: The Proof Press, 1937.

Shorter Works

Adams, Leonie. "Winter Bloom." *Poetry* 44 (April 1934): 40–41.

Benet, William Rose. "Poets in Collected Editions." *The Yale Review* (January 1928): 373–74.

Davis, Rebecca Harding, et al. "Are Women to Blame?" *North American Review* 148 (April 1889): 622–42.

Davis, Rebecca Harding. "In the Gray Cabins of New England." *Century Magazine* 27 (February 1895): 620–23.

Degler, Carl. "What Ought to Be and What Was: Women's Sexuality in the Nineteenth Century." *The American Historical Review* 79 (December 1974): 1467–90.

Deland, Margaret. "The Change in the Feminine Ideal." *Atlantic Monthly* 105 (March 1910): 289–302.

Dietrich, Mae. "Lizette Woodworth Reese." *Emily Dickinson Bulletin* 15 (December 1970): 114–20.

Gregory, Eliot. "Our Foolish Virgins." *Century Magazine* 63 (November 1901): 3–15.

Guiney. Louise Imogen. "The Point of View: On Being Well-Known." *Scribner's* 49 (January 1911): 121–24.

Hariss, Robert P. "April Weather: The Poetry of Lizette Woodworth Reese." *South Atlantic Quarterly* 29 (April 1930): 200–207.

Kaufman, Emma B. "The Education of a Debutante." *Cosmopolitan* (September 1903): 499–508.

Kindilien, Carlin T. "The Village World of Lizette Woodworth Reese." *South Atlantic Quarterly* 56 (January 1957): 91–104.

Lucey, William L., S. J. "Louise I. Guiney on American Woman Poets." *Boston Public Library Quarterly* 12 (1960): 110–14.

"The Passing of the Old Lady." *Atlantic Monthly* 99 (June 1907): 874.

Pittock, Malcolm. "In Defence of Ella Wheeler Wilcox." *Durham University Journal* 65 (December 1972): 86–89.

Repplier, Agnes. "The Repeal of Reticence." *Atlantic Monthly* 113 (March 1914): 297–304.

Rogers, Anna A. "Why American Marriages Fail." *Atlantic Monthly* 100 (September 1907): 289–98.

"Sex O'Clock in America." *Current Opinion* 55 (August 1913): 113–14.

Shade, William G. " 'A Mental Passion': Female Sexuality in Victorian America." *International Journal of Women's Studies* 1 (1978): 13–29.

Ticknor, Caroline. "The Steel-Engraving Lady and the Gibson Girl." *Atlantic Monthly* 88 (July 1901): 105–108.

Wells, Kate Gannett. "The Transitional American Woman." *Atlantic Monthly* 46 (December 1880): 817–23.

Index

Entries for women poets treated at length in this book first show where discussion of the poet is concentrated and then group scattered references to her by subject. Some or all of these subjects may also be treated in the main discussion.

In the Emily Dickinson entry, I have used the Thomas Johnson numbering system for the poems.